Bruno Latour

Modern European Thinkers
Series Editors: Anne Beech and David Castle

Over the past few decades, Anglo-American social science and humanities have experienced an unprecedented interrogation, revision and strengthening of their methodologies and theoretical underpinnings through the influence of highly innovative scholarship from continental Europe. In the fields of philosophy, post-structuralism, psychoanalysis, critical theory and beyond, the works of a succession of pioneering writers have had revolutionary effects on Anglo-American academia. However, much of this work is extremely challenging, and some is hard or impossible to obtain in English translation. This series provides clear and concise introductions to the ideas and work of key European thinkers.

As well as being comprehensive, accessible introductory texts, the titles in the 'Modern European Thinkers' series retain Pluto's characteristic radical political slant, and critically evaluate leading theorists in terms of their contribution to genuinely radical and progressive intellectual endeavour. And while the series does explore the leading lights, it also looks beyond the big names that have dominated theoretical debates to highlight the contribution of extremely important but less well-known figures.

Also available:

Hannah Arendt
Finn Bowring

André Gorz
Conrad Lodziak and Jeremy Tatman

Alain Badiou
Jason Barker

Félix Guattari
Gary Genosko

Georges Bataille
Benjamin Noys

Jürgen Habermas
Luke Goode

Jean Baudrillard
Mike Gane

Herbert Marcuse
Malcolm Miles

Walter Benjamin
Esther Leslie

Guy Hocquenghem
Bill Marshall

Pierre Bourdieu
Jeremy F. Lane

Slavoj Žižek
Ian Parker

Gilles Deleuze
John Marks

Bruno Latour

Reassembling the Political

Graham Harman

www.plutobooks.com

First published 2014 by Pluto Press
345 Archway Road, London N6 5AA

www.plutobooks.com

Copyright © Graham Harman 2014

The right of Graham Harman to be identified as the author of this work
has been asserted by him in accordance with the Copyright, Designs and
Patents Act 1988.

British Library Cataloguing in Publication Data
A catalogue record for this book is available from the British Library

ISBN   978 0 7453 3400 4   Hardback
ISBN   978 0 7453 3399 1   Paperback
ISBN   978 1 7837 1197 0   PDF eBook
ISBN   978 1 7837 1199 4   Kindle eBook
ISBN   978 1 7837 1198 7   EPUB eBook

Library of Congress Cataloging in Publication Data applied for

10   9   8   7   6   5   4   3   2   1

Typeset by Stanford DTP Services, Northampton, England
Text design by Melanie Patrick
Simultaneously printed digitally by CPI Antony Rowe, Chippenham, UK
and Edwards Bros in the United States of America

Contents

Abbreviations for Latour's Works Cited in the Book

AIME   *An Inquiry into Modes of Existence* (2013)
BAB   "Redefining the social link" (1987)
BEC   "Whose Cosmos, Which Cosmopolitics?" (2004)
COP   "Coming out as a philosopher" (2010)
DBD   "Let the dead (revolutionaries) bury the dead" (2014)
EWC   "The Enlightenment Without the Critique" (1987)
GIFF   "Facing Gaia" (the Gifford Lectures) (2013)
INT   "On Interobjectivity" (1996)
NBM   *We Have Never Been Modern* (1993)
PA   "The Powers of Association" (1986)
PF   *The Pasteurization of France* (1988)
PFM   "How to Write '*The Prince*' for Machines as Well as for Machinations" (1988)
PH   *Pandora's Hope* (1999)
PIC   *Paris: Invisible City* (1998)
PN   *Politics of Nature* (2004)
PRG   "Pragmatogonies" (1994)
PW   *The Prince and the Wolf* (2011)
RAM   "On the Partial Existence of Existing and Non-Existing Objects" (2011)
RD   "From Realpolitik to Dingpolitik" (2005)
RGDV "Turning Around Politics" (2007)
SA   *Science in Action* (1987)
TPL   "What if we *Talked* Politics a Little?" (2003)
TSD   "Technology Is Society Made Durable" (1991)
UNS   "Unscrewing the big Leviathan" (1981)

A Note on the Life and Thought of Bruno Latour

Given that some readers of this book might be unfamiliar with its central character, a brief introduction is in order. Bruno Latour was born on June 22, 1947 in the charming town of Beaune, roughly 50 kilometers south of Dijon in the Burgundy region of France. He is the youngest child of a large family belonging to the prominent Louis Latour wine dynasty (not to be confused with Château Latour wines from the vicinity of Bordeaux). Latour knew early that his vocation was intellectual life rather than wine production, and he chose to study philosophy in the face of a certain degree of family resistance. Perhaps the first sign of future world prominence came in the early 1970s, when he achieved first place in the whole of France in the Agrégation examination in philosophy. Given this brilliant result, an outside observer might have expected the young Latour to opt for a standard career as an academic philosopher. Instead, the always unorthodox tendencies of his mind prevailed, leading him on a path that to this day remains hard to describe in terms of the known university disciplines. Latour's national service work in Africa sparked an interest in anthropology, leading to his idea of an anthropology of the sciences that would describe Western science in the same terms as those used by anthropologists to describe the isolated and "primitive" peoples of the world. This project led him to the Jonas Salk Institute in San Diego, where his observations of scientists at work led to the publication of his first book *Laboratory Life*, co-authored with the British sociologist Steve Woolgar. Seemingly on the verge of a sparkling career, he nonetheless found himself blackballed by one prestigious institution in the United States, just as he would be shunned decades later by another at home in France. Latour landed instead at the Center for the Sociology of Innovation at the School of Mines in Paris, where he found a sympathetic colleague in Michel Callon; together, the two would do crucial collaborative work. Latour did not leave the School of Mines until more than twenty years later, by which time he was an international celebrity and the author of such influential books as *The Pasteurization of France*,

Science in Action, We Have Never Been Modern, and *Pandora's Hope.* In 2006 he moved to the ambitious Paris Institute of Political Studies, better known by its affectionate nickname: Sciences Po. During this period Latour has further solidified his reputation as one of the world's most prominent figures in the human sciences, having received such prestigious awards as the 2008 Siegfried Unseld Prize in Germany and the 2013 Holberg Prize in Norway. Latour lives in the Latin Quarter of Paris with his wife Chantal, with whom he has two adult children: a daughter named Chloë and a son named Robinson.

Latour is one of the founders of a method in the social sciences known as actor-network theory (ANT), which rejects sweeping categories of analysis such as "society" or "capitalism" in favor of a laser-like focus on the specific *actors* or *actants* at work in any situation. As the word suggests, actors are defined by their *actions* and nothing else. This has two immediate consequences. The first is that Latour empties the world of the traditional objects or essences that one might think lie hidden behind the overt actions they perform. Stated differently, Latour's is a world of verbs rather than nouns, relations rather than substances. Perhaps the chief philosophical parallels here are the American pragmatist thinker William James,[1] who joined C.S. Peirce in proclaiming that a thing without consequences is simply not a thing, and the English metaphysician Alfred North Whitehead,[2] who held that entities are constituted by their relations (or "prehensions"), and that any notion of an underlying substance hidden behind the actions or relations of an entity is a mere "vacuous actuality."

The second consequence of Latour's version of actor-network theory is the breakdown of the typical modern distinction between humans and the world, or culture and nature. The collapse of this difference is pivotal for Latour, as indicated by the title of his brilliant 1991 treatise *We Have Never Been Modern.* Rather than starting with an arbitrary taxonomy that declares one type of entity to be "natural" (existing independently and working with clockwork mechanical precision) and another to be "cultural" (resulting from the projection of relativistic human meanings and values onto cold, dead physical matter), we must start by considering all entities in exactly the same way. Namely, whatever *acts* in some way is real: whether it be neutrons, trees, mountains, armies, politicians, unicorns, stick figures, or flying saucers. Unicorns cannot be excluded from the picture, since they obviously have an *effect* on the structure of fairy tales and the stuffed animal collections of children. We cannot say that neutrons are *more real* than unicorns, only that they are *stronger* than unicorns. After all, neutrons simply have more and better animate and inanimate *allies* testifying to their existence than do unicorns. Truth is primarily a matter of strength in assembling allies, not of immaculate point-for-point correspondence with some external reality. In terms of political philosophy, this view of truth is connected with Latour's early fondness for the philosopher Thomas Hobbes. We recall that for Hobbes the Leviathan is the supreme authority, and any transcendent appeal to religious or scientific truths runs the risk of freelance dissidents claiming access to a higher truth than that of society. For Hobbes such claims can only plunge us into civil war. For Latour as well, any claim to pass beyond the various relational networks of actors to make direct contact with a transcendent truth is merely an attempt to short-circuit the unavoidable negotiations between human and nonhuman actors, which make up the only reality we have.

With their unyielding insistence that entities be considered solely in terms of their effects, Latour and his colleagues give us a powerful method that has swept like wildfire across the social sciences and spawned thousands of disciples. Yet this very same method has earned Latour the scorn of many scientific realists, who loathe his elimination of truth as correspondence with a transcendent outer world, and equally loathe his insistence that the networks that produce scientific truth are no different in kind from those found in political struggle. More generally, Latour has been pigeonholed as a "social constructionist," a term that makes sense only if we add that "society" for Latour includes photons, planets, and mushrooms no less than language and disciplinary practice. For a more complete defense of Latour's contributions to philosophy, readers are referred to my 2009 book *Prince of Networks*.[3]

Yet none of this is the final word on Latour's philosophy, since he has recently published a weighty systematic book entitled *An Inquiry into Modes of Existence*, in which his former actor-network approach is repositioned and subjected to strict limits. While the early Latour flattened all human and nonhuman entities onto a single plane of actions, the later Latour insists that reality is also broken up into numerous different zones or "modes" that must not be conflated with each other. To give just one example, it is easy to draw the following contrast between science, religion, politics, and law. Science functions by trying to establish reference to something existing in the outside world, and is judged according to how well it meets this criterion. Yet this same criterion would be absurd in politics, which is obviously not a simple exercise of making political statements that correspond to an outer reality, since it is often necessary to be duplicitous or blandly shake hands or whip up the emotions of the public in order to succeed. Nor is correspondence with the outside world a good criterion even in law, which is concerned with linking together documents, precedents, and evidence rather than establishing a correspondence with external fact. A perfectly justified legal appellant can still lose a judgment due to apparent trivialities such as missed deadlines or tedious failings in procedure, as seen in extreme form in Franz Kafka's novel *The Trial*. There is also the strange case of religion, however low its prestige among Western intellectuals today. Here too, Latour as a practicing Catholic ventures the heretical-sounding statement that religion is not a matter of corresponding to a real God that exists autonomously in the outer world; religion is concerned instead with purely immanent rituals and processions. The key principle of Latour's later philosophy is that each mode of existence has its own "felicity conditions," its own way of establishing truth, which must not be confused with the conditions applicable to the other modes. Science must no longer be allowed a monopoly on claims to truth.

This initial summary should be sufficient for understanding the chapters that follow. For newcomers to Latour who are interested in reading his books, I would recommend *We Have Never Been Modern* as a good starting point (I started there myself). *Science in Action* and *Pandora's Hope* also provide good general overviews of Latour's actor-network theory phase, as does the later work *Reassembling the Social*. His newest book, *An Inquiry into Modes of Existence*, is probably not the best hill to climb first, since it will make far more sense to those who are already familiar with the earlier period of Latour's career.

Introduction
Truth Politics and Power Politics

When Pluto Press asked for advice on who should write a book on Bruno Latour's political philosophy, I insisted on doing the job myself. This was not because I imagined myself an expert on the topic. Despite having spent fascinated years with the works of Latour, and despite having written an entire book reconstructing his metaphysics,[1] I still had no clear sense of Latour's political philosophy. Sometimes his political ideas were scattered like seed throughout his writings, though rarely in concentrated form; at other times, his politics seemed to coincide with reality as a whole, identified with the struggle of actants coupling and uncoupling from networks. In both of these cases it seemed doubtful whether a coherent political philosophy could be reassembled from Latour's works. Yet by the conclusion of this project, all doubts were removed, and I had become convinced of the following three points. First, Latour's work is thoroughly political from the beginning of his career all the way to the present. Second, the usual critiques of Latour's political philosophy (which normally come from the Left) have failed to engage him on any but the most peripheral issues. And third, however much practical detail may be missing from Latour's politics, he is closer to the future of political philosophy than much of the better-known work conducted under that heading.

Despite my initial perplexity, the research for this book did not begin in utter darkness. In *Prince of Networks* I argued for Latour's historic importance as a philosopher, and this importance was reason enough to suspect that his magic box of innovations might lead us (explicitly or not) to a new model of the political landscape. It had long seemed to me that our basic political spectrum of Left vs. Right was hopelessly entangled with a modern ontology that Latour effectively destroyed in his 1991 classic *We Have Never Been Modern*, even if most philosophers and activists are still guided by this Left/Right schema. As Latour sees it, modernity is grounded in a taxonomical rift between a mechanistic nature on one side and an arbitrarily constructed society on the other. Ontology has consequences, and the effect of this modern ontology is that the dualism of nature and culture suggests a scheme in which politics is based either on a knowledge of the true nature of human things, or on the conviction that knowledge does not exist and must therefore be replaced by a struggle for dominance. As a temporary placeholder for these two options we might speak not of "Left" and "Right" politics, but of "Down" and "Up" politics, in the same whimsical spirit as the classification of quarks in particle physics. But it should already by clear that the division between Down and Up does not coincide with the distinction between Left and Right, since the latter orientations can and do exist under both models of politics.

Down politics sees itself as a political philosophy of knowledge as opposed to ignorance. It comes in both Left and Right forms. On the Left, it consists in the revolutionary view that humans are equal as thinking things and as bearers of inalienable rights. If humans do not currently enjoy such rights, if they fall prey to enduring inequality, it is because they are blocked by some ulterior force: the accidental accretions of history, the self-serving ideologies of privileged groups, and perhaps even their own ignorance, such that they may need an educated vanguard to liberate them from darkness. Under this model the key political act is *opposition*, since the existing state of power will almost never coincide with truth, and must therefore be confronted and replaced. The weak are generally more right than the strong: "The stone the builders rejected has become the cornerstone," as the Bible puts it.[2] The West, still the seat of economic and military power, must subject itself to masochistic self-condemnation as a historical site of monstrous crimes and vested interests that prevent our rebuilding the world in the image of egalitarian truth. Protest, sarcasm towards authority and tradition, refusal to participate, and "speaking the truth to power" become the tokens of a genuinely political attitude. Over the past decade, this form of Leftism has been resurgent in the continental philosophy subfield in which I work. Radical hard Left positions have largely replaced the social constructionist liberal-Leftism of the 1990s, now widely dismissed as the sophistry of suburban language games. Alain Badiou and Slavoj Žižek, both of them revolutionary firebrands, have become the emblematic continental thinkers of our time.

But Down politics also comes in a Right version, if less frequently so. Here the supposed political knowledge leads us not to universal human equality, but to the evident superiority of philosophers over the masses. These beleaguered heroes must somehow exist amidst a multitude of inferiors who are blinded by facile commitment to national flags and permissive lifestyles, and even to religion, "considered by the people as equally true; by the philosopher, as equally false; and by the magistrate, as equally useful."[3] The central political question becomes how to prevent the masses from discovering how dangerous philosophers really are, so that philosophers will not be ostracized or even poisoned. This requires shrewd public rhetoric joined with coded esoteric writing, and sometimes outright political deception. This view of things can be found in Plato's *Republic* (though only if taken literally), and is also found today among numerous disciples of Leo Strauss, whose influence on recent American policy has been considerable.

What the Left and Right versions of Down politics share is the notion that politics ought to be built in the image of *truth*, and that truth faces various unfortunate obstructions that must be dealt with either through revolutionary violence or prudent aristocratic innuendo. Both versions presuppose that *someone* has access to the truth: the working class as a whole, the revolutionary avant garde, or the superior philosopher. Hence, both of these political philosophies must collapse if we discover that there is no such thing as unmediated political knowledge. And given that Latour is the mortal enemy of all forms of unmediated knowledge, it should be clear that he shares nothing in common with either of these positions. For Latour there is no transcendent truth that might be embodied in some ideal form of society. We can thus rename Down politics as "Truth Politics": not because it is true, but because it *thinks* it has the truth. Viewed from the Truth Politics of both Left and Right, Latour can only look like a sophist, since he denies all claims to direct knowledge of the truth.

This brings us to Up politics, named thus because it does not base politics on some underlying truth that governs appearance. Instead, politics becomes a power struggle without any transcendent court of appeal: a war of all against all in which seizing power for one's own standpoint becomes an end in itself. The Left version of the Up standpoint is familiar both from the identity politics of postmodernist intellectuals and from claims that desire is infinitely creative and must be subject to no sublimating social constraint. The Right version can be found in Thomas Hobbes, with his fear that transcendent appeals to religion or science will produce civil war by outflanking the somber power of the sovereign Leviathan. It can also be found in the dark German thinker Carl Schmitt, for whom politics begins when all common ground ends, when a "state of exception" is declared and politics is revealed for what it always is: a mortal struggle that separates all contenders into friends and enemies. The enemies are simply to be defeated, not annihilated as evil degenerate Satans, since any moralistic view of the enemy would require a transcendent viewpoint on justice and goodness that does not exist according to the partisans of Up.

What the Left and Right versions of Up politics share is the sense that politics cannot appeal to a truth lying elsewhere in order to settle its disputes, since politics itself *is* ultimately the truth. All struggle is a struggle for power or survival, with the hope that our friends may win and our enemies lose; it is not a struggle for truth against falsity. Note that both versions of Up political philosophies must collapse if it is shown that *there is* some standard of right and wrong or good and bad beyond the struggle itself. Up politics can be renamed as "Power Politics," already a widely familiar term. But whereas Latour's distance from Truth Politics is so obvious that no one would ever accuse him of belonging to that group, his relations with the Power Politics camp display much more complicity and ambiguity. Indeed, for long portions of his career Latour was not only mistaken for a Power Politician, but in many respects actually *was* one. We might even read Latour's entire career as a long effort to free himself from the mere power struggle of actants in order to regain some sort of access to a reality beyond power.

We now face a modern deadlock between Truth Politics and Power Politics, both of them coming in Left and Right forms and both of them emanating from the modernist dualism that Latour devotes his career to destroying. Truth Politics favors the truth of human nature over the shallowness of human culture, while Power Politics favors the immanence of human culture over the illusory depth of human nature. Later in the book we will consider whether Latour's attempted destruction of Truth Politics and Power Politics also leads to the dissolution of the political Left and Right. In the meantime, it will not do to dismiss Latour as a "bourgeois neoliberal Catholic," or some other piece of grandstanding rhetorical fuzziness. Though it is a prominent vice of the revolutionary Left to depict nearly every alternative view as "reactionary," Latour is simply not a reactionary. The case is far subtler than this. What he tries to do is to replace the modernist dilemma of Truth Politics and Power Politics with what I shall call "Object Politics," a reference to his use of terms such as *Dingpolitik* (thing politics) and object-oriented political philosophy. Is Latour able to define an Object Politics that does not succumb to the vices of Truth or Power Politics? Is he successful in establishing a pragmatist lineage for Object Politics by running it through John Dewey? Does the coming era of ecological troubles really entail Object Politics in the way Latour suggests? More generally, is Object Politics a viable program with concrete political consequences rather than just broad metaphysical ones? These are some of the questions that guided the writing of this book.

Yet I have also suggested that Latour is not an entirely neutral broker with respect to the four political positions outlined above (Left and Right Truth Politics, Left and Right Power Politics). When in doubt, Latour's political philosophy can be summarized roughly as follows: he is a liberally minded Hobbesian who adds inanimate entities to the political sphere. If forced at gunpoint to choose between the four positions above, he would probably choose the Hobbes/Schmitt pole of Right Power Politics, though without the remorseless dose of authoritarianism and reaction found in these authors. Having known Latour personally for fifteen years, I can safely describe him (*qua* voter, citizen, and reader of the news) as a politically benevolent French centrist with progressive tendencies, not as a sinister Machiavellian chess player. Yet Latour *qua* political philosopher is fascinated by Hobbes and Schmitt, insofar as his philosophy leaves no room for any transcendent truth that could guide political action. His science is a science of immanent networks devoid of things-in-themselves, just as his Catholicism is a borderline heretical religion of rituals and processions without a transcendent God. It would be nonsensical to call Latour a disciple of Marx, but not so ridiculous to call him a disciple of Schmitt. Yet Hobbes is an even better point of comparison. In July 2012, during a chance encounter with Latour on a sidewalk in Copacabana, we briefly discussed my plans for the present book. I asked about his earliest enthusiasm in political philosophy, and without hesitation he answered: "Hobbes." In retrospect, it was a question that hardly needed to be asked. If we take the word "King" in a figurative rather than literal sense, Latour might just as well have been speaking of himself in his 1991 summary of Hobbes:

> Civil wars will rage as long as there exist supernatural entities that citizens feel they have a right to petition when they are persecuted by the authorities of this lower world. The loyalty of the old medieval society—to God and King—is no longer possible if all people can petition God directly, or designate their own King. Hobbes wanted to wipe the slate clean of all appeals to entities higher than civil authority. He wanted to rediscover Catholic unity while at the same time closing off access to transcendence. (NBM 19)

Religion is not the only problem, since Hobbes also refuses transcendent appeals to nature by way of science. Consider his rejection of Robert

Boyle's experiment demonstrating the existence of a vacuum, as recounted by Latour:

> How can a society be made to hold together peacefully, Hobbes asks, on the pathetic foundations of matters of fact? He is particularly annoyed by the relative change in the scale of phenomena. According to Boyle, the big questions concerning matter and divine power can be subjected to experimental resolution, and this resolution will be partial and modest. Now Hobbes rejects the possibility of the vacuum for ontological and political reasons of primary philosophy, and he continues to allege the existence of an invisible ether that must be present, even when Boyle's worker is too out of breath to operate his pump. (NBM 22)

Each of the four political philosophies mentioned above runs obvious risks. There are Stalinist or Platonist dangers when the elites of Truth Politics try to rebuild society in the name of their purported truth, all consequences be damned. And Power Politics faces both Machiavellian and Relativist dangers when truth is thrown to the wind and we are left with nothing but struggles, without recourse to anything beyond struggle itself. My conception of Latour's political philosophy is that after beginning with a basically Hobbesian framework lacking transcendent courts of appeal, he gradually faces up to the drawbacks of this position. Latour's increasing insistence on our political *ignorance* is one index of his struggle to find standards that could soften the hard edge of Power Politics without recourse to a transcendent world of absolute knowledge. This leads him through Schmitt to the debate between Walter Lippmann and John Dewey, and thus to an "object-oriented" politics in which struggles are prompted by external irritants rather than feeding solely on themselves. Yet I shall also argue that Latour's solution remains too confined within his initial Hobbesian horizon to make a full escape from Power Politics, so that he always remains more tempted by Schmitt than by Marx or Rousseau. Nonetheless, there is a sense in which Latour is closer to being right than those who swallow Truth Politics whole. And furthermore, however much the critics have scratched their heads over Latour's importation of nonhumans into the political sphere, the age of climate politics is already upon us, and Latour's Object Politics is surely a more promising route to Gaia than any of the various brands of modern political philosophy.

Chapter 1 sets the basic terms of the discussion, reviewing the problems and clues that must guide us in the search for a Latourian political philosophy. Chapters 2, 3, and 4 consider the political philosophy of what

I shall term (admittedly with some appearance of cliché) early Latour, middle Latour, and late Latour. Though most philosophers have been robotically divided into early, middle, and late phases at some point in the scholarship about them, it will be shown in Latour's case that the division is justified. Chapter 5 considers various critiques of Latour from the Left, which I shall reinterpret as critiques based on Truth Politics. These critiques are fewer in number than might be expected, since the vast literature on Latour is not yet so vast where politics is concerned. The topic of Chapter 6 is Carl Schmitt as a good right-wing exemplar of Power Politics, and here we consider how various Left and Right treatments of Schmitt differ from Latour's own. Chapter 7 turns to the debate between Lippmann and Dewey, now one of the keystones of Latour's understanding of politics. The concluding Chapter 8 ties together the various threads of this book and looks ahead to how political philosophy might change in Latour's wake.

One of my guiding principles has been not to put words into the mouth of Bruno Latour. Since he is alive and well and still very much in his intellectual prime, it is not my place to speculate how Latour *might* speak about the political philosophies of Arendt, Grotius, Jefferson, Locke, Xenophon, or others about whom he has said little or nothing. Nor will I speculate about what he *might* say in the course of a longer engagement with Marx. In practice, this means that I have spoken mostly about those political philosophers discussed by Latour himself. One of the effects of this decision is that, while Chapter 6 deals directly with Schmitt and Chapter 7 directly with Lippmann and Dewey (all of them posthumous dialogue partners with Latour), Chapter 5 is concerned with Leftist commentators critical of Latour rather than with Marx and Foucault directly (since Latour has so far dealt with these figures only in passing).

The country where Latour is taken most seriously as a philosopher is still the Netherlands, the only place on earth where his books are usually sold together in the "Philosophy" section rather than dispersed through a confusing variety of shelves. Thus it is surely no accident that three Dutch authors have taught me more about Latour's political philosophy than anyone else: Gerard de Vries, Noortje Marres, and Peer Schouten. Since I am fortunate to know all three in person, my debt to them goes beyond those of their works cited below.

Will Viney at Pluto Press is the one who approached me about this project, and is also responsible for suggesting its catchy subtitle, a reference to Latour's own *Reassembling the Social*. His successor David Castle was unusually patient in enduring some unexpected delays in the completion of the book. Anthony Winder's remarkably alert copyediting greatly enhanced the quality of my prose. I should also thank the staff of the George A. Smathers Libraries at the University of Florida in Gainesville, who treated me as if I were a member of their own faculty. The American University in Cairo, my employer since the turn of the century, also deserves gratitude for generous research funding for this book.

But my greatest debt is to my wife, Necla Demir Harman, for enduring my manic writing schedule and many other things. Commuting from Ankara to Cairo would be an impossible arrangement if not for her constant support.

1

In Search of a Latourian Political Philosophy

At the time of this writing in early 2014, Bruno Latour is firmly established as one of the world's leading intellectuals. Not yet 70 years old, he has reached the point where his battles for influence have mostly been won. His work has been cited tens of thousands of times in so many disciplines that we have to regard Latour himself as personifying a new discipline. He has received Norway's lucrative Holberg Prize, that emerging Nobel of the human sciences. He has delivered the prestigious Gifford Lectures in Edinburgh, thus joining the ranks of such canonized philosophers as Hannah Arendt, Henri Bergson, William James, and Alfred North Whitehead. He has ranked as the tenth most cited book author in the humanities, just ahead of the formidable quartet of Sigmund Freud, Gilles Deleuze, Immanuel Kant, and Martin Heidegger.[1] Nor has Latour gone unappreciated at his home institution, having served as Vice President for Research at Sciences Po in Paris, one of Europe's most dynamic universities.

While none of this proves Latour's ultimate historical weight as a thinker, it certainly earns him the right and the burden of comparison with the names mentioned above. The names I have chosen are mostly those of philosophers; as a philosopher myself, I am more concerned with Latour's contributions to my own discipline than with his already celebrated achievements in the social sciences. And in philosophy, I am sorry to report, results are still delayed. Here Latour's battle for influence has barely begun, and is likely to continue beyond his own natural lifespan. It is sufficient to note that the same list that ranked Latour as the tenth most cited author in the humanities described him only with the headings "sociology, anthropology," though the "philosophy" tag was awarded freely to Michel Foucault, Jacques Derrida, and Judith Butler (all of them dismissed by some academic philosophers as charlatans) along with Noam Chomsky, Jean Piaget, and Roland Barthes (all of them further from disciplinary philosophy than Latour himself). Though academic categories are of little long-term importance, the problem is not just one of categories, since philosophers still do not seem to be reading Latour's books in significant numbers. In 2009 I published *Prince of Networks*, the first treatment of Latour as a pivotal figure in contemporary philosophy.[2] The primary aim of that book was to alert philosophically trained readers to a neglected major figure living in their midst. But so far, at least, the evidence suggests that *Prince of Networks* has served to introduce more social scientists to philosophy than philosophers to Latour. While I am delighted that *Prince of Networks* has reached such a large interdisciplinary audience, it is puzzling that Latour remains unread and sometimes even unknown in the continental branch of philosophy, where recent French authors can usually count on a warm reception and an optimistic hearing. Even so, his status in France has improved to the point where Patrice Maniglier could risk describing Latour as "the Hegel of our times" in the pages of *Le Monde* without sounding ridiculous.[3]

But since *Prince of Networks* has already made a detailed case for Latour as a philosopher, I shall not repeat the exercise here, and will behave in what follows as if Latour's recognition by philosophers were a *fait accompli*. The question guiding the present book is different: granted that Latour is a philosopher, can we find a political philosophy in his works? So far he has not written an explicit treatise on politics in the usual sense of the term, nor does he seem in any rush to do so. Yet the word "politics" can often be found in Latour's books, and not just in explicit titles such as *Politics of Nature* or "From Realpolitik to Dingpolitik." His work abounds with intriguing references to such political philosophers as Machiavelli, Hobbes, Schmitt, and more recently Dewey and Lippmann. In his early period Latour shows a tendency to identify the political sphere with reality as a whole, to such an extent that he is often accused of reducing truth to politics.[4] Yet the place of politics in his work remains visibly unsettled. In his more recent writings on the "modes of existence," Latour claims to renounce his earlier ontologization of politics, reframing it as just one mode among numerous others. These changes in his conceptions of politics, along with his evident worry over the possible overuse of political metaphors in his earlier work, indicate that the nature of the political sphere remains one of Latour's central concerns.

FOUR DANGERS

Before beginning, we should be aware of four pressing dangers that threaten political philosophy in the field that I shall call, without qualification or irony, "continental philosophy"—as opposed to the Anglo-American analytic philosophy that dominates university departments in most of the world. Reports of the death of the analytic/continental divide are highly premature, and the rampant claims that this division is "merely sociological" seem to imply (in rather un-Latourian fashion) that sociology deals only with figments of the imagination. Although Latour's star is probably still brighter in the Anglophone countries than in Germany and his native France, it is the continental philosophers of the latter nations with whom he is ultimately destined to be weighed: with Heidegger, Derrida, Foucault, and Deleuze, rather than analytic philosophers such as Saul Kripke, David Lewis, and W.V.O. Quine.

The first danger is that of relative silence about political philosophy, which is more common than might be expected. For while there have obviously been numerous works of political philosophy over the past century and a half, some of them quite memorable, many of the greatest philosophers during this period have had little to say about politics at all. Here I must agree with Leo Strauss, who complained that the most significant thinkers of the first half of the twentieth century (he meant Bergson, Whitehead, Husserl, and Heidegger) had offered surprisingly little to political philosophy in comparison with past figures of comparable rank.[5] We need not accept Strauss's call for a return to the ancients to accept his point that the major figures of philosophy had reached a political deadlock by the middle of the twentieth century: it is enough to compare Bergson with Spinoza, Husserl with Plato, Heidegger with Hegel, or Whitehead with Locke to grasp Strauss's point. Does Latour avoid this first danger? The answer is mixed. It is true that we find no detailed theory of government in his writings, and if you ask Latour in person about his political philosophy, his answer will not be as decisive as that of a Straussian or a Marxist.[6] In this respect he faces the same deadlock that continental philosophy has long faced in trying to pass from a general ontology of the world to the drawing of specific political consequences. Nonetheless, Latour's works are saturated with political concepts in a way that is obviously not true of Bergson, Husserl, or Whitehead, and in my view is not true of Heidegger either (despite the shrill charges of Emmanuel Faye that Heidegger's *entire philosophy* consists solely of Nazi propaganda).[7] In the writings of Latour such terms as force, alliance, and delegation are so ubiquitous that when we attempt to reconstruct his political philosophy, the trail is not altogether cold.

The second possible danger—the polar opposite of the first—is that of finding politics *everywhere* in philosophy rather than nowhere. This common defect takes on one of two possible forms. The first is to treat philosophy as the handmaid of politics, a problem often encountered on both the Left and the Right. On the Left there are those who hold philosophy to be worthless unless it messianically liberates humanity from the depredations of capital, as in McKenzie Wark's demanding lament that "perhaps the problem is not with correlationist philosophies but with philosophy *tout court*. If the philosophers were going to save us they would have done so already."[8] On the Right we find those who dismiss the supposed conceptual innovations of philosophy as "poetry," while treating philosophy in its own right primarily as a tool for the political hierarchizing of perennial human types. The late Stanley Rosen (a disciple of Strauss) is a good representative of such a position, revealing his private views in what looks at first like a summary of Nietzsche: "[T]here cannot be a radically unique creation … The fundamental task is one of rank-ordering types that have always occurred and will always exist."[9] For all the generational and political distance between Wark and Rosen, they are brothers in viewing philosophy as the servant of an ultimate political order known only to themselves and a handful of privileged masters and peers. This particular danger is not the one facing Bruno Latour, who is not sufficiently committed to any particular vision of political life to subordinate the rest of his thinking to it. Yet there is another way of mistakenly finding politics everywhere in philosophy: through the *ontologizing* of politics. Rather than treating philosophy as the vassal of a favored political cause, one might describe the whole of reality with political metaphors in a manner that blurs the distinction between the political and the non-political. We shall see that this danger, unlike the Wark-Rosen danger, haunts Latour throughout his early career. It is surely one of the chief motives for his more recent insistence that politics is merely one mode of existence among thirteen others. Latour's manner of navigating this danger, whether successfully or not, will be our concern in Chapter 4.

The third danger facing political philosophy in present-day continental circles comes from what Francis Bacon called the *Idola teatri*, or Idols of the Theater. It is always hard to step outside one's time and challenge the reigning political doctrine of the moment, which since the wonder year of 1989 has been a largely unchallenged model of representative democracy combined with a market economy. Yet we always frequent more than one theater at a time, and hence our idols can assume opposite forms simultaneously. For while it may be true that it is easier to imagine the end of the world than the end of capitalism (a remark often attributed to Frederic Jameson), it is now equally difficult to imagine a continental philosophy that would not be robotically committed to the axiom that capitalism must be reversed, destroyed, mocked, abhorred, or accelerated to the point of suicide. In short, if the Left remains sadly beleaguered in the contemporary world of malls and elections, continental philosophy faces the opposite problem of a crushing peer pressure under which everyone competes to rush to the left flank of everyone else, and to be seen in public as doing so more radically than everyone else.

Only recently did this atmosphere fall upon us once again. For several decades the mainstream political position of continental philosophers was a sort of unsurprising left-leaning liberalism. Those who counted as the leaders of continental philosophy in the 1980s and early 1990s spoke little of revolution, and limited themselves to taking often admirable stands on issues relatively un-risky among intellectuals: Apartheid, capital punishment, imperialism, greater opportunities for women. But the situation has now changed to the point where the hard Left is the only respectable place to be found. This may have begun with the mid-1990s ascendance of Deleuze, whose irreverent style and personal political track record seemed to hint at the wildest revolutions of desire. But over the past decade *de facto* rulership of continental philosophy has been assumed by Badiou and Žižek, communist sparkplugs who are willing to defend, respectively, Mao's Cultural Revolution and Stalin's forced collectivization. In this new intellectual climate there is immediate social payoff for proclaiming oneself a militant, calling for a total overthrow of the existing order, referring to mainstream liberals as "reactionaries," and airing gloomily nihilistic claims about the present human situation. Since Latour will never be mistaken for a radical Leftist, he provides a valuable source of intellectual friction for those who subscribe too easily to the views just mentioned. We consider Latour's relation to the Left in more detail in Chapter 5.

The final danger is one that confronts Latour specifically rather than continental philosophers as a whole. My original proposal for this book received unusually thorough and helpful feedback from four anonymous referees. One of them remarked a little skeptically that while it would be interesting to see what I had to say about Latour's political philosophy, it would probably just boil down to Latour arguing that "might makes right." This concern is understandable. After all, Latourian actor-network theory has little place for right that fails to acquire might by linking up with allies and arranging other entities in efficacious fashion. By Latour's own admission, he has often been unfair to the losers of history; his philosophical commitment to immanence often verges on a commitment to *victory*, since he allows little room for a transcendent right that would console the losers on a rainy day.

FOUR CLUES

Along with these four dangers, we also have four intriguing clues to guide us in piecing together Latour's political philosophy. The first has already been mentioned: the fact that Latour recently signalled a drastic change in the place of politics in his thinking. This was heralded in 2008 in his remarks at the London School of Economics:

> [W]e should not confuse ... the idea of multiplicity of beings and the consequent abandonment of the human-nonhuman distinction with any position about how to organize the polity. This is an entirely different question and ... relies on the specification of what is original in the political mode of existence, as different from laws as it is from reference, and so on. (PW 97)

Whereas the early Latour ably employs such terms as "democracy" to describe the ontological equality of humans and nonhumans, the later Latour seems to regret this flattening of all actors onto a single plane, and tries to re-establish distinctions between various different modes of existence. It is necessary to account for this shift in Latour's views on politics from the early phase to the late. Though normally I detest the method of cleanly dividing a thinker's career into discrete periods, we shall need to cut Latour's career not into two parts, but into three. If the Latour of the 1980s shows a snare-drummer's delight in depicting animate and inanimate entities as locked in a Machiavellian duel to the death, his emphasis in the 1990s and early 2000s shifts to politics as the careful fabrication of fragile networks in the name of civil peace. We treat these early and middle phases in Chapters 2 and 3, respectively, before shifting in Chapter 4 to Latour's late conception of politics as a rare and specific mode of existence.

A second clue can be found in Latour's great respect for politicians, quite unusual among intellectuals. As he puts it, "contempt for politicians is still today what creates the widest consensus in academic circles" (PF 245). But Latour could hardly disagree more with this consensus: "It takes something like courage to admit that we will never do better than a politician [... Others] simply have somewhere to hide when they have made their mistakes. They can go back and try again. Only the politician is limited to a single shot and has to shoot in public" (PF 210). We will never do better than a politician. Latour has no time for those beautiful souls who cling to the supposed purity of their principles while unable to bring victory to their cause. "What we despise as political 'mediocrity' is simply the collection of compromises that we force politicians to make on our behalf" (PF 210). A more common Latourian term for compromise is *mediation*, and mediation is at the heart of Latourian political philosophy just as it is at the heart of everything else he has written. For Latour we are mediocre not when we assemble actors in networks of associations, but when we strike poses in the name of principles without doing what it takes to have them win. An old military maxim tells us that amateurs talk strategy but professionals talk logistics. While these words are already Latourian enough, we might make them even more Latourian by writing: "Amateurs talk ends but professionals talk means." The mediations required to bring something about inevitably lead to a translation of our initial goals. Here Latour strikes a *realist* note that is clearly audible throughout his political theory, and that immediately puts him at odds with the ultimately Rousseauian notion that the primary meaning of politics is the removal of oppression.

This brings us to a third and related clue, found in an even more candid statement by Latour from the 2008 event at the London School of Economics:

> Can I add one more thing? Because usually it's true, I mean this is a common thing in political philosophy, that reactionary thinkers are more interesting than the progressive ones [*Laughter*] in that you learn more about politics from people like Machiavelli and [Carl] Schmitt than from Rousseau. And the exceptions are extremely rare, like [Walter] Lippmann (an example I owe to Noortje [Marres]). (PW 96)

If we were to hear Machiavelli or Schmitt say that "reactionary thinkers are more interesting than progressive ones," it would be cause for grim reflection rather than laughter. But the audience at the LSE can laugh rather than cringe precisely because Latour *is not* himself one of the reactionaries, despite finding them "interesting." This raises the following question: how might we find reactionary thinkers more interesting than progressives without joining the reactionaries ourselves? Or should we simply join them, if they are so much more interesting than the progressives? We discuss these questions in Chapter 6.

A fourth clue can be found in Latour's 2007 response to his longtime friend Gerard de Vries, who had tried to apply Aristotle to the tasks of Latourian philosophizing:

> In contrast to [de Vries], I do not believe that returning to Aristotle is helpful. I don't find much in the Greek ideal of the city that can be reused, unless one is giving commencement addresses in the neoclassic aula of so many of our campuses. Nodding to the busts of Demosthenes and Pericles once in a while can't do any harm, but the adequate resources might [lie] much closer at hand: instead of Aristotle, let's turn to the pragmatists and especially John Dewey ... [who], taking his cue from Walter Lippmann, [spoke of] "the problem of the public." Here is a Copernican Revolution of radical proportions: to finally make publics turn around topics that generate a public around them instead of trying to define politics *in the absence* of any issue. (RGDV 814–815)

This passage contains several noteworthy elements. We find an apparent lack of interest in ancient political philosophy, leading Latour to make the rather un-Latourian suggestion that ancient civilization lies too far in the past to be of use to us today. We also find Latour's enthusiasm (inspired by his former student Noortje Marres) for the American thinkers Dewey and Lippmann, which leads him to the equally un-Latourian claim that these authors enacted a "Copernican Revolution" of "radical" proportions in political philosophy. Third and most importantly, we find Latour's additional Marres-inspired view that politics is generated by *issues* rather than arising in a vacuum. In Chapter 7 we discuss Latour's desired synthesis of Lippmann and Dewey, before considering the prospects of post-Latourian political philosophy in Chapter 8.

A SOCIETY OF HUMANS AND NONHUMANS

Abraham Païs, the formidable biographer of Niels Bohr, shares the secret of Bohr's intellectual success in a charming passage: "[Bohr] explained how he had to approach every new question from a starting point of total ignorance."[10] Let's follow the illustrious example of Bohr, and start our discussions of Latour and political philosophy from zero. I can think of no better zero point than the ruins of the ongoing Congolese Civil War, where we find one of the most helpful analyses of Latour's politics so far. Peer Schouten, a young Dutch researcher at the University of Gothenburg in Sweden, has tried to apply the lessons of actor-network theory to the failure of the Congolese state. Concealed in the midst of Schouten's 2013 article on the materiality of state failure is a clear-headed assessment of Latour's relation to the well-known social contract tradition of modern political philosophy. Though contract theories come in many flavors, they agree in treating society as an artificial construction rising from a prior "state of nature," which was either brutal (Hobbes) or wondrous (Rousseau) depending on which tradition one favors.[11] The implications of one's choice are profound. The Hobbesian tradition views order as lucky salvation from global mortal combat, with the implication that political institutions are fragile constructions amidst environing chaos and therefore must not be flouted. By contrast, the Rousseauian tradition views order as inherently oppressive, and this turns *opposition* into the basic praiseworthy attitude towards the existing powers of society. Given this choice, Latour must be placed squarely on the Hobbesian side of the ledger given his constant emphasis on the fragile contingency of networks, such that critical opposition to them somehow misses the point.

Let's now turn to Schouten's helpful analysis of Latour in terms of social contract theory. The key for us is the second section of the article, "The 'Social' Contract," running from pages 555 through 563. Schouten's ironic use of quotation marks around the word "social" are meant to indicate Latour's well-known remodelling of the term. Whereas the social usually means people and excludes inanimate nature, Latour extends the term "society" to include every possible entity—whether humans, animals, machines, atoms, concepts, or fictional characters. Once "society" is refashioned in this extremely broad sense, it is clear that the usual meaning of "social contract" cannot survive, since this tradition takes little to no account of inanimate entities. Schouten first surveys the basic assumptions of his own academic field, international relations (usually abbreviated IR).

> IR as a discipline typically builds on the work of classical political philosophers and hinges fundamentally on understandings of sovereignty that derive from classical social contract theory. For the first and most famous of social contract theorists, Thomas Hobbes, in the state of nature—a state of being where interactions were unmediated by the state—life was literally a state of anarchy. (p.555)

In keeping with this Hobbesian picture, "IR metaphorically transposed the individual in the state of nature to the 'macro' level of the state in the anarchical international system—consider [Kenneth] Waltz's famous assertion that 'states in the world are like individuals in the state of nature'" (p.556). If we are committed to an actor-network approach, as seems to be the case with Schouten, what is wrong with the picture painted by IR? According to the traditional IR view, the anarchy of the state of nature is tamed by the sovereign state through various policing instruments, but this sovereign state then immediately enters a new state of nature, competing with other states using military instruments. In the sovereign state we find the sole locus of order, with anarchy swirling below and above. Moreover, the only ordering agent on the scene is *people*, in the form of the sovereign human or humans. In other words, the problem with this model is that it focuses on humans generally, and the state specifically, as the privileged sites of political order.

The Latourian contribution to this picture follows naturally from his basic innovation in ontology, which consists of a "flat" model in which all entities are equally real (though not equally *strong*) as long as they have some sort of effect on other entities. Latour is one of the great critics of modernism, which he defines as an artificial taxonomy splitting the world into "facts" on one side and "values" on the other: (1) rigid, inert objects of nature acting with clockwork mechanical precision, and (2) free and arbitrary human cultural projections ungrounded in external reality. This dualism still haunts much of present-day philosophy, and clearly haunts the tradition of modern political philosophy, which imagines (against the ancient tradition of society as always already there) an orderless state of nature tamed by the application of human culture. As Schouten complains about his own academic field:

> Classical political contract theory provided IR with the building blocks of a distinctively *social* political realm, and a *social* explanation of how modern societies can exist as stable spatio-temporal phenomena. This ontological commitment to the "social" in IR means that governmental power and its opposite, state failure, are understood exclusively in terms of pure human interactions. (pp.556–557)

Schouten's basic point about Latour (and about the present-day Congo) is that political stabilization relies on nonhuman actors even more than human ones. A group of naked people standing in a field would find it difficult to create durable institutions or power hierarchies. In Schouten's words, "[nonhuman] artefacts such as statistics, vessels, maps and sextants start to explain how humans can arrive at keeping relations stable and controlling them from a distance, allowing colonial expansion, state domination and 19th-century empires" (p.560). Rousseau already saw this in his *Discourse on the Origin of Inequality*, when discussing the need of chains and weapons to enslave one's fellow humans; though, true to form, he viewed such mediations merely negatively as instruments of oppression.[12] In Latour's case, on the contrary, it will turn out that only mediations can save us from the state of nature.

But here we have an apparent contradiction. At first it seemed as if Latour were opposed to the concept of the state of nature altogether, since social contract theory appears to inherit the most un-Latourian of all dualities: that between uncivilized nature and civilized culture. In fact Latour's relation to the Hobbesian tradition is ambivalent, and I will argue throughout this book that his tension with Hobbes is the engine of his entire political philosophy. Though Latour departs from Hobbes in important respects, he does so in the way that one departs from a cherished mentor or rival. Though it would be absurd to say that "Latour is a Rousseauian" or "Latour is a Marxist," the alternative statement that "Latour is a Hobbesian" hits on something close to the truth. We might even parrot Whitehead and say that "Latour's political philosophy is a series of footnotes to Hobbes," if not that it also needs to be read as an attempted mutation of Hobbes.

Schouten notes that despite Latour's incompatibility with the nature/culture divide that underlies social contract theory, "Latour most explicitly positions himself in terms of, and vis-à-vis, social contract theory."[13] Several Hobbesian elements are embedded in Latour's basic principles, including the background model of a power struggle between entities (a "war of all against all" in a broader sense than Hobbes intended), and the notion that any transcendence would threaten peace by allowing recourse to something beyond the sovereign political settlement. Perhaps more importantly, there is even the trace of a state of nature in Latour. As Schouten cleverly notes, this state of nature can be found in Latour's co-authored work on baboons: "Throughout his oeuvre, Latour consistently invokes baboons … In baboons, Latour found what comes closest to pure 'society,' that is, devoid of objects that interfere with interactions. Baboons are to Latour what Amerindians were to the classics" (p.558). In baboon society life consists of an endless series of direct, personal interactions, unmediated by structures or artefacts extending beyond the individual. Society exists, but lacks stability, since it must be renegotiated each time an encounter between baboons occurs. As Schouten notes, this leads Latour to a delightfully perverse theoretical inversion: "paradoxically, then, Latour's state of *nature* is purely 'social,' that is, made up only of interactions between humans (or baboons). What we have here is Latour's reconstruction of 'society' as IR wants us to believe it is: entirely composed of social processes and human (or baboon) politics" (p.559). That is to say, IR's classical solution to the state of nature (the emergence of politics among living creatures) represents for Latour the very state of nature that we should hope to exit. So the only way to escape the unmediated interactions of primitive pure society is through mediated interactions, and this mediation is more durable when it occurs by way of inanimate things. Let's quote from Schouten's fine article one last time: "[Latour's] Leviathan—or political society—is in the first place the result of introducing *nonhuman* entities that give durability and 'body' to social arrangements" (p.559).

BABOONS AND THE STATE OF NATURE

Latour's interest in baboons was sparked by his early collaboration with the primatologist Shirley Strum of UC San Diego; the results of their joint work are nicely summarized in a co-authored 1984 symposium paper. Strum and Latour begin their paper with what might be read as a comical dig at the Hobbesian state of nature: "Pre-scientific folk ideas about baboons claimed that they were a disordered gang of brutes, entirely without social organization, roaming around at random" (BAB 786). Yet over time an increasing amount of social order was observed among them: "The trend has been in the direction of granting baboons more and more social skill and more social awareness ... These skills involve negotiating, testing, assessing and manipulating" (BAB 788). Rather than stating glibly that baboon society is structured by male dominance, or something along those lines, we must ask, "how do baboons know who is dominant or not? Is dominance a fact or an artefact?" (BAB 788). Stated differently, "baboons are not *entering into a stable structure* but rather negotiating what the structure will be, and monitoring and testing and pushing all other such negotiations ... If there were a [pre-existent social] structure to be entered, why all this behavior geared to testing, negotiating, and monitoring?" (BAB 788). Here we find one of the key aspects of Latourian political philosophy never found in Hobbes, since Latour (along with co-author Strum) "shifts the emphasis from looking for the social link in the *relations between actors* to focusing on *how* actors achieve this link in their search for what society is" (BAB 785). Or again, "shifting or stable hierarchies might develop not as one of the principles of an overarching society into which baboons must fit, but as the provisional outcome of their search for some basis of predictable interactions" (BAB 789). Whereas state-of-nature theorists tell a once-and-for-all story about how nature gave way to culture (whether for good or ill), it is typical of Latour that the nature of the political always remains somewhat *unknown*. This links Latour with the philosophical tradition of politics inaugurated by Socrates (philosophy in the sense of *love* of wisdom, not wisdom) despite Latour's consistent misreading of Socrates as an epistemological tyrant. Latour should at least prefer Socrates' political philosophy of uncertainty to the false certainty of Émile Durkheim, for as the young Latour writes in 1986: "[S]ince Durkheim, social scientists have considered political philosophy to be the prehistory of their science. Sociology had become a positive science only once it stopped bickering about origins of society and instead *started with* the notion of an all-embracing society that could then be used to explain various phenomena of interest" (PA 269). Here we see what political philosophy really means for Latour: the insight that the *polis* is not pre-given, but is an ongoing problem or mystery even for those who inhabit it.

Let's concede, at any rate, that baboons no longer seem to be a disordered gang of brutes roaming around at random. If this is true then there is no state of nature even among baboons, let alone among humans. All societies are always already complex. But if all are complex, not all are *complicated*, a subtle terminological distinction that for Strum and Latour marks the threshold separating humans from baboons. The plight of baboons is signalled early in the article: "If actors have only themselves, only their bodies as resources, the task of building stable societies will be difficult" (BAB 790). The intensity of interactions among individual baboons makes for obvious volatility. But already with hunter-gatherer humans, something new has occurred. These hunter-gatherers "are rich in material and symbolic means to use in constructing society compared to baboons, although impoverished by comparison with modern industrial societies. Here, language, symbols and material objects can be used to simplify the task of ascertaining and negotiating the social order" (BAB 791). As human society grows more complicated, it is paradoxically simplified: "modern scientific observers replace a complexity of shifting, often fuzzy and continuous behaviors, relationships and meanings with a complicated array of simple, symbolic, clear-cut items. It is an enormous task of simplification" (BAB 791). Already with sedentary agricultural civilization, "the social bond can be maintained in the relative absence of the individuals" (BAB 792). Human society is in no way made solely or even principally of people, but requires fences, coins, uniforms, monuments, ships, flags, wedding rings, and highways in order to stabilize itself. Nonetheless, the scope of the word "social" has continually narrowed: "Starting with a definition which is coextensive with all associations, we now have, in common parlance, a usage [of 'social'] that is limited to what is left after politics, biology, economics, law, psychology, management, technology and so on, have taken their own parts of the associations" (BAB 794).

In other words, though all societies are mediated, some are more mediated than others. Relying on this tacit principle, Strum and Latour proceed to offer a remarkably ambitious theory of the different degrees of both animal and human society, as summarized in a table on page 794 of their paper. A first division is made between asocial animals that flee other individuals and social animals that respond more constructively to the behavior of others of the same species. The latter type can be split into those that diversify by way of body types rather than social realities: "Insect societies are an example where the actors' own bodies are irreversibly molded," whereas in other animals "the genotypes produce similar phenotypes [and] these phenotypes are then manipulated by the ever-increasing social skills of individuals" (BAB 795). The latter sort are divided, in turn, into two further kinds: "Baboons provide an example of the first ... They have nothing more to convince and enlist others in their definition than their bodies, their intelligence and a history of interaction built up over time" (BAB 795). By contrast, "we have the human case where the creation of society uses material resources and symbols to simplify the task" (BAB 795). Nor does the branching cease once we enter the human sphere: "'primitive' societies are created with a minimal amount of material resources; increasing such resources produces 'modern' societies. Thus technology becomes one way of solving the problem of building society on a larger scale. In this sense even modern technology is social" (BAB 796).

Here we encounter an ambiguity that haunts Latour's entire philosophy, and especially his political philosophy. On the one hand "mediation" is an ontological category for Latour, since even at the purely physical level we never find any interaction that is not mediated by some third entity. On the other hand, "mediation" also functions as a criterion for measuring the degree of complication of any specific scenario. The first horn of this dilemma defines the status of politics in Latour's early period, as when Strum and Latour write: "Politics is not one realm of action separated from the others. Politics, in our view, is what allows many heterogeneous resources to be woven together into a social link that becomes increasingly harder and harder to break" (BAB 797). In this sense *absolutely everything* is political, since we have already learned that in Latour's universe absolutely everything consists of "heterogeneous resources woven together into a social link." If everything is political in this early stage of Latour's thinking, one might suspect that *none* of it is actually political. As we shall see, Latour tries over the years to resolve this lingering problem. But for now at least, we have secured one of the key Latourian political innovations: the way in which nonhuman entities are woven into the political fabric as agents of stabilization.

This theme is so important for Latour's political philosophy that we should take a moment to note how ubiquitous it is in Latour's early and middle periods. In 1986, with Latour not yet 40 years old, we read his rather typical call for

> an alternative way of defining sociology [by making] it the study of *associations* rather than of those few ties that we call social ... [The analyst] can use all the forces that have been mobilized in our human world to explain why we are linked together and that some orders are faithfully obeyed and others are not. These forces are heterogeneous in character: they may include atoms, words, lianas or tattoos. (PA 277)

An important article of 1991, the time of Latour's manifesto *We Have Never Been Modern*, begins as follows:

> For a long time social theory has been concerned with defining power relations, but it has always found it difficult to see how domination is achieved. In this paper I argue that in order to understand domination we have to turn away from an exclusive concern with social relations and weave them into a fabric that includes non-human actants, actants that offer the possibility of holding society together as a durable whole. (TSD 103)

In 1994, following another tip of the hat to Shirley Strum, Latour asks:

> Why would the enrollment of nonhumans be of any use? Because they can *stabilize* social negotiations ... They are at once pliable and durable; they can be shaped very fast, but, once shaped, they last much longer than the interaction that has fabricated them. Social interactions, on the other hand, are extremely labile and transitory. (PRG 803)

So much the worse for baboons. There is also the marvelous 1996 article "On Interobjectivity," which despite its title has nothing to say about object-object interactions, but which lucidly rephrases the lesson of ape society while linking it with the theme of the social contract. For instance: "[T]he new sociology of simians ... depicts actors who cannot attain anything without negotiating at length with others. The simplest case is that of a chimpanzee that does not dare to continue eating at a rich food source it has discovered because the troop is moving on and it cannot stay behind alone" (INT 228). And further: "Each monkey poses itself the question of knowing who is stronger or weaker than itself, and develops trials that permit it to decide the matter" (INT 232). Whereas "monkeys almost never engage with objects in their interactions ... for humans it is almost impossible to find an interaction that does not make some appeal to technics" (INT 238). Better yet, nonhuman entities serve as firewalls protecting us from the constant social anxiety that plagues our primate cousins: "While I am at the counter buying my postage stamps and talking into the speaking grill, I don't have family, colleagues, or bosses breathing down my neck. And, thank heavens, the server doesn't tell me stories about his mother-in-law, or his darlings' teeth" (INT 233). Rather than having to construct society out of a formless state of nature, humans are involved in a systematic process of *desocialization*, using nonhuman entities to mediate interaction with our fellows. In turn, this frees us from the false modern mystery of how society emerged from brute nature: "By finding already present 'in nature' such a high level of sociability, human sociology finds itself freed from the obligation to found the social, contrary to the hoary tradition in political philosophy and to theories of the social contract" (INT 229). If Latour is in some sense a Hobbesian, he nonetheless remains a Hobbesian with no state of nature—not even as a minimal thought experiment. Though Schouten is right to identify baboon society as embodying the state of nature for Latour, this is true only in a comparative sense. Mediations are present in baboon society just as everywhere else, but some mediations (those involving nonhuman entities such as contracts, uniforms, names, and property rights) are more mediated than others.

A DISPERSED LEVIATHAN

Yet we can find even more direct references by Latour to Hobbes. At the astonishingly early date of 1981 (when Latour would have been a cherubic 34 years old) he and Callon published an important essay entitled

"Unscrewing the Big Leviathan." This devilish little piece gives us further orientation as to Latour's early debt to Hobbesian political philosophy. The basic strategy of Callon and Latour's article is to claim that Hobbes already knew what actor-network theory now knows, with just a few important omissions. Hobbes is misunderstood when read as giving greater ontological status to the Leviathan state than to anything else, since in fact there is no difference of scale for Hobbes no matter what entity we might be considering. While this may be a stretch as a reading of Hobbes, it is rather illuminating as to how the young Latour and Callon view their own work.

How can the *bellum omnium contra omnes*, the war of all against all that typifies the state of nature, be brought to an end? "Everyone knows Hobbes's reply: through a contract that every man makes with every other and which gives one man, or a group of men bound to no other, the right to speak on behalf of all" (UNS 278). But while the Leviathan is usually depicted as a monstrous central power, "the construction of this artificial body is calculated in such a way that the absolute sovereign is nothing other than the sum of the multitude's wishes ... He says nothing without having been authorized by the multitude, whose spokesman, mask-bearer, and amplifier he is" (UNS 278). Or stated more colorfully, "he is the people itself in another state—as we speak of a gaseous or a solid state" (UNS 278). The way the multitude becomes a single Leviathan has to do with processes of *translation*, that most Latourian of all Latourian concepts. If Hobbesian political philosophy involves a single translation of right from the multitude to the sovereign, Latour's political philosophy wants to spread translation throughout the universe, between all sizes of human social bodies and even between humans and inanimate beings. The difficulty is that Hobbes's solution has overshadowed the *problem* he uncovered: the problem of translation itself. "The originality of the problem posed by Hobbes is partly concealed by his solution—the social contract—which history, anthropology, and now ethology have proved impossible" (UNS 279). The problem with the social contract theory is that it "displays, in legal terms, at society's very beginnings, in a once-and-for-all, all-or-nothing ceremony, what processes of translation display in an empirical and a reversible way, in multiple, detailed, everyday negotiations" (UNS 279). If we can just turn Hobbes into a general theorist of translation then all will be well, and we can explain how many actors are able to act as one: not just in the case of multitudinous humans combining in a single state, but in any case where multiple entities act as a single force. The problem is urgent, since "no sociologists at present examine macro-actors and micro-actors using the same tools and the same arguments" (UNS 280), a claim that was no doubt true at the time.

Already in 1981, baboons appear at the founding of Latour's political theory. Hobbes assumed that society and politics first appear in the human realm. Animals were regarded as merely a "herd of brute beasts—eating, mating, howling, playing and fighting one another in a chaos of hair and fangs—[which] surely tallies closely with the 'state of nature' postulated by Hobbes. Without any doubt at all, the life of a baboon is 'poor, nasty, brutish, and short'" (UNS 281). But as we already learned from Strum, a rather different picture emerged once baboons were studied: they turned out to be even more painfully social than humans, and utterly lacking in non-baboonish mediators. "One animal does not go close to just any other; an animal does not cover or groom another by chance; nor does it move aside just at random; animals cannot go just where they wish" (UNS 280). And further, "the famous elementary impulses which fuel the war of all against all—eating, copulating, domination, reproduction—have been observed to be constantly suspended, halted and diffracted by the play of social interactions. There is no chaos, but no rigid system either" (UNS 282). To create a more durable society than this, as we have seen, means going beyond direct baboon interactions and incorporating stronger and more inert materials into our society: "in the state of nature, no one is strong enough to hold out against every coalition. But if you transform the state of nature, replacing unsettled alliances as much as you can with walls and written contracts, the ranks with uniforms and tattoos and reversible friendships with names and signs, then you will obtain a Leviathan" (UNS 284). And again:

> The primatologists omit to say that, to stabilize their world, the baboons do not have at their disposal any of the human instruments manipulated by the observer ... The ethnomethodologists forget to include in their analyses the fact that ambiguity of context in human societies is partially removed by a whole gamut of tools, regulations, walls and objects of which they analyze only a part. We must now gather up what their analysis leaves out and examine with the same method the strategies which enlist bodies, materials, discourses, techniques, feelings, laws, organizations. (UNS 284)

The world is not made up of nature on one side and culture on the other, but only of actors. "What is an 'actor'? Any element which bends space around itself, makes other elements dependent upon itself and translates their will into a language of its own" (UNS 286). Though all actors are born equal, they do not die equal: some actors manage to establish asymmetries that make themselves stronger than the others, turning themselves into obligatory passage points that others must traverse. Callon and Latour show this with a brief case study of the duel in France between Renault and EDF (the French electric utility) over the future of electric cars, a duel in which Renault initially looks like the loser but is able to reverse its fortunes and emerge triumphant by undercutting EDF's allies and empowering its own. Through this case study we see that, "contrary to what Hobbes states … certain actors become the Form of the Leviathan's body and certain others its Matter" (UNS 289). Initially, the situation is as follows:

> an actor like EDF clearly displays how the Leviathan is built up in practice—and not juridically. It insinuates itself into each element, making no distinction between what is from the realm of nature (catalysis, texture of grids in the fuel cell), what is from the realm of the economy (cost of cars with an internal combustion engine, the market for buses) and what comes from the realm of culture (urban life, Homo automobilis, fear of pollution). (UNS 288–289)

But with a few deft reversals, Renault again becomes master of the situation: "Renault discovers that, by using electronics, [the internal combustion engine] can be perfected so as to be unbeatable for several decades" (UNS 291). This constant reversibility of power is one of those features of Latour's philosophy that is most incompatible with the views of the political Left, which tends to fix poles of power as asymmetrical "oppressor" and "oppressed" terms.

As seen earlier, we cannot make humans the sole locus of politics without considering the role of nonhumans. That is to say, "we cannot analyze the Leviathan if we give precedence to a certain type of association, for example associations of men with men, iron with iron, neurons with neurons, or a specific size of factors. Sociology is only lively and productive when it examines *all associations with at least the same daring as the actors who made them*" (UNS 292). This foreshadows Latour's later infatuation with the forgotten French sociologist Gabriel Tarde, who (unlike Durkheim) found societies even amidst the ostensibly inanimate realm of chemicals, atoms, and stars.[14] Against the single super-sovereign Leviathan of nightmare, "there is not just *one* Leviathan but many, interlocked one into another like chimeras, each one claiming to represent the reality of all, the programme of the whole" (UNS 294). This is roughly the same Nietzschean vision of will to power expressed aphoristically by Latour a few years later in his crucial work *Irreductions*. Though it is "impossible not to be terrified ... by the flood of speeches Leviathans make about themselves" (UNS 295), they are actually weak and mutable, often losing power more quickly than their sad detractors expect. Yet at other times they can be maddeningly stable, "being encumbered and weighed down with the enormous technical devices they have secreted in order to grow ..." (UNS 295). Leviathans are no more or less stable than a city, in which "constantly—but never at the same time—streets are opened, houses razed to the ground, watercourses covered over. Districts previously thought out-of-date or dangerous are rehabilitated; other modern buildings become out of fashion, and are destroyed" (UNS 295).

In this way, Hobbes is reinterpreted as a general theorist of translation. Callon and Latour admit that there are limits to this reading: "Hobbes restricted this process of translation to what we now call 'political representation'... And yet it is a very long time now since 'political representation' was alone sufficient to translate the desires of multitude" (UNS 296). Even political critique requires that we remove the focus on human political sovereigns and representatives, since doing so leaves the ruling powers safely ensconced: "[analysts] 'restrict themselves to the study of the social.' They then divide the Leviathan into 'reality levels' leaving aside ... the economic, political, technical and cultural aspects in order to restrict themselves to what is 'social'... The Leviathans purr with relief, for their structure disappears form view, whilst they allow their social parts to be sounded" (UNS 298). Sociologists have no privileged vantage point on this process, for "there is no 'metadiscourse'—to speak archaically—about the Leviathan ... Sociologists are neither better nor worse than any other actors" (UNS 298–299). If they confine themselves to the social, they "[affix] seals onto the black boxes, and once again [guarantee] that the strong will be secure and the cemeteries peaceful—filled with lines of hermetically closed black boxes crawling with worms" (UNS 300). What the theory of translation teaches us, by contrast, is that "it is no more difficult to send tanks into Kabul than to dial 999. It is no more difficult to describe Renault than the secretary who takes telephone calls at the Houston police station" (UNS 299). Callon and Latour aim this same arrow at the Marxist Left, though they bury their bold remark deep in a footnote, as so often happens with young researchers: "It is not Marxism that helps interpret what is beneath Hobbes's theory; it is, on the contrary, the latter that might explain what is beneath the former" (UNS 302, note 10).

GENERAL REFLECTIONS

This opening chapter was meant to set the stage for our inquiry into Latour's political philosophy. We have seen that Latour can fruitfully be viewed as a political descendant of Hobbes, though with all the signs of protracted struggle usually found in the dependence of any gifted thinker on a previous one. In the next three chapters we follow this struggle through three periods of Latour that I have termed early, middle, and late, a classification that will prove to be justified despite its surface banality. In the first place, the existence of a late period is even more obvious in Latour's case than in those of Heidegger or Wittgenstein, since his recent "modes of existence" project begins with an explicit limitation on the earlier actor-network theory. And as concerns political philosophy (if not ontology), the actor-network period needs to be split in half in its own right. The reason is that Latour's early love affair with Hobbes fades abruptly in 1991 with *We Have Never Been Modern,* in which Hobbes is suddenly treated as no better than his opponent, the natural scientist Robert Boyle. For the first time in Latour's career, there is an explicit sense that Hobbesian Power Politics is no better than Boylean Truth Politics. On this basis, we can take 1991 as the turning point between early and middle Latour. Yet we still cannot pinpoint a start or end date for the late Latour. For on the one hand, as long as Latour is alive and well and working at the peak of his powers, we cannot predict whether the "modes" period will lead to yet another new phase in the years to come. And on the other hand, we cannot even point to an exact start date for the late period, for a reason that is probably unique in the history of philosophy. Namely, since the work of the late Latour began in secret in the late 1980s, it was actually simultaneous with the early and middle periods. As an analogy, imagine that Heidegger had already written the *Contributions to Philosophy* during his youthful Marburg years but not published it, or if Wittgenstein had penned the *Philosophical Investigations* early and in secret right under Bertrand Russell's mentoring nose. For the purposes of this book, I shall take *The Pasteurization of France* (1984) to be typical of the early Latour's political philosophy, *Politics of Nature* (1999) as emblematic of the middle period, and *An Inquiry into Modes of Existence* (2012) as the obvious exemplar of Latour's late period.

But before moving on to the early Latour, let's review some of the landmarks established so far. By my count, we are already in a position to deduce at least eight key features of Latour's political philosophy:

1. Latour's rejection in ontology of the modern dualism between mechanical nature and arbitrary culture entails, politically, a rejection of the modern split between the state of nature and a society constructed *ex nihilo*. There was never a state of nature, not just because it is a highly unlikely or unverifiable fiction (many critics have already said this) but because there cannot be any situation that is free of mediation. Even baboons are not just drooling, copulating gluttons, but already live in a painfully complex society.

2. If there was never any state of nature, then *a fortiori* there was never a "bad" or "good" state of nature. No decision between these is either possible or relevant. Hence, Latour cannot advocate either the strongly authoritarian politics that tends to follow from theories of a bad state of nature, or the romantic and revolutionary politics that opposes a basically good state of nature to a basically corrupt and unequal society. In short, Latour cannot accept either Right or Left politics in their standard modern forms.

3. For the very same reason, neither "reaction" nor "revolution" are adequate models of politics for Latour. The former seeks to ground politics either in natural right or in unquestionable sovereign authority, while the latter tries to ground it either in natural human equality or the irreducible character of diversity in a world devoid of absolute truth. If viewed through Latourian lenses, neither of these can be considered a valid analysis of the world.

4. Latour has a paradoxical attitude towards mediation. On the one hand, there is always and only mediation: not just in baboon society but (in the manner of Tarde) all the way down through insect society into the realm of inanimate matter itself. Mediation is a global ontological category. But on the other hand, there are degrees of mediation, since the more mediations that exist, the more advanced the society. Latour and Strum are partly able to address this paradox by pointing to specific *kinds* of mediation that entail various jumps in types of society. Insects use different body types as mediators, baboons use purely social relations, hunter-gatherers use things, agricultural societies use durable markers, and industrial societies use machines and higher-order symbolic mediations. Yet the basic tension remains. There has never been anything other than mediation, yet at the same time it is good to create *even more* mediation.

5. Whereas Hobbes speaks of an overarching sovereign Leviathan expressing the will of its subjects, Latour and Callon invoke a multitude of distributed Leviathans found in countless locations. The question

of sovereignty occurs not just at one political point, but everywhere. This runs the obvious risk of an ontologization of politics. As Gerard de Vries will later teasingly put it, Latour seems committed to a politics of "mini-kings."[15]

6. Despite his widespread distribution of sovereignty among countless actors, Latour in his early period remains committed to something like a Hobbesian "war of all against all," or a Nietzschean duel of centers of power in which each tries to master the others without appeal to any higher authority. This is the grain of truth in the charges that for Latour, "might makes right."

7. Since neither the unique sovereign nor the free human subject can serve as the center of political philosophy for Latour, *institutions* must form that center. Only institutions can provide some durability against the backdrop of drooling baboon society. It follows that our *primary* attitude towards institutions should be to build and extend them rather than critique or destroy them. This is the grain of truth in occasional complaints from the Left that Latour is a basically conservative thinker. His *primary* political concern is not that oppressive injustices need to be torn to the ground so that we may start from scratch (the basic attitude of the Left), but that stronger and better connections need to be built between actors. As might be expected from the title of his most famous book, Latour is as resolutely non-modern in his politics as in everything else. He does not aspire to rebuild the world in the shape of some particular idea of how things ought to be built (as the Left generally wishes).

8. Perhaps the most important reason that Latour has no such aspiration is that in his view *we never really know* what actors are, or what their best possible links might be. We must test these links no less carefully than baboons do, rather than ripping down whole political neighborhoods in the name of some perfect model. Revolutionary aspirations in politics tend to go hand-in-hand with philosophical *idealisms* (and materialism is just another form of idealism, as Latour argues in "Can We Get Our Materialism Back, Please?"), which hold that truth is directly accessible to rational procedure. Latour is deeply committed to the notion that actors always *outrun* our conceptions of them. This entails a politics of careful experimentation, not fiery outbursts of indignation.

2

Early Latour: A Hannibal of Actants

For the purposes of political philosophy, the spirit of the early Latour can be detected not only by publication date (roughly through 1991), but also from the tone of carefree celebration with which Latour depicts the power struggles of human and inhuman entities. During this period, as a general rule, appeals to anything over and above the successful assembling of networks of allies are viewed with suspicion. The actor-network heroes of the early Latour may not be Machiavellian dictators or military butchers, but there are numerous smiles for those entrepreneurs of theory who know how to mix inanimate scientific entities with other sorts of non-theoretical allies. James Watson's self-portrayal in *The Double Helix* comes to mind, with his successful fusion of theory, hunches, laboratory politics, grant report technicalities, and gossip.[1] Even for the early Latour, it is less a matter of "might makes right" than the view that right that never takes the trouble to attain might has a futile or even pathetic character about it. Consider the following passage from Latour's famous book of 1987, *Science in Action*:

> No matter what a paper did to the former literature, if no one else does anything with it, then it is as if it never existed at all. You may have written a paper that settles a fierce controversy once and for all, but if readers ignore it, it cannot be turned into a fact; it simply cannot. You may protest against the injustice; you may treasure the certitude of being right in your inner heart, but it will never go further than your inner heart; you will never go further in certitude without the help of others. (SA 40)

It is less a matter of contempt for those who fail to assemble the needed allies than of realizing that there is simply *no room* in Latour's philosophy for a transcendent right that could be cheated by might.

LATOUR ON MACHIAVELLI

Having already considered Latour's relation to Hobbes, we might also reflect on his relation to an even more sinister figure in the history of philosophy: Niccolò Machiavelli. There are already numerous methods available either for excusing Machiavelli outright or diminishing the threat represented by his most famous book. One way is to join Whitehead in asserting that if Machiavellian behavior seems to work, it will not work for very long. Referring in conversation either to Mussolini or Stalin (it is unclear from the context), Whitehead remarks: "He has read Machiavelli … and Machiavelli wrote the rules for a short-term success, of from five to fifteen years."[2] There is also Machiavelli's own excuse for *The Prince*, which is that he portrays people as they are rather than as they ought to be—a statement of serious philosophical significance, given its step towards a politics of "immanence." There is also the more usual absolution of Machiavelli, which is to say that his "true" political views are found not in *The Prince* but in his *Discourses on Livy*, where the stereotypical Machiavelli of deceptions and strangulations is not to be found.

In 1988 Latour puts an interesting spin on this old *Prince* vs. *Discourses* trope, insisting that the two books contain the same teaching:

Machiavelli, a republican at heart, established the foundations of democracy in his *Discourses on the First Decade [Ten Books] of Livy*. In spite of this he is often taken as a dangerous and amoral cynic because he wrote *The Prince*. In practice, however, the two works are one and the same: if democracy is to be stable the harsh realities of power have to be understood. (PFM 1)

Machiavelli as a democratic theorist! The theory of democracy Latour offers here is intriguing. Though Hannibal used both strategy and inhuman cruelty to keep his massive North African army together in Italy for more than a decade, we should not draw an arbitrary distinction between the strategy part of Hannibal and the cruelty part: "In his book [*The Prince*] Machiavelli offers a set of rules which go beyond the distinction between good and evil made by moralists, citizens, or historians … For example acting virtuously should be neither the rule nor the exception but one possibility among others" (PFM 1–2). The passage is pitched as a description of Machiavelli, but we can already detect the early Latour's own position as well. Though Latour himself is a perfectly agreeable twenty-first century man who would never imitate Hannibal's reported cruelties (robberies, murders, forcing a captive to fight an elephant), his early political philosophy also has a "beyond good and evil" flavor to it, even if the Machiavellian moments in his case histories never strike us as morally vile.

Latour's real objection to Machiavelli, like his objection to Hobbes, is not to the lack of any moral standard. Instead, he objects to the failure of the two thinkers to grant a sufficient role to nonhuman actors. Latour at this early stage seems allergic to any moralistic conception of politics: "If you want to be virtuous, [Machiavelli] says, you need much more than your self-righteous sense of morality, you need many more allies, many of whom will betray you. Instead of concerning yourself with ethics, enlist allies, fight enemies and beware of all" (PFM 2). In Latour's eyes, the real defect of Machiavelli is to be found in his excessively human-centered conception of the world: "The machinations [Machiavelli] described are based on passions and manipulations of other men. The only non-human allies that he explicitly adds to the *combinazione* are fortresses and weapons" (PFM 2). And again: "Machiavelli builds his plots by keeping men in check through the handling of other men who are in turn kept in line by other men. Thus his world is a *social* one. To constantly repair the decaying social order, social forces are, if not the only, at least the main resource" (PFM 2). In today's world this is not true, "and this is why Machiavelli's world, no matter how troubled and bloody, appears to us, by contrast, a fresh and easy one to understand, and why his astute stratagems seem to us disarmingly naïve compared to those we have to entangle today" (PFM 2). It is no longer just a question of popes, generals, mercenaries, and princesses. Instead, "to the age-old passions, treacheries and stupidity of men or women, we have to add the obstinacy, the cunning, the strength of electrons, microbes, atoms, computers, missiles. Duplicity indeed, since the Princes always have two irons in the fire: one to act on human allies, the other to act on non-human allies" (PFM 3). After quoting Machiavelli to the effect that humans are so wretchedly fickle that they must be kept in line by fear, Latour remarks humorously but sincerely:

> Clever indeed, but how [much more clever] it is to bind together men, these wretched creatures that are always ready to break their contracts and go to gas companies or to competitors, by wires, meters, copper, and filament lamps. Instead of a tiny list that includes love and fear, the modern Prince has a long mixed list that includes many other elements in addition to love and fear. (PFM 9)

Having established a greater "biodiversity" of struggling actors than Machiavelli's human-centered vision allowed, Latour takes aim at the Marxist tradition for similar errors. "[Marx] placed the Prince—renamed capitalist—in a class struggle so that whenever a machine or a mechanism was introduced in the production process, it was to displace, replace, unskill, humiliate, and discipline the workers" (PFM 7). The primary function of machines was supposedly to replace rebellious workers and thereby keep them in line. But in cases where the opposite happens, Marxists are at a loss:

> Whenever the introduction of a machine does *not* attack the workers, many Marxists are left speechless and start talking about technical factors and other determinisms. When a machine does deskill textile workers they know what to say; when companies create new highly skilled workers they see this as a puzzling exception, or even, in [Donald] MacKenzie's terms as an "obverse trend." (PFM 7)

Marxism is a philosophical idealism ("materialism" for Latour being just another form of idealism) that, at least as much as Machiavellianism, treats the entire world in terms of a struggle between people:

> Marxists have moved only reluctantly from the tenet that the only way to prove that "technology is socially shaped"—their words—is by showing the class struggle at work. The idea rarely dawns on them that a Prince might have more than two enemies—the workers and other Princes—and that, struggling on many fronts at once, he might from time to time need highly skilled and independent-minded collaborators to resist, for instance, other Princes. (PFM 7–8)

Latour's reading of Machiavelli is similar to his reading of Hobbes, with a mostly appreciative attitude visible in both cases. Both Machiavelli and Hobbes avoid a model of politics in which truth is distorted by regrettable political factors, since trials of strength are all that exist. Reality means that which resists such trials. There is no dualistic opposition between natural right and cultural might, but a single immanent plane where mightless right may as well not even exist. All consoling appeals to a transcendent authority are pointless as long as we fail to amass the needed allies to allow our position to prevail. Hobbes and Machiavelli fail not through immorality, but through their modernist ontology of people in opposition to nature. The struggle between actors must include nonhuman ones as well: not just forts and weapons, but atoms, machines, rainbows, buses, and tar. We no longer accept a two-world physics of superlunary and sublunary realms; by the same token, we should not accept a two-world politics in which human power struggles are treated differently from the duels between humans and nonhumans.

A critic might now say, with some justification, that Latour has completely reduced politics to a power struggle among competing forces. In turn, this would seem to put him on the side of the Sophists, such as Thrasymachus in Plato's *Republic*, who defines justice as "the advantage of the stronger." With no court of appeal available to Latour beyond the duel among actants, it might well seem that the advantage of the stronger is the only principle in play. Here as always it is Ray Brassier who airs the charges against Latour most abrasively: "Latour's texts are designed to do things: they have been engineered in order to produce an effect rather than establish a demonstration. Far from trying to prove anything, Latour is explicitly engaged in persuading the susceptible into embracing his irreductionist worldview through a particularly adroit deployment of rhetoric. This is the traditional modus operandi of the sophist."[3] What is most ironic about this charge is that Latour himself might be the first to embrace it: for he spends a considerable portion of his 1999 book *Pandora's Hope* defending the cosmopolitan political tact of the Sophists against Socrates, whom Latour portrays as a captain of the rationalist "epistemology police" along the lines of Brassier himself. But in this respect, Latour and Brassier are merely united in a shared misreading of Socrates. The Greek *philosophia* of Socrates has nothing whatsoever to do with the "enlightened" dogmatic rationalism that Brassier and his circle habitually and grimly defend. After all, it is the Sophists who claim a *knowledge* that motivates their rhetorical labors, however flimsy that knowledge may seem ("everything is true"; "nothing is true"). As I argued in *Prince of Networks*, the proper maneuver is to align Latour with Socrates and the rationalists with the Sophists, since claiming knowledge is the last way to join the Socratic camp; his professions of ignorance are no mere ironic game, but the very heart of what philosophy means. Philosophy is neither successful epistemology nor successful natural science. Philosophy differs from both of these in demanding the incorporation of *non-knowledge* into one's view of the world, including one's view of politics. And here it is Latour who remains true to the meaning of philosophy, despite his somewhat perverse decision in *Pandora's Hope* to side with the Sophists. As we shall see, Latour's mature political philosophy is not Truth Politics but something more like Ignorance Politics, and in the good old Socratic sense of ignorance.

On this note, let's consider briefly the conflicting meanings of the term "realism" in philosophy and in politics. While there are a number of different senses of "realism" in philosophy, the leading sense is the notion that reality exists independently of the mind. Now, it is often blithely assumed that philosophical realism means something more: namely, that "there is a world independent of the mind, *and that world can be known.*" However, the view that the real can be *known* is perhaps the most insidious form of idealism, since it believes it can replace the real with some epistemic *model* of it. Against this false traditional realism of knowledge, we must choose reality and the *philosophia* that never claims to reach it, but only to strive towards it. Latour's critique of materialism makes largely the same point: materialism thinks it *knows* what matter is (the extension of physical stuff in space) and thereby prematurely replaces matter with a theory of matter. In this sense, realism and rationalism in philosophy must be viewed as polar opposites rather than as brothers. When Latour treats actors as trials of *strength*, he is not realist enough, since he is telling us that actors are nothing other than force. But when he says that actors can only be measured imperfectly by way of *trials* of strength, then he is a realist, since he is tacitly leaving open the question of what lies behind the trials. By disavowing any things-in-themselves beyond the relational networks of actors, Latour undercuts the metaphysical foundations for realism. Yet there remains in his thinking a grain of realism, even in those early years when he sometimes seems to indulge in an orgy of Machiavellian power plays.

Let's now turn to *political* realism, where all talk of transcendent principle gives way to a ruthless calculation of power and national interest. While this standpoint might seem to fit the early Latour's political philosophy fairly well, we should ask how well it maps onto philosophical realism as just described. And here we need to distinguish between *three* levels rather than two. Level One is that of transcendent principle, more or less abolished by the early Latour, whether it takes the form of moralistic appeal to standards of goodness, or of "scientific" trump cards played by Marxists and other Truth Politicians. In either case, we remain stranded at the level of principle without staying attuned to the sometimes surprising resistance of actors placed in networks. Level Two is that of political realism as usually defined, which for the early Latour covers the cosmos as a whole. Here moral or revolutionary complaints are useless. We must build the rail infrastructure quickly to empower the economy to be re-elected. We must acknowledge that our opponent has deviously outmaneuvered us, and instead of crying about it, outmaneuver him in turn. Perhaps we make flattering remarks to the governor while handing him a bottle of his favorite cognac. Perhaps we frighten our bellicose neighbor with naval exercises of our own. This political realism entails recognition that the world is made of realities or of "how things are" (Machiavelli) and not "how things ought to be." But there is also a Level Three, which does not exist for the early Latour any more than for the rationalists: a real beneath the knowable real. This is the genuine Socratic real, the only one that exposes Thrasymachus as wrong, since the nature of the "advantage of the stronger" must always elude us.

For another take on this problem, we turn to one of those "interesting reactionaries" not mentioned by Latour himself: Leo Strauss. The usual tendency, of course, is to identify Machiavelli with the Sophists. Yet Strauss takes a novel position on this question, a position that initially seems inscrutable or outright sinister. As Strauss puts it in his "Machiavelli" article in his co-edited *History of Political Philosophy* volume:

> Toward the end of the *Nicomachean Ethics* Aristotle speaks of what one may call the political philosophy of the Sophists. His chief point is that the Sophists identified or almost identified politics with rhetoric. In other words, the Sophists believed or tended to believe in the omnipotence of speech. Machiavelli surely cannot be accused of that error … But Xenophon, who was a pupil of Socrates, proved to be a most successful commander precisely because he could manage both gentlemen and nongentlemen [unlike Proxenos, who was unable to punish]. Xenophon, the pupil of Socrates, was under no delusion about the sternness and harshness of politics, about that ingredient of politics which transcends speech. In this important respect Machiavelli and Socrates make a common front against the Sophists.[4]

In one sense it is difficult to know what this means. Our first reaction may be that it is simply a dark form of Straussian elitism, in which some people can be persuaded to do the right thing by speech while others ("nongentlemen") must be ruled by force. Our second reaction may be to lament Strauss's slippery logic, which identifies Xenophon with Machiavelli through shared belief in the insufficiency of speech, then Xenophon with Socrates through the mere fact of discipleship, thus yielding an unlikely match of Machiavelli with Socrates. But it is more interesting to read the passage as a recognition of the force of reality beyond any claims of knowledge. What the Sophists and rationalists have in common is their claim to knowledge and the demand for everything that follows from this supposed knowledge. (Alain Badiou: "*A truth affirms the infinite right of its consequences, with no regard for what opposes them.*")[5] But viewed from a Straussian standpoint, what the early Latour would have in common with Machiavelli and Socrates is the notion of politics as a trial of force that is largely impenetrable to ideas.

IRREDUCTIONS

One of Latour's key philosophical works is the short treatise *Irreductions*, published as an appendix to his 1984 study *The Pasteurization of France*. Though I have already considered this treatise in detail at the beginning of my book *Prince of Networks*, it is worth examining here for its specifically political implications. The origins of *Irreductions* can be found in Latour's picturesque road-to-Damascus intellectual conversion in the winter of 1972. Driving his Citroën van one day through the Burgundy countryside, the young Latour was jolted by the realization that all theories perform some sort of *reduction*. He pulled the van to the side of the road and daydreamed about what it would be like if we refrained from reducing anything to anything else: "I knew nothing, then, of what I am writing now but simply repeated to myself: 'Nothing can be reduced to anything else, nothing can be deduced from anything else, everything may be allied to everything else … And for the first time in my life I saw things unreduced and set free" (PF 163). The world is filled with all shapes and sizes of actors, and to convert or reduce one to another is a work of translation that can never do full justice to the original. This is the meaning of the term "irreduction." The class struggle "explains" World War I no more and no less than wishes explain dreams or Foucauldian surveillance explains prisons.

This flat cosmos of mutually irreducible actors is the rock on which Latour has built his astounding intellectual career. Not everyone has been impressed by this career, of course. Let's again cite Brassier, the least inhibited of Latour's critics:

> It is instructive to note how many reductions must be carried out in order for irreductionism to get off the ground: reason, science, knowledge, truth—all must be eliminated. Of course, Latour has no qualms about reducing reason to arbitration, science to custom, knowledge to manipulation, or truth to force: the veritable object of

his irreductionist afflatus is not reduction per se, in which he wantonly indulges, but explanation, and the cognitive privilege accorded to scientific explanation in particular.[6]

Brassier's annoyance stems directly from his own rationalist proclivities. The terms "reason," "science," "knowledge," and "truth" are for Brassier the only guarantors we have against a relativist free-for-all of poetic and rhetorical self-indulgence. In Brassier's rationalism, there is a real world outside the mind. This real world must be approached by human knowledge, even if only as a desirable *telos* rather than an actually attainable state, though primarily in the negative form of successively annihilating every model of reality that the human mind has ever conceived. The natural sciences are the most successful means we have of performing this operation, and thus of replacing gullible pre-scientific fetish with rational, scientific conceptions.

While it is by no means true that Latour aims to "eliminate" reason, science, knowledge, and truth, it is certainly the case that he wishes to reinterpret them as exercises in translation. By spending several decades in the study of scientific practice, Latour was not trying to eliminate science except in the narrow scientistic sense of "the cognitive privilege accorded to scientific explanation in particular," a privilege that Brassier merely asserts in table-pounding fashion without providing further reason as to why we should join him in extending this privilege. But this in itself is not especially interesting. What is more interesting is Brassier's claim that Latour's *Irreductions* is a reductionist work in spite of itself. This charge is sometimes raised even by Latour's supporters, though in fact it was first aired by Latour himself in Interlude III of the very same treatise: "Why should [irreduction] be preferred to [reduction]? I still do not know, but I do not like power that burns far beyond the networks from which it comes ... I want to reduce the reductionists, escort the powers back to the galleries and networks from where they came" (PF 191). His answer is merely provisional and not entirely satisfying. My own view is that Latour *does* in fact perform reductions in his *Irreductions*, though this is neither as important nor as devastating as the evident logical contradiction might suggest. Here we should simply pay attention to what Latour does rather than to what he says. Though the explicit claim of *Irreductions* is that nothing can be reduced to anything else, in practice Latour does perform one master reduction that typifies his intellectual career. Namely, that to which all else is reducible, that which cannot be further reduced without some more or less disfiguring translation, is *actors*. Presumably it is impossible to do theoretical work without some sort of reduction, in the sense of taking certain aspects of reality to be more important than others. The sole alternative would be to perform "Zen" gestures such as raising a finger, or Dadaist maneuvers such as shouting random syllables and performing wild masked dances in response to philosophical questions. What Latour really means when he says "nothing can be reduced to anything else" is this: *actors* cannot be reduced to anything else. This is not an arbitrary decision on Latour's part, but is simply his own attempt to do justice to the global scope of philosophy's subject matter. It follows directly from his pragmatist-flavored *metaphysics of effects*, according to which anything is real insofar and *only* insofar as it has some sort of effect on something else. Given that wastebaskets, clowns, unicorns, a Pepsi bottle, King Lear, and square circles already clear this rather low hurdle for reality, we should not begin our inquiry by eliminating them in favor of their presumed underlying natural subcomponents as revealed by the hard sciences. If Latour's metaphysics is rejected, this should not be due to finding an artificial logical problem with how the project of *Irreductions* is formulated ("Latour says not to reduce, but then makes a blunder by reducing anyway"). Instead, a critic would need to address the root of the issue by showing that there are inherent problems with taking actors to be the fundamental layer of reality, which is precisely what I tried to do myself in *Prince of Networks*.

At the beginning of *Irreductions*, Latour reports that empirical fieldwork never seemed to convince anyone of his views about science and society: "Knowing that empirical studies would never do more than scratch the surface of beliefs about science, I decided to shift from the empirical and, as Descartes advised us, to spend a few hours per year doing philosophy" (PF 153). What he decided during those "few hours per year" (it was much more than that, of course) is that the world is best understood as being made of actors. This is another way of saying that the world is made of forces, effects, or relations, or with heterogeneous forces of different types, "and all of these forces together seek hegemony by increasing, reducing, or assimilating one another" (PF 154). Some pages later, he backtracks from this Nietzschean vision of a global will to power: "[C]ertain forces constantly try to measure rather than be measured and to translate rather than be translated. They wish to act rather than be acted upon. They wish to be stronger than the others. I have said 'certain' rather than 'all,' as in Nietzsche's bellicose myth" (PF 167). In any case, the real comes to be defined as that which affects other realities.

There are only trials of strength, of weakness … Whatever resists trials is real. The verb "resist" is not a privileged word. I use it to represent the whole collection of verbs and adjectives, tools and instruments, which together define the ways of being real. We could equally well say "curdle," "fold," "obscure," "sharpen," "slide." There are dozens of alternatives. (PF 159)

All entities are inherently equal, or mutually symmetrical. The way to create an asymmetry is to "lean on a force slightly more durable than [oneself]" (PF 160). Latour even tries to state the equality of essences and relations: "Is an actant essence or relation? We cannot tell without a trial. To stop themselves being swept away, essences may relate themselves to many allies, and relations to many essences" (PF 160). But this is somewhat misleading, since Latour has already defined reality as force, and force consists in its relations to other forces; there is no non-relational essence in Latour's universe, hiding outside its relations to other things. The world simply *is* relational in structure.

But if the world is made of forces, we are nonetheless ignorant of what these forces are. Our inherent ignorance about actors is Latour's most Socratic idea (despite his unfortunate distaste for Socrates), and will even turn out to be his most important political principle. As he puts it, "since we all play with different fields of force and weakness, we do not know the state of force, and this ignorance may be the only thing we have in common" (PF 155). This is what separates Latour from every form of philosophical rationalism and every form of Truth Politics. We cannot know what the Roman Republic really is, whether we are Roman politicians or latter-day historians. In order to find out, we must subject Rome to various trials of strength, which may teach us much but can never teach everything. As Latour puts it, "there are no equivalents, only translations" (PF 162). There is no direct access to reality either actually or in principle, despite the long-cherished dreams of rationalists. Every interaction is an interpretation: "Whatever the agreement, there is always something upon which disagreement may feed. Whatever the distance, there is always something upon which an understanding may be built. In other words, everything is negotiable" (PF 163). This is the sense in which logic is "a branch of public works or civil engineering" (PF 171).

Striking one of his frequent Hobbesian notes, Latour concludes that "we cannot distinguish between those moments when we have might and those when we are right" (PF 183). Hence, there seems to be no surplus beyond the tribunal of power, no higher court of reality where losers in the struggle for might could lodge an appeal. This does make the early Latour's world sound a bit like an unprincipled power struggle between human and inhuman forces, without any "normative" guidance to separate good powers from bad. Yet we cannot forget that *ignorance* is one of Latour's central political principles, in a way that is not true for Thrasymachus and other Sophists. Latour does not claim to know where "the advantage of the stronger" can be found, but quite the contrary. Along with ignorance there is another recurrent Latourian theme—the surprising fragility of power. "Power is the flame that leads us to confuse a force with those allies which render it strong ... We can avoid being intimidated by those who appropriate words and claim to be 'in power'" (PF 186). Stated differently: "*We always misunderstand the strength of the strong.* Though people attribute it to the purity of an actant, it is invariably due to a tiered array of weaknesses" (PF 201).

We must also never forget that the political side of Latour's theory of force encompasses the nonhuman realm as well:

I know neither who I am nor what I want, but *others* say they know on my behalf ... Whether I am a storm, a rat, a rock, a lake, a lion, a child, a worker, a gene, a slave, the unconscious, or a virus, they whisper to me, they suggest, they impose an interpretation of what I am and could be. (PF 192)

Or again: "Things in themselves?... You complain about things that have not been honored by your vision? You feel that things are lacking the illumination of your consciousness? ... Things themselves lack nothing, just as Africa did not lack whites before their arrival" (PF 193). The general breakdown of the human/nonhuman distinction can best be seen in science itself, which makes use of every possible type of entity: "If science grows, this is because it manages to convince dozens of actants of doubtful breeding to lend it their strength: rats, bacteria, industrialists, myths, gas, worms, special steels, passions, handbooks, workshops ... a crowd of fools whose help is denied even while it is used" (PF 204–205). Arranging such forces is the best we can ever do, simply because translation is the best we can ever do. "Machiavelli and Spinoza, who are accused of political 'cynicism,' were the most generous of men. Those who believe that they can do better than a badly translated compromise between poorly connected forces always do *worse*" (PF 211).

The main principle of *Irreductions* is always *force*, in a sense that includes natural, political, and all other kinds of forces: "To force I will add *nothing*"

(PF 213). This ought to be more widely believed, since "if people did not believe in 'science,' there would be nothing but trials of strength" (PF 214). If you complain that this dispenses with any conception of truth as correspondence with an external reality, Latour will simply celebrate this fact: "We can say that whatever exists is real. The word 'truth' adds only a little supplement to a trial of strength. It is not much, but it gives an impression of potency, which saves what might give way from being tested" (PF 227). Despite Latour's frequent talk of trials as translations, there is a sense in which the translation has no original: "The trials of strength are all whole and complete, exact precisely to the extent that this is possible. *They are not approximate*" (PF 233). Force is without supplement: "Demonstrations are always of force, and the lines of force are always a measure of reality, its only measure. We never bow to reason, but rather to force" (PF 233). In sum, "to oppose might and right is criminal because it leaves the field free for the wicked while pretending to defend it with the potency of what is right ... Like Spinoza, we look cruel in order to be fair" (PF 234).

Despite all of this, Latour still insists on a difference between science and politics, apparently because he wants to avoid the *human*-centered connotations of politics:

> If it were possible to explain "science" in terms of "politics," there would be no sciences, since they are developed precisely in order to find other allies, new resources, and fresh troops. This is why the sociology of science is so congenitally weak ... Science is not politics. It is politics by other means. But people object that "science does not reduce to politics." Precisely. It does not reduce to power. It offers *other means*. (PF 229)

These other means do not prevent science from being realistic, as well as rather strong. For while it is true that "the idealists were right: we can only know insofar as we draw things to ourselves," it is just as true that "[the idealists] forgot to add that things have to be drawn together to topple us" (PF 231). The fact that they *can* be drawn together shows that they somehow exist outside us and are not just immanent in human political calculation. Nor does Latour have any sympathy for those who claim to be *superior* to science:

> The sciences have always been criticized in the name of superior forms of knowledge that are more intuitive, immediate, human, global, warm,

cultivated, political, natural, popular, older, mythical, instinctive, spiritual, or cunning. We have always wanted to criticize science by claiming that an alternative is superior, by adding a court of appeal to the court of first instance, by asking God or the gods to puncture the pride of the learned and to reserve the secret of things for the humble and lowly. But there is no knowledge superior to the sciences because there is no scale of knowledge and, in the end, no knowledge at all. (PF 231–232)

We are now in a position to summarize the philosophy of *Irreductions* and its political consequences, an important step given Latour's claim that the nucleus of his entire philosophy can be found in this treatise.[7] We cannot begin by taking some entities as more real than others. Entities are actors, meaning that they are real as long as they resist trials of strength. Actors in turn are *forces*, and Latour accepts the existence of nothing over and above forces. In this connection we hear the basic Latourian principle that we must not "treat the winners and the losers asymmetrically" (PF 218), as rationalist history of science tends to do: treating Pasteur as a luminous genius and his defeated rivals Liebig, Peter, and Pouchet as untutored retrograde clowns. Latour holds instead that we should simply treat Pasteur as *stronger* than the other three, as more successful than they are in amassing animate and inanimate allies for his program. This is enough to convince Latour that he is proceeding "symmetrically" in his treatment of Pasteur. But note that there is another sense in which Latour's methods are not symmetrical at all, since *Irreductions* is really a philosophy of victory. Since there is no court of appeal beyond winning and losing, there is a basic asymmetry present from the start. And in this connection we are led to the truly problematic asymmetry in Latour: not the one between winners and losers *per se* (after all, Latour is far more generous to Liebig, Peter, and Pouchet than most historians of science) but the asymmetry between *deserving* losers and *undeserving* losers. Two failed painters are equally failed, yet we all concede that the critic might "discover" one of them later as a neglected great painter, and we normally do not think that unknown great painters are simply produced by the critic who discovers them. In other words, *objects are not just actors*, not just score sheets of victories and defeats. To force we must always add something, however loud the objections of the early Latour. Namely, to force we must add a supplement of *reality* that expresses different forces at different times, sometimes stronger and sometimes weaker.

The political implications of this should be obvious. Latour is surely right not to let trials of strength be reduced to *knowledge*. When he says that "there is no scale of knowledge and, in the end, no knowledge at all" (PF 232), he is not echoing the Sophists, as Latour himself and his critic Brassier both seem to believe. Instead he is really echoing Socrates, as becomes clear in Latour's later thoughts on the crucial role of ignorance in the political sphere. The reason politics cannot be grounded in knowledge is because knowledge can only be loved, not possessed, a point never taken seriously enough by rationalists who want to turn philosophy into science or geometry. It is hardly original to warn that attempts to rebuild the political sphere in terms of transcendent rational ideas often lead to disaster, but since Badiou has recently returned to mocking this point in his recurrent diatribes against Bernard-Henri Lévy, it is useful to do so once more. An awareness of ignorance needs to be built into political philosophy. Unfortunately, the early Latour seems excessively fond of the *immanence* of the political and the impossibility of any outside standards, which leaves him with only a weak sense of political ignorance. At this stage he is still a devotee of Hobbes and Machiavelli, and somewhat later of Schmitt, for all of whom politics is primarily a struggle for victory rather than the appeal to a higher common standard.

PASTEUR: A CASE STUDY

Having looked at *Irreductions*, we should also consider the famous study of Pasteur, to which *Irreductions* was attached as an appendix. Latour treats Pasteur as a milder sort of Machiavelli who makes use of every means at hand to consolidate his discoveries, rather than as the torch bearer of medical enlightenment against drooling hordes of irrational obscurantists. Latour takes as his model *War and Peace*, a novel that famously depicts military actions as happening chaotically, outside the control of commanding officers. This notion creates obvious friction with the usual account of Pasteur's career. If Pasteur's research activity is viewed in political terms at all (which is rare enough), it tends to be depicted as follows: "The strategy was conceived entirely in advance; Pasteur concocted it and had every detail figured out; it went according to plan, following a strict order of command from Pasteur to the sheep by way of his assistants and the caretakers. [However,] following Tolstoy's advice, we can say that such an account has to be false" (PF 5). Unfortunately, "we do not know how to describe war and politics any better than we know how to explain science. To offer well-conceived Machiavellian strategies to explain science is as meaningless as to write ['The first column marches, the second column marches.']" (PF 6)

All the marvelous detail of Latour's reading of Pasteur's career can be boiled down to perhaps two major steps. In the first step, Pasteur enrolls the support of the hygienists. In the second, he gains the support of his former enemies the doctors. Pasteur's period of medical dominance then comes to a close with the discovery of parasitical diseases in the tropics, which can no longer be explained by his microbes. As Latour demonstrates, the hygiene movement arose in the nineteenth century as a response to widespread demand for better workers and soldiers, meaning those not wracked with disease. But lacking a unified principle for their field, the hygienists were initially limited to offering masses of disconnected *ad hoc* advice. It seemed to be generally good to avoid open sewers and pestilential neighborhoods, to wash one's hands, to avoid spitting in the street, and not to eat dinner from the same plate as the family cat. But not only was the sheer number of disjointed rules unmanageable, they did not even work without fail:

> A salesman sends a perfectly good beer to a customer—it arrives corrupted. A doctor assists a woman to give birth to a fine eight-pound baby—it dies shortly afterward. A mother gives perfectly pure milk to an infant—it dies of typhoid fever. An administrator regulates the journey of Moroccan pilgrims to Mecca—cholera returns with the sanctified pilgrims and breaks out first at Tangiers, then at Marseille. A homemaker takes on a Breton girl to help the cook—after a few months the cook dies of galloping consumption. (PF 32)

Such unpredictable incidents led to a certain fatalism: "Indeed, the doctrine of 'morbid spontaneity' was the only really credible one" (PF 32). But once Pasteur had established the microbe as the root of infection, the situation was completely reversed. Previously "hygiene's style was cumulative and precautionary, since it set out to embrace everything," but following the appearance of the microbe "they redeployed their forces [and] eliminated a lot of knowledge ... Once they had given their advice on everything; now they decided on a few things" (PF 49).

As for Pasteur himself, "it is enough to speak of 'displacement.' The Pasteurians *place* themselves in relation to those forces of hygiene that I have described, but do so in a very special way: they go out to meet them, then move in the same direction, then, pretending to direct them, deflect them very slightly by adding an element that is crucial for them, namely the laboratory" (PF 60). Whereas the physiologists worked in serene isolation at the Collège de France, sure of their status as an exact science, Pasteur's laboratory "claimed to dictate its solutions directly to pathology" (PF 61). As to how Pasteur was able to accomplish such a thing, Latour tells us in almost Machiavellian tones that "the general principle is simple, being the principle of any victory: you must fight the enemy on the terrain that you master" (PF 61). In Pasteur's case the terrain was that of *experiment.* "The movement of the Pasteurian research program could be seen as a takeover that, as always, *diverted* the problem toward the place where the Pasteurians knew they were strongest: the laboratory" (PF 66). In words that will not surprise any reader of *Irreductions*, Latour concludes that "it would be pointless to say that there was, on the one hand, Pasteur the man of science, locked away in his laboratory, and on the other, Pasteur the politician, concerned with getting what he had done known. No, there was only one man, Pasteur, whose strategy was itself a work of genius" (PF 71).

Unlike the hygienists, the doctors were not favorably inclined to Pasteur at the outset: "As Léonard has shown, the doctors were skeptics. Even more than skeptics, they would be called 'grumblers,' if that category were accepted in sociology" (PF 116). For "the doctors found disputable what for the hygienists was indisputable" (PF 117). The doctors were not "corrupt" or "irrational," though it is safe to say that the threat to their professional position encouraged them to see weaknesses in Pasteur's case where the hygienists saw only strengths. "The entire Pasteurian takeover of medicine was aimed at redefining pathology so that disease would be *prevented* instead of *cured,*" which might put the doctors out of business (PF 122). Almost as bad, the Pasteurians wanted to declare disease to be contagious, which meant that the patient's illness was now a matter of public safety rather than of the traditional discreet confidence between patient and doctor. "But what of individual liberty? The presence of the microbe redefined it: no one had the right to contaminate others ... *Disease was no longer a private misfortune but an offense to public order*" (PF 123). The doctors did not like the idea of being transformed from guides of their patients to agents of a public health authority. We can hardly blame them for this anti-Pasteurian skepticism, since in Latour's words "we only believe what may be of benefit to us" (PF 123). Eventually the doctors were willing to go along with the new arrangement, but only as part of a wider deal: "[T]he physicians would serve the state, but the state would then rid the physicians of their traditional enemies ... the pharmacists, the charlatans, the nuns and so forth" (PF 126). Latour notes that before we accuse the doctors of narrow-minded corruption, we should not forget that the hygienists jumped on Pasteur's bandwagon more quickly for reasons of equal self-interest. In the doctor's case, self-interest and Pasteurism eventually joined hands due to "the serum, invented by Roux and his colleagues ... a therapy that was used *after* a patient had been diagnosed sick" (PF 127). While vaccines had threatened to put doctors out of business by preventing all disease in advance, serums were to be administered in the doctor's office itself.

As we have seen, there is no strong distinction in the early Latour between politics and science. Pasteur's actions are all alike; all involve the assembly of animate or inanimate allies in a chain that does the work Pasteur needs. In that sense, "politics" is simply a metaphor for reality as a whole rather than a specific domain of a sort that would allow us to accuse Latour of "reducing science to politics." Nonetheless, it still feels as if there were a grain of truth in the distaste felt for Latour by scientific realists. There is something in Latour that they never quite like, and this same concern even seems to drive Latour himself forward in his evolving conception of politics.

Perhaps the chief index of this mysterious something is the somewhat evasive way Latour deals with the question of whether microbes existed before Pasteur discovered them. The easy realist answer to this question would be "of course," while the easy social constructionist answer would be "of course not." Clearly uncomfortable with both alternatives, Latour tries to find a middle-ground position. "Since microbes saw their forms stabilized before the period under study, it is difficult to recall the time when they were being forged and tested, like Siegfried's sword" (PF 79). He continues: "The Greek name [microbe] should not make us forget the tests, for it is the name of an action, like Indian names. Instead of He-Who-Fights-the-Lynx, we have He-Who-Separates-Starch. The object has no other edges, apart from these tests" (PF 80). Just as David Hume holds that "objects" are nothing but bundles of qualities, Latour seems to think they are simply bundles of actions. Still, he hedges on the question of whether they pre-exist their discovery by humans: "Did the microbe exist before Pasteur? From the practical point of view—I say practical, not theoretical—it did not" (PF 80). Like a present-day Averroës, Latour comes close to advocating two different types of truth, in a division of labor between the "theoretical" (realism) and "practical" (anti-realism). But after a dozen-page delay, he comes down clearly enough on the anti-realist side of the question, without ever taking a stand directly: "'Well, Mister

Know-It-All, did Pasteur discover the cause of anthrax or not?' Now I should like to reply at last in the affirmative. But this affirmative is also accompanied by a lot of accessories … I would be prepared to say that Pasteur had 'really discovered' the truth of the microbe at last, if the word 'true' would add more than confusion" (PF 93).

A generation later, in *Pandora's Hope*, Latour simplifies this response about Pasteur with the sort of ontology that Quentin Meillassoux would dismiss as "correlationist."[8] The middle Latour of 1999 sarcastically notes, with a "we" that does not include himself, that "we imagine microbes must have a substance that is a little bit *more* than the series of its historical manifestations" (PH 167). Quite the contrary, he tells us: "Each element is to be defined by its associations and is an event created at the occasion of each of those associations" (PH 165). A radical claim indeed, for it leads Latour to claim that microbes pre-existed 1864, but only *beginning in 1864*. In other words, Pasteur "retrofitted the past with his own microbiology: the year 1864 that was built after 1864 did not have the same components, textures, and associations as the year 1864 produced during 1864" (PH 170). Latour even has the audacity to call this standpoint "commonsensical" (PH 145) when it is clearly anything but that.

Though Latour's reading of Pasteur in 1999 is seemingly much more radical than that of 1984, it is really just a more fearless statement of what was already his position in *The Pasteurization of France*. Given Latour's replacement of autonomous substance with a series of actions, a non-acting microbe could hardly be called real. Its reality must await its action, though Latour seems here to conflate action on human knowledge with action *tout court*, since we could easily speak of the microbe having acted before any human became aware of the fact. The situation is similar to the controversial argument Latour later made about the cause of death of the Egyptian pharaoh Ramses II: "The attribution of tuberculosis and Koch's bacillus to Ramses II should strike us as an anachronism of the same caliber as if we had diagnosed his death as having been caused by a Marxist upheaval, or a machine gun, or a Wall Street crash" (RAM 248). Though Latour tries to finesse the problem with an alternative third position, his conclusion is essentially that Ramses cannot have died of tuberculosis prior to its discovery. For as he puts it, "There is indeed a *supplement* in the notion of substance, but we should not, following the etymology of the word, 'what lies underneath,' imagine that this supplement resides 'beneath' the series of its manifestations" (RAM 262). But here Latour puts a crucial political spin on the theme: "Sociology offers a much better definition of substance with its definition of *institution*, that which is above a series of entities and makes them act as a whole" (RAM 262). Let's remember these words about "institution," an important theme in Latour's middle and late political philosophy.

"NO, HOBBES WAS WRONG"

The end of the early Latour's political philosophy can plausibly be dated to his 1991 classic *We Have Never Been Modern*. We have seen repeatedly that the early Latour is deeply under the influence of Hobbes. In 1991, Latour writes at some length about Hobbes in connection with a famous book by Steven Shapin and Simon Schaffer that provided inspiration for Latour's own work.[9] In so doing, Latour takes a distance from Shapin and Schaffer's overtly Hobbesian claims, which makes this one of the key moments for our analysis of the stages of Latour's political philosophy. In one sense, the early Latour demolishes the nature/culture divide, replacing it with a neutral ontology of actants: clearly a move towards a "symmetrical" ontology. But in another sense, it can be doubted whether the neutral ontology that results is really all that neutral. For even if Latour gets rid of the nature/culture divide, the resulting neutral terrain looks a lot more like the old "culture" pole than it does like the "nature" pole. When confronted with Shapin and Shaffer's advocacy of the constructionist Hobbes over his naturalist rival Boyle, Latour seems to recoil in the horror of self-recognition, denying that Hobbes could possibly be right. Let's take a brief look at Latour's partial disowning of the Hobbesian tradition, the very moment that marks the passage from early to middle Latour.

Latour first expresses great admiration for the work of his colleagues: "At first glance, [Shapin and Schaffer's] book does nothing more than exemplify what has been the slogan of the Edinburgh school of science studies and of a great body of work in the social history of science and in the sociology of knowledge: 'questions of epistemology are also questions of social order'" (NBM 15–16). And yet, "in part unwittingly," they "[ruin] the privilege given to the social context in explaining the sciences" (NBM 16). In doing so, "they come to grips with the very basis of political philosophy" (NBM 16). Instead of showing the mutual influence of two separate zones called nature and politics, they use the conflicting interpretations by Boyle and Hobbes of an air-pump to "examine how Boyle and Hobbes fought to invent a science, a context, and a demarcation between the two" (NBM 16). By resurrecting Boyle's forgotten political philosophy and Hobbes's discredited scientific theory, they "outline a rather nice quadrant: Boyle has a science and a political theory; Hobbes has a political theory and a science" (NBM 17). Boyle and Hobbes turn out to be surprisingly similar in both their political and scientific views: "they want a king, a Parliament, a docile and unified Church, and they are fervent subscribers to mechanistic philosophy" (NBM 17).

Boyle invents the empirical method by inviting trustworthy witnesses to take note of the air pump's functioning, but "Hobbes rejects Boyle's entire theater of proof" (NBM 18). Recall that Hobbes opposes any form of transcendence, which he regards as a threat to peace. "Civil wars will rage as long as there exist supernatural entities that citizens feel they have the right to petition when they are persecuted by the authorities of this lower world. The loyalty of the old medieval society—to God and King—is no longer possible if all people can petition God directly, or designate their own King" (NBM 19). In Latour's view this need not lead to authoritarianism, since "[t]here is no divine law or higher agency that the Sovereign might invoke in order to act as he wishes and dismantle the Leviathan. In this new regime in which Knowledge equals Power, everything is cut down to size: the Sovereign, God, matter, and the multitude" (NBM 19). To summarize, "such is Hobbes's generalized constructivism designed to end civil war: no transcendence whatsoever, no recourse to God, or to active matter, or to Power by Divine Right, or even to mathematical Ideas" (NBM 19). The danger of Boyle's procedure is that it tries to produce scientific facts that transcend the civil authority. Even worse, they are facts about the vacuum, an immaterial entity of precisely the sort that Hobbes also believes threatens peace. As a result, "Knowledge and Power will be separated once more. You will 'see double' as Hobbes puts it. Such are the warnings he addresses to the King in denouncing the goings-on of the Royal Society" (NBM 20).

While Latour is impressed by the initial Boyle/Hobbes symmetry set up by Shapin and Shaffer, he is disappointed by their asymmetrical conclusion. It looks at first as though we have a division of labor between Boyle and Hobbes, with Boyle inventing "one of the major repertoires for speaking about nature ('experiment,' 'fact,' 'evidence,' 'colleagues')" and Hobbes creating "the chief resources that are available to us for speaking about power ('representation,' 'sovereign,' 'contract,' 'property,' 'citizens')" (NBM 24–25). But instead of treating Boyle and Hobbes symmetrically, Shapin and Shaffer come down rather clearly on the side of Hobbes, despite some moments of hesitation late in their book. "Strangely enough, they seem to adhere more steadfastly to the political repertoire than to the scientific one" (NBM 28). Like the Edinburgh school of sociology of science from which they come, Shapin and Shaffer seem to hold that "if all questions of epistemology are questions of social order, this is because, when all is said and done, the social context contains as one of its subsets the definition of what counts as good science" (NBM 26). As they conclude, "knowledge, as much as the State, is the product of human action. Hobbes was right."[10] Latour offers an immediate rejoinder: "No, Hobbes was wrong." He follows this up with characteristic wit:

> [Shapin and Shaffer] offer a masterful deconstruction of the evolution, diffusion and popularization of the air pump. Why, then, do they not deconstruct the evolution, diffusion and popularization of "power" or "force"? Is "force" less problematic than the air's spring? ... unless one adopts some authors' asymmetrical posture and agrees to be simultaneously constructivist where nature is concerned and realist where society is concerned! But it is not very probable that the air's spring has a more political basis than English society itself ... (NBM 27)

Latour is convincing when he argues that to privilege society as the wider context encompassing science is no better than explaining society as built from the atoms of natural science. It is necessary to offer a symmetrical ontology that gives fair treatment to both. Yet it remains doubtful whether Latour does this any better than Shapin and Shaffer. What he says of these two colleagues sounds disturbingly similar to what some of his scientistic critics say about Latour himself: "Strangely enough, [Latour seems] to adhere more steadfastly to the political repertoire than to the scientific one." Indeed, this is a fairly standard critique of Latour by now, and not always an uneducated one. I have tried to suggest that the critique is at once both fair and unfair. It is unfair insofar as Latour does not treat human society as taxonomically more significant than the entities of nature. In no way does Latour hold, as some of his more superficial critics maintain, that scientific truth is purely constructed by human society. Indeed, "society" does not even exist for Latour as an all-embracing framework, and he has carried on a long-running polemic with the Durkheimian tradition on precisely this point.

And yet, if he does not think that scientific truth is a construction of human society, he *does* think it is the construction of relational networks of humans and nonhumans. Though Latour would surely concede that Boyle's trustworthy witnesses do not construct a vacuum in the tube *ex nihilo*, he also does not believe in a vacuum-in-itself that would be unwitnessed by any human or nonhuman entities. This is what allows Latour to say, in the case of Ramses II, that we cannot extract tuberculosis from the network that produced it and then project the disease retroactively into ancient Egypt. Things for Latour are incapable of undergoing adventures in time and space (to use Whitehead's delightful phrase), because for Latour as for Whitehead, a thing happens in one place and one time only. There is no substratum lying beneath a series of actions, but only a "superstratum" that unifies them from above—an "institution" that links multiple distinct actions together and determines that they all lie on the "same" trajectory of the "same" actor, just as Hume thinks that the successive profiles of an apple are linked only through the customary conjunction that binds them together. Though Latour avoids the Shapin/Shaffer problem of subordinating natural entities (the vacuum, protons, matter) to social entities (society, language, power), he nonetheless makes a different subordination. Namely, the non-relational side of things is subordinated to the relational side. This is the grain of truth in scientists' continuing complaints about Latour's position.

Since this is a book on Latour's political philosophy, it is tempting to consider his motives as political in nature. In fact, most of what Latour says about Hobbes's political concerns may also apply *mutatis mutandis* to Latour himself. If Hobbes holds that "civil wars will rage as long as there exist supernatural entities that citizens feel they have a right to petition when they are persecuted by the authorities of this lower world" (NBM 19), this sounds a great deal like Latour's complaints about people who appeal to truths outside the networks in which they are fabricated. Latour is no less allergic to transcendence than Hobbes himself.

In closing, if I say that scientific rationalists have a legitimate concern about Latour, I do not mean to let them off the hook. For it is also true that Latour's concerns about scientific rationalists strike the target quite heavily. No matter how "transcendent" natural things may seem to be for Boyle and his modern-day heirs, they are in fact perfectly *immanent*. After all, the whole point of the sciences is that their objects can be *known*, turned into accessible knowledge useful (in the hands of dogmatists) for shutting up other people and bringing a premature end to political conversation. By the same token, Hobbes wants to use the Leviathan to shut up those who speak of the transcendent vacuum and other scientific facts, not to mention those who call on God against the state. Stated differently, both Truth Politics and Power Politics are theories of immanence that take no account of our basic ignorance. And though Latour often moves in this direction himself through his sympathies for Hobbes, he is also aware that we are never sure in what the polity consists. Latour attempts to make room for surprise and surplus in his politics no less than in his ontology. With his 1991 critique of Shapin and Shaffer, Latour takes a first step away from his early notion that reality is equivalent to force.

3

Middle Latour: The Parliament of Things

We have seen that Latour's early preference for Power Politics of the Hobbesian variety begins to shift with the phrase "No, Hobbes was wrong," his 1991 rejoinder to Shapin and Schaffer. The term "middle Latour," for all its flaws, can be used to name the intervening period between this partial disowning of Hobbes and the gradual emergence of the modes of existence project, which was partially revealed in a 2003 article (TPL), shared in draft form at Cerisy-la-Salle in 2007, then finally published in French in 2012 and in English the following year (AIME). The most emblematic work of political philosophy by the middle Latour is surely *Politics of Nature*, which appeared in French in 1999 and English in 2004. According to Gerard de Vries, "*Politics of Nature* presents [Latour's] political philosophy."[1] I would not give such a clean verdict myself, precisely because I *agree* with de Vries's assessment of the vast scope of the book, whose "aim is no less than to outline 'due process' for cosmopolitics. The key problem addressed is how to bring a collective of humans and non-humans together into a common world." Yet it is not clear how a work of political philosophy can be a cosmopolitics without ballooning into a global ontology pertaining to non-political matters as well. While the post-1991 and pre-modes project Latour seems less intoxicated by his earlier vision of a Nietzschean struggle of forces between all animate and inanimate things, he still tacitly equates politics with a sweeping metaphysical doctrine. The model of power struggles between networks of allies is replaced by that of carefully assembled institutional networks, but the tendency to ontologize the political largely remains. Though Latour notes that the title *Politics of Nature* also toys with its own inversion, verging on a treatise on the "Nature of Politics," there is something metaphysical or at least metapolitical about the book, and little that could find immediate practical use in the political sphere, despite its explicit references to ecology.

This chapter proceeds in three steps. First, we consider *Politics of Nature* in as much detail as we can. Second, we discuss Latour's 2004 article on the prominent German sociologist Ulrich Beck, which shows us Latour's understanding of peace as a deal between enemies rather than the result of a shared, impartial rationalism. Finally, we look at Latour's 2007 response to the critique of *Politics of Nature* by his old friend de Vries.

A NEW SEPARATION OF POWERS

Though the first two chapters of *Politics of Nature* are clear and useful, they are largely a recapitulation of the central ideas of Latour's earlier career. For this reason, we must ruthlessly compress our treatment of those chapters, mentioning only those portions that are indispensable for understanding the rest of the work. The key term of the book is "political ecology," not to be confused with the ideology of existing environmental movements. For such movements have always shipwrecked on their commitment to the very nature/culture modernist dualism that Latour aims to destroy. "Let me put it bluntly: *political ecology has nothing to do with nature* ... the belief that political ecology is interested in nature is the childhood illness of the field" (PN 3). More importantly, Latour often defines "ecology" as the opposite term to "modernism." To ecologize is not to remove all meddling human hands from the pristine virginity of nature, but to compose the common world that comprises natural, cultural, real, imaginary, animate, inanimate, and all other actors by means of "due process" (PN 8), which simply means not assuming that we know in advance what actors are. This requires a certain acknowledgment of *ignorance* that marks Latour's Socratic heritage. But given that Latour does not allow for a transcendent world lying beyond all access, it remains a puzzle what exactly our ignorance is supposed to be ignorance *about*. Indeed, this will prove to be the deepest challenge facing Latour's political philosophy: how to maintain his Hobbesian hostility to transcendent reality without slipping into a Hobbesian power play that fails to account for the resistance of the surprising and the new. What distinguishes political ecology from both deep ecology and power struggles is precisely its position of ignorance: "This is its great virtue. It *does not know* what does or does not constitute a system. It does not know what is connected to what" (PN 21). As we read in another important passage: "Political ecology does not shift attention from the human pole to the pole of nature; it shifts from *certainty* about the production of risk-free objects

... to *uncertainty* about the relations whose unintended consequences threaten to disrupt all orderings, all plans, all impacts" (PN 25).

It should not escape our notice that Latour views *relations* as the place of all possible surprise. He makes the same point later in the chapter: "[B]y abandoning the notion of nature, we are leaving intact the two elements that matter the most to us: the multiplicity of nonhumans and the enigma of their association" (PN 41). The wording in these passages is not accidental. It is not actors themselves who surprise us due to a hidden internal surplus, a notion that would be anathema to Latour. Instead, actors only surprise us when brought into new and unforeseen *combinations*. Surprise is necessary to free us from the burden of Hobbes, whose legacy is now beginning to weigh more heavily on Latour. "Just as we have distinguished Science from the sciences, we are going to contrast power politics, inherited from [Plato's] cave, with politics, conceived as *the progressive composition of the common world*" (PN 18). As we saw earlier, this is the reason why we must distinguish between the political philosophies of early and middle Latour. Though the younger Latour reveled in swashbuckling claims to be the Machiavelli of inanimate things, he now shifts his concern to the fragile composition of a common space for all.

The reason Latour must locate all surprise in relations and associations is because he utterly rejects any attempt to place it in some hidden reserve in the things themselves, a purely nonsensical notion in his relational metaphysics. Thus his distaste for traditional realism in philosophy: "Henceforth when we hear censors ask 'big' questions on the existence of an objective reality, we shall no longer make a huge effort to respond by trying to prove that we are 'realists' no matter what" (PN 17). Matters of fact, which exist in themselves, are now to be replaced by matters of *concern*, which exist only in relation to other actors that register their presence. The externality of the world demanded by Latour is not that of shadowy hidden beings, but only of actors that happen never to have come into relation with us before now:

> Yes, there is indeed an objective external reality, but this particular externality is not definitive: it simply indicates that new nonhumans, entities that have never before been included in the work of the collective, find themselves mobilized, recruited, socialized, domesticated ... There is indeed an external reality, but there is really no need to make a big fuss about it. (PN 38)

The main critical question raised by the present book is whether the sort of political ignorance that Latour incorporates into his political philosophy is really ignorant enough. His justified disdain for the "epistemology police" amounts to contempt for any privileged external reality that could be brought into politics to silence the supposed babblers and power players. Yet it is my view that Latour conflates this issue of the *knowability* of the real with the entirely different question of whether the real *exists* beneath the current relational networks of actors. This can be seen from his ambiguous complaint that in the modern period, as for example with asbestos before its cancerous side effects were known, "the object produced had *clear boundaries*, a well-defined essence" (PN 22). What worries Latour here: the claim that objects have an essence, or simply that the essence can be "well-defined"? These are actually two different problems, since the contention that things have an internal character prior to entering relations is not the same as holding that we can know this character and thus be empowered to tell ignorant people to shut up. This issue is no mere quibble, since it points to the central ambiguity in Latour's entire philosophy, his political philosophy included.[2] In a first gesture he brilliantly undercuts the modern taxonomy that places mechanistic nature on one side and arbitrary human perspectives and values on the other. But in a second gesture, he tacitly conflates this distinction with an entirely different one between the "in-itself" and the "for-us." Having undercut nature as a separate domain of mechanistic reality, he assumes he has also undercut "things-in-themselves," even while not performing the same sabotage of "things-for-us." In other words, the nature/culture duality is successfully replaced by a neutral third term ("actants"), while the rather different duality of "in-itself"/"for-us" is not replaced by a third term at all. Instead, the "for-us" wins out over the "in-itself," though this is effectively obscured by Latour's admirable expansion of the "us" to include all animate, inanimate, and fictional entities. As he puts it, "the belief that there are only two positions, realism and idealism, nature and society, is in effect the essential source of the power that is symbolized by the myth of the Cave and that political ecology must secularize" (PN 34). Notice the pairing of realism with nature, an entirely unnecessary bond, given that one can be a realist about the social domain no less than the natural. Quarks and moons have a reality that their relations and associations do not exhaust, but so do princes, jesters, and lawyers.

Latour's needless worry that realism entails naturalism can be seen in his call for a "Collective Without *Outside* Recourse" (PN 37, emphasis added). This continued allergy to the Outside signals that Latour remains committed to the Hobbesian model of a politics without transcendence. Thus his sole option for allowing political surprise to exist is by way of the shuffling of existing relations between things. This would indeed be wise on Latour's part if non-relational reality were inherently *knowable*, for then the epistemology police could easily crush politics, replacing it with a Science opposed only by corrupt or gullible reactionaries. What Latour never considers, in his politics or in his metaphysics, is the possibility of a transcendence that *cannot be known*. With this single step, he could have avoided the complementary pitfalls of Truth Politics and Power Politics. Instead, he tries to modify or hotwire the Hobbesian/Schmittian power play, with results that can only be called insufficient.

We have seen that Latour's strategy is to "associate the notion of external reality with *surprises and events*, rather than with the simple 'being-there' of the warrior tradition, the stubborn presence of *matters of fact*" (PN 79). At times he seems to place surprises more on the side of nonhumans than humans: "The only thing that can be said about [nonhumans] is that they *emerge in surprising fashion*, lengthening the list of beings that must be taken into account" (PN 79). But more often the surprises seem to come from the *connection* between humans and nonhumans, as when Latour speaks of "these human and nonhuman actors whose *association* is sometimes surprising" (PN 79, emphasis modified) and of how ecological and health crises "can be spotted through the ignorance of *connections* between the actors" (PN 79, emphasis modified). Politics thus becomes experimental in a way that it cannot be for either Truth Politics or Power Politics. For the early Latour, nonhuman things were important for their role in *stabilizing* human society. But for the middle Latour, their primary role is to *destabilize* society by confronting it with unexpected controversies: "The venerable word Republic is admirably suited to our task, if we agree to bring out the overtones of the underlying Latin word *res*, 'thing'" (PN 80). And during modernity, we tended "to forget that a thing emerges before anything else as *a scandal at the heart of an assembly that carries on a discussion requiring a judgment brought in common*" (PN 80).

Despite the claims of Science with a capital S that "the facts/things speak for themselves," this is far from accurate. Things cannot speak directly to humans, but can only do so through mediators. "In politics, there is a very useful term for designating the whole gamut of intermediaries between someone who speaks and someone else who speaks in that person's place, between doubt and uncertainty: spokesperson" (PN 64). We must reconceive politics in such a way that nonhumans are allowed to speak, in mediated fashion, through spokespersons: "By defending the rights of the human subject to speak and to be the sole speaker, one does not establish democracy; one makes it increasingly more impracticable every day" (PN 69, emphasis removed). Indeed, civilization itself requires that nonhumans have a voice: "[I name] the extension of speech to nonhumans Civilization, [thereby] finally solving the problem of representation that rendered democracy powerless as soon as it was invented, because of the counter-invention of Science" (PN 71). Yet however clearly we conceive this new idea of the political role of nonhumans, "the conceptual institution that would make it fruitful does not yet exist. This institution is what we have to invent" (PN 68). The remainder of *Politics of Nature* is a provisional attempt to invent just such an institution.

Chapter 3, "A New Separation of Powers," proposes replacing the modern bicameral system of nature and culture. Latour now claims (in tacitly anti-Hobbesian fashion) that the political problem with nature is not to be found in its externality, "for it is only thanks to such an externality that public life survives: the expanding collective is constantly nourished through all its pores, all its sensors, all its laboratories, all its industries, all its skills by such a vast exterior" (PN 91). Neither is the supposed *unity* of nature the problem, for "it is normal, in fact, for public life to seek to collect the world that we hold in common, and it is normal for it to end up obtaining this world in partially unified forms" (PN 91). Instead, nature is blameworthy "solely because of the short-circuits that it authorizes when it is used to bring about this unity once and for all" (PN 91). What we need is "due process" (PN 91), not a power play or nature play that would silence the political task of composing the world by saying: "Therefore, just shut up!" (PN 91). Externality remains crucial for Latour in softening the hard edges left over from his Hobbesian origin. Facts are not invincible cudgels to be used in bullying the ignorant, but "signal the existence of surprising actors" (PN 103). The matter of fact is really a matter of concern: "it agitates, it troubles, it complicates, it provokes speech" (PN 103). Entities, or "propositions" as Latour calls them following Whitehead, "propose their *candidacy* for common existence and subject themselves to trials whose outcome is still uncertain. Let us say that, under the name of fact, new entities appear in the form of that which leaves those who are discussing them *perplexed*" (PN 104). It is not a matter of aiming towards external things-in-themselves, but of extending the number of stakeholders in the collective (PN 106). If people remain attached to the modern distinction between unshakeable facts and arbitrary values, "it is because it seems at first to guarantee a certain transcendence over the redoubtable immanence of public life" (PN 121). In short, it is the *collective* that distinguishes between immanent and transcendent rather than these themselves forming some sort of basic ontological rift, and the collective will often need to reconsider for admission those candidates it has rejected. In one of his more vivid examples, Latour notes that we continue to view the 8,000 annual French fatalities in auto accidents as politically acceptable. We exclude this concern as a decisive factor in debates (if such even exist) over the continued use of motor vehicles and their infrastructure (PN 113). Yet we might imagine a situation in which this changes. What if it were 200,000 deaths per year? Or what if a safer alternative were already within reach? In these cases the victims of French car crashes might be readmitted as legitimate speakers in the political collective. This unstable state of the collective leads Latour to speak of an "experimental metaphysics" that displays the following advantage: "The old system allowed shortcuts and acceleration, but it did not understand dynamics, whereas ours, which aims at slowing things down and fosters a great respect for procedures, does allow an understanding of movement and process" (PN 123).

But the real aim of Chapter 3 is to begin to lay down the institutions required by Latour's *nonmodern* (not anti-modern) conception of the world. The old distinction between fact and value cannot be jettisoned altogether, since it expresses something of use in its reference to outside and inside. But it ought to be transformed. Instead of fact and value, we must distinguish between the "power to take into account" and the "power to arrange in rank order" (PN 111). The power to take into account has the responsibility of detecting entities currently excluded from the collective. Its tacit question is "How many are we?" and its moral injunction is "Thou shalt not simplify" (PN 104; emphasis removed). This is the function of *complexity* in the collective, which requires that the collective not bury its head in the sand as to what eludes it. A good example is the work of the sciences, which constantly bring new beings to light. By dealing with external realities, perplexity occupies the "fact" side of the Old Regime, and does so in the manner of "taking into account." Though Latour does not always make this point explicitly, he is essentially doubling the old fact/ value dualism into a fourfold structure. The power to take into account is split into "fact" and "value" poles, and so is the power to arrange in rank order (PN 115). These will later be associated with four professional skill sets, each of them called upon to deal with all four of the main poles of the world, and all of them overseen by a fifth skill set to be discussed below. In any case, perplexity is what takes "facts" into account.

But what takes "values" into account? Latour's name for this zone of the world is *consultation*. If we find ourselves complaining about an ethical problem in any situation, "we express our indignation, as we affirm that powerful parties have neglected to take into consideration certain associations of humans and nonhumans; we accuse them of having put a *fait accompli* before us by making decisions too quickly, in too small a committee" (PN 106). Its tacit question is still "How many are we?", but its maxim is "thou shalt listen to many voices" (PN 106; emphasis removed). Politically speaking, "the only real difference is between the few and the many; there are those who meet in secret to unify prematurely what is and those who demonstrate publicly that they wish to add their grain of salt to the discussion, in order to compose the Republic" (PN 106). And here Latour explicitly notes that "this third requirement *resembles the first one* on perplexity … the two have a most striking family resemblance, even though tradition has placed them in different camps, dressing one in the white coat of 'Science,' the other in the white toga of 'values'" (PN 106). If perplexity is concerned with not artificially limiting the *quantity* of recognized beings, consultation is concerned with their *quality*.

We turn now to the power of arranging in rank order, which under the old system overlapped entirely with the "value" side of the world. Here again there is a fact/value split of sorts. The first of these functions is *hierarchization*, whose guiding question is "Can we live together?" and whose maxim is "Thou shalt discuss the compatibility of the new propositions with those which are already instituted" (PN 108; emphasis removed). Concerning candidates for entry into collective life, it must be asked whether they fit with that collective life as it now exists. "Do these propositions that come to complicate the fate of collective life in large numbers form an inhabitable world, or do they come on the contrary to disturb it, reduce it, crush it, massacre it, render it unlivable?" (PN 107). We might think once more of the 8,000 annual auto fatalities in France. While the power to take into account might give us reams of medical data and moral objections to the ongoing slaughter of innocents, how can the collective take these scruples fully into account without destroying the transportation system of France? How can France possibly ban all cars just to save 8,000 people per year? The hierarchical function thus leads France to retain motor vehicles and shrug off the death toll as the unfortunate cost of doing business. There may be moral and even geopolitical objections to allowing Putin to seize portions of the Ukraine in 2014, but what would be the price to the American and European collectives of a punitive strike against the nuclear power Russia, enlivened by its belief in historic claims on its neighbor? In a sense, hierarchization is the moment that opposes Hegel's "beautiful soul" and its presumed moral superiority to everything that actually happens in the world. There comes a moment when certain chickens are left to the wolves because the collective itself cannot face the wolves, under penalty of disruption.

The second function in this group, and the last of the four overall, is *institution*. It too asks the question "Can we live together?" and is guided by the following maxim: "Once propositions have been instituted, thou shalt no longer debate their legitimate presence within collective life" (PN 105; emphasis removed). Institution can be viewed as both the mirror image and the twin brother of perplexity. Whereas perplexity tries to keep the number of candidate entities open, institution tries to bring discussion to a close. "Once the candidacy of the new entities has been recognized, accepted, legitimized, admitted among the older propositions, these entities become states of nature, self-evidences, black boxes, habits, paradigms" (PN 104). Such black boxes "serve as indisputable premises to countless reasonings and arguments that are prolonged elsewhere" (PN 104). Once established or institutionalized, entities take on the form of "essences" (PN 104). This is not because they truly exist outside the collective, but because no good reason currently exists to open them up and examine their internal components. The inability of the United States to control gun violence, so appallingly mysterious to most Europeans, becomes easier to grasp once we consider America's reverence for its Constitution, whose blunt statement that "the right to bear arms shall not be infringed" is a powerful counterweight even to the most subtle legal hermeneutics. The Constitution could always be reopened for amendment or thorough revision, but perhaps at a terrifying cost on other fronts.

The lengthy Chapter 4 of *Politics of Nature*, entitled "Skills for the Collective," adds even more diversity to Latour's new quadripartite political realm. Whereas Heidegger contented himself with a mere fourfold structure of earth, sky, gods, and mortals,[3] Latour now advances nothing less than a sixteen-fold structure. The reason for this is that he identifies four professional "skills," each of them needed to discuss every one of the four functions of perplexity, consultation, hierarchization, and institution. Before doing so, he offers a spirited defense of metaphysics and an equally spirited polemic against economics. The chapter begins as follows: "Metaphysics has a bad reputation. Politicians mistrust it almost as much as scientists do. Speculations of philosophers sitting alone in their rooms, imagining that they can define the essential furniture of the world—just what no serious person should be indulging in any longer" (PN 128). But here Latour gives a rare and interesting twist to the notion of metaphysics. While this discipline is usually accused of making sweeping absolute knowledge claims that are deaf to the lessons of experience, Latour sees metaphysics as precisely the opposite: as the guarantor of our basic *ignorance* versus the know-it-all claims of Absolute Science and Power Politics. As he puts it, "[i]f we were to abstain from all metaphysical meditation, it would be tantamount to believing that we already know how the world is furnished: there is a nature *common to all*, and on top of that there are secondary difference that concern each of us as a member of a particular culture or as a private individual" (PN 128). In this sense Latour identifies metaphysics with political ecology itself, since both are tasked with building a collective in the face of an exteriority that can never be fully known but only taunts us with agitations and surprises.

Latour is less favorable towards economics, which is subjected to deep criticism here, as it is again later in *An Inquiry into Modes of Existence*. The key passage in *Politics of Nature* (PN 134) is too long to quote in full. But the heart of the critique is that economics plays a double game, playing the "fact" card against those who complain of its amorality ("Shh! I'm calculating ..." PN 134) and the "value" card against those who demand that it describe things in detail ("it will reply that it does not have time to be descriptive, because it has to move on to the normative judgment that is indispensable to its vocation," PN 134). On the whole, economists receive harsher blows from Latour than even the scientists and politicians, for whom he has plenty of residual admiration. As Latour states optimistically, "it must be possible to liberate economics from its failure to dissimulate the search for values under already-established facts, and the search for facts under already-calculated values ..." (PN 135). And more generally, "[t]here is no such thing as an economy, just as there is no such thing as *Homo oeconomicus* ... We do not find, at the bottom, an economic infrastructure that the economists, situated above, would study" (PN 135). Instead, there is only "a progressive economization of relation ... the economizers ... *performed* the collective by stabilizing the relations between humans and nonhumans" (PN 135–136). Or again, "Political ecology is quite clearly not soluble in the gastric juices of political economics" (PN 136). The problem is that economics does a great deal of work to make so many incommensurable things commensurable in terms of exchange value, but then forgets that this was merely a work of translation that left many properties of the things uneconomized. Despite these objections, economists will soon join scientists, politicians, and moralists among the four basic professions empowered by Latour to deal with the four ecopolitical functions.

We saw earlier that Latour sees two functions as "taking into account" (perplexity, consultation) and two others as "putting into order" (hierarchization, institution). In each of these four zones, a known profession finds its most comfortable home. Scientists correspond to *perplexity*, since it is they who continuously unearth previously unknown claimants to reality. Moralists match up with *consultation*, for they are the ones who insist that the rights of the unheard no longer go unheard. It is politicians who hail from the zone of *hierarchization*, since they are the ones who must deal with putting in order the accepted and rejected appellants from the world outside the present collective. And finally, economists are linked to *institution*, since they are the ones who stabilize the current boundaries between humans and nonhumans. Yet these four professions, which Latour is at pains to tell us should not be taken too literally, do not remain confined to the sphere from which they originate. For that would be the bad, modern version of the division of labor: a taxonomical quarantine in which politicians were supposed to speak about humans but keep their mouths shut about the facts of nature, while scientists were supposed to speak about nature but keep their noses out of politics and values. Instead, Latour conceives of a new model in which all professions must speak about all four zones of reality, in each case by using the different skills that are their own. The results are summarized in an encyclopedic chart (PN 162–163) that is too detailed to summarize here. As if that were not enough, all four professions have two additional tasks: separation of powers (preventing the different zones from encroaching on one another) and scenarization of the whole (bringing coherence to the common world). This gives Latour's diamond 24 facets in all, though in the next chapter he increases it by at least one: the "power to follow through," granted to the profession of the *administrator*, including both bureaucrats and the state.

Modernity always had dreams of annihilating its enemies, of tossing them into the "dustbin of history" where all archaic garbage was destined to go. Modernity delighted in casting witches, pirates, slaves, leeches, religions, and dictators into the outer darkness of non-being, only to see all of these figures return to haunt the collective at a later date. In part this was inevitable, since every collective must reject certain claimants to reality: "There remains the most difficult, the most painful, the cruelest of tasks ... the explicit and formal *rejection* of those with whom one has not been able to come to terms ... in short, the risk of committing an injustice" (PN 177). But one of the features of Latour's political ecology, with its refusal of the modernist narrative of linear progress, is that it throws nothing away forever. Under the modern system, "excluded parties did not take the form of enemies but that of nonexistent beings who had never belonged to the real world" (PN 177). According to Latour, rejection should now mean only a "process of excluding certain entities *for the time being as incompatible* with the common world" (PN 179). Like the Taliban of Afghanistan, the Irish Republican Army, Colorado marijuana smokers, or death row inmates freed by DNA evidence, all of them placed on a black list of inhumanity but then approached in negotiation, excluded entities are never beyond the pale of all possible settlement. We simply exclude entities from the collective, we "[do] not claim to humiliate them by withdrawing existence" (PN 179). Latour imagines us addressing the rejected as follows: "In the scenarios attempted up to now, there is no room for you in the common world. Go away: you have become our enemies" (PN 179). But he does not tell them this: "You do not exist; you have lost forever any right to ontology; you will never again be counted in the construction of a cosmos" (PN 179). It is necessary to keep the door open in this manner, since "all Republics are badly formed, all are built on sand. They hold up only if they are rebuilt at once and if the parties excluded from the lower house come back the next morning, knock at the doors of the upper house, and demand to participate in the common world" (PN 183).

That brings us to the concluding Chapter 5 of *Politics of Nature*, entitled "Exploring Common Worlds." Latour returns to the theme of the outside or the exterior, the very means by which he hopes to avoid the Power Politics he inherited from Hobbes. "Through construction, the collective feeds on what remains outside, which it has not yet collected. But how can we talk about that which escapes it entirely?" (PN 184). Any nature-in-itself is now out of the question, since "there is no longer the unified transcendence capable of putting an end to the logorrhea of public assemblies" (PN 185). Instead, there are countless transcendences, as many as there are entities currently excluded from the collective. A good number are destined to appear or return, since nature and politics are to be replaced by "the distinction between enemies and appellants, between the current stage of the collective *and its re-collection in the next round*" (PN 186). Those that have been rejected "will return in any event to haunt the collective at the next stage" (PN 186). We cannot make things too easy for ourselves by short-circuiting the collective with either natural law or violence (PN 187). Yet we hardly need to do so, since "transcendences abound in the propositions that are external to the collective" (PN 187).

Latour now introduces a *topological* idea that will later prove to be of great importance for his political philosophy: the notion of politics as a *loop*. Speaking of the upper house that replaces Politics and the lower house that replaces Science, Latour notes that "it no longer suffices to exist in the upper house in order to exist in the lower one. It no longer suffices to have been rejected by the lower house to cease to exist in the upper one. *Provided that they work in a loop*, the two assemblies have as their result the production, at a given moment, of provisional assemblies" (PN 188). This theme of the loop will return later. For now, we need only consider that such a passage of entities into and out of the collective threatens the modern notion of continual progress in which the old is never brought back from the dead. For modernity, rejected entities amounted to "fantasies that were driven out of the real world and pushed back into a vast dump, a cemetery filled with archaisms and irrationalities" (PN 189). For Latour there is no longer such a garbage dump, since the rejected return to haunt us: "Must political ecology then refrain from plunging into history? Must it abandon forward movement? For want of being modern, must it resign itself to the postmoderns' running in place? Or, worse still ... will it have to accept the designation 'reactionary'?" (PN 191). The answer is no, since the collective will still be driven forward, though now by repeatedly responding to an excluded exterior rather than annihilating reactionary and archaic irrationalities. "It is thus quite capable of showing a difference between past and future, but it obtains that difference *by way of the gap between two successive iterations* and no longer by way of the old distinction between facts and values" (PN 191). In other words, no collective can stay motionless, since every Republic is always a bad piece of work and the unformatted exterior always a looming threat. Indeed, it is the special gift of politicians to be drenched with worries over what might arise at any moment to disrupt the collective. Yet there is a sense in which Latour does find himself in diametrical opposition to the modern sense of progress. For the moderns, the increasing purification of nature and society from one another means that progress entails becoming less and less attached to the world, rising above it in critical superiority. Latour takes the opposite tack: "We no longer expect from the future that it will emancipate us from all our attachments; on the contrary, we expect that it will attach us with tighter bonds to more numerous crowds of *aliens* who have become full-fledged members of the collective that is in the process of being formed" (PN 191). Along with death and taxes, there is a third certainty: "tomorrow, the collective will be more intricate than it was yesterday" (PN 192).

We now come to the heart of Latour's final chapter, his introduction of a third power to join taking into account and arranging into order: it is the "power to follow through." This is the natural site of the administrative profession, though the other four skills are granted the power to follow through as well, bringing the total number of professional contributions on Latour's political map to 29. The power to follow up might also be called "the power to *govern*, if everyone agreed to use this expression to designate the relinquishment of all mastery" (PN 200). He tells us that this should not be confused with the state, which is far too implicated in the modernist form of politics (PN 201). Instead, we might compare the power to govern with *science policy* rather than political science. If we take science policy in a sufficiently broad sense, it becomes "a function that makes it possible to *characterize the relative fruitfulness* of collective experiments, without its being monopolized right away by either scientists or politicians" (PN 202). We should not despise administrators or even bureaucrats, since "we do not see how to get along without [the latter] for the elaboration of a public life that would finally unfold according to due process, for the excellent reason that bureaucrats are *masters of processes and forms*" (PN 204). As for administrators, they "ensure the continuity of public life" (PN 205). Moreover, "[h]ow can we detect new phenomena at the extreme limit of the sensitivity of instruments, without a meticulous accumulation of data over a very long time?" (PN 205). Put differently, "the State ensures the comparison between matters of concern n and $n+1$" (PN 207), much like the God of continuous creation imagined by the occasionalist philosophers. Latour seems aware that his defense of administrators and bureaucrats could try the patience of those, from the Left or the Right, who might hope for a more risqué political agenda: "If this definition appears too weak to those who believe they must be heirs of Louis XIV, Rousseau, Danton, Hegel, Bismarck, or Lenin, they should recall the importance attached [by *Politics of Nature*] to the fragile envelope that separates the inside of the collective from the outside" (PN 207). Be careful what you wish for, since the seeds of transformation surround us in all directions, with lurking claimants to reality already at the walls of the collective. There will always be change enough to satisfy all of us: "the one who is rejected ... will come back the next day to put the collective at risk: today's enemy is tomorrow's ally" (PN 207). But above all, do not be afraid, since the enemy is "as frightened as you are!" (PN 209).

Latour closes his final chapter with a new overarching professional figure—the diplomat. The first advantage of the diplomat is his or her lack of a false neutrality: "contrary to the arbiters who always rely on a superior and disinterested position, the diplomat always belongs to one of the parties to the conflict" (PN 212). Or even more vividly: "a potential traitor to all camps, he does not know in advance in what form those whom he is addressing are going to formulate the requirements that may lead to war or peace" (PN 212). The key function of the diplomat is to probe for the difference between the essential and inessential interests of his interlocutors, which neither he nor they know perfectly in advance. Is the status of Jerusalem really a non-negotiable point for both Israelis and Palestinians, or can one side or both be persuaded that this is not essential and that something else is the essence of the dispute? Is the military defense of Taiwan an essential commitment for the United States, or is this negotiable in the name of better relations with China? Is Egypt really prepared to go to war with its African neighbors over a specific percentage of Nile water rights? The parties to such disputes may think they know where their essential commitments lie, but the diplomat realizes these are matters for testing, probing, and the art of the deal. In other words, "diplomacy has to carry out a triage between what is expendable and what is essential" (PN 214), but "only on condition that the other will agree to the same triage" (PN 214; emphasis removed). If everything is essential, then we must be prepared to go to war over absolutely anything, which is absurd. The diplomat is uncertain of everything: "she agrees to engage with collectives that find themselves, with respect to the precise distribution of requirements and expressions, *in the same uncertainty* as the one in whose name she is dealing" (PN 215). This passage echoes Socrates in the *Meno* when he differentiates himself from the torpedo fish (which only stings others) by saying that he stings himself as well, not knowing what virtue is any better than those with whom he speaks. The diplomat's greatness "is that he imposes *on the very ones who sent him* this fundamental doubt about their own requirements" (PN 216).

AGAINST BECK'S COSMOPOLITANISM

In 2004 Latour wrote a response (BEC) to the German sociologist Ulrich Beck, most famous for his book *Risk Society*. At issue is Beck's call for a new cosmopolitanism, which, after a few opening pleasantries, Latour fights as ardently as he can. Though Beck's proposals for contemporary peace are welcome, "peace proposals make sense only if the real extent of the conflicts they are supposed to settle is understood" (BEC 450). Latour holds that this is not the case with Beck, and he pulls no punches in explaining why. The key point for Latour is his familiar complaint about the pairing of multiculturalism with what he calls "mononaturalism." One cannot imagine anything less Latourian than the usual modern dyad that pits a single world outside the mind against the numerous views on that world from different arbitrary cultural standpoints. "Beck takes his key term ['cosmopolitanism'] and its definition, off the shelf, from the Stoics and Kant. Those definitions (Beck's, Kant's, the Stoics') are problematic: none shows understanding that the cosmos itself is at stake" (BEC 453). Latour now takes a stand with anthropology against Beck's own discipline, sociology: "Like most sociologists, Beck suffers from anthropology blindness. For the sociologist, nature, the world, the cosmos, is simply there; and since humans share basic characteristics, our view of the world is, at baseline, the same everywhere" (BEC 453). If we have so much in common, then why do conflicts occur? Latour is disappointed with Beck's answer to this question: "Perversity, acquisitiveness, undisciplined instincts account for the fact that we do not—we rarely have—peace" (BEC 453). This is just another sample of the rationalist model of Truth Politics that Latour detests: a model proclaiming that the political truth would already be incarnate if not for the superstitious religions, irrational desires, criminal impulses, and gullible fetishes of all the corrupt and naïve resisters of enlightenment. The term "cosmopolitan" was brought up in the same rationalist crib as rationalism and scientism, and it ought to be replaced with a more general "cosmopolitics," the term of Isabelle Stengers that Latour loves so well.[4]

Latour contends that unlike Stengers, Beck holds that "wars rage because human cultures have (and defend) differing views of the same world. If those views could be reconciled or shown to differ only superficially, peace would follow automatically" (BEC 454). In other words, multi-culturalism must be tamed by mononaturalism, the underlying doctrine on which everyone should agree. Against this view of conflict, which Latour sees as far too mild, he invokes the "awesome multiplicity" of the *pluriverse* as defined by William James (BEC 454). He salutes the Stengers of *Cosmopolitics*, Volume 7 for opposing "the malady of tolerance" (BEC 454), which arises quite naturally once human conflict is misunderstood as superficial. And now at last, we begin to see why Latour takes such an interest in the discomforting political philosophy of Schmitt. Perhaps Beck's central problem is that he wishes to define warfare out of existence, dismissing it as the result of petty human failings. And that is one problem that Schmitt obviously does not have:

> As is well known from Carl Schmitt's definition, any conflict, no matter how bitter, that is waged under a common arbiter is not a war but what he calls a "police operation." If there exists one cosmos, already unified, one nature that is used as the arbiter for all our disputes, then there are, by definition, no wars but only police operations. (BEC 455)

In this respect, the West has been too condescending to take its enemies seriously. "To use Schmitt again: Westerners have not understood themselves as facing on the battlefield an enemy whose victory is possible, just irrational people who have to be corrected ... As I have argued elsewhere, Westerners have until now been engaged in *pedagogical wars.*"[5] (455)

Pedagogical wars are no longer equal to the times, since "things have changed of late and our wars are now wars of the worlds, because it's now the makeup of the cosmos that is at stake. Nothing is off limits, off the table, for dispute" (BEC 455). Science and rationalism effectively depoliticize the world: "The settlements that nature offers are reached without due process—they put 99 percent of what is up for grabs off limits, and the result is always another round of conflict" (BEC 455). Or even more bluntly, "politics is moot if it is not about (what John Tresch calls) 'cosmograms'" (BEC 455).[6] In other words, "we perhaps never differ about opinions, but rather always about things—about what world we inhabit. And very probably, it never happens that adversaries come to agree on opinions: they begin, rather, to inhabit a different world" (BEC 455). Implicit here is a new view of peace, one already heralded by Latour's views on how to emerge from baboon society: just as nonhuman entities stabilize the *polis*, they may also form the basis of peace between different polities. The rather different view that prevails in much political philosophy leads Latour to a high pitch of sarcasm: "When men of good will assemble with their cigars at the Habermas Club to discuss an armistice for this or that conflict and they leave their gods on hooks in the cloakroom, I suspect that what is under way is not a peace conference at all" (BEC 456). And as for Beck himself:

> How is it that Beck believes religion is ignorable? Again, there is no cosmos in his cosmopolitanism: he seems to have no inkling that humans have always counted less than the vast population of divinities and lesser transcendental entities that give us life ... Beck appears to believe in a UNESCO koine, a sociological Esperanto, that lies hidden behind stubborn defects, whether social or psychological, in our representations. Men of good will, he would say, must agree that gods are no more than representations ... [But] peace settlements are not, as Stengers emphasizes, between men of good will who have left their gods (their narrow attachments) behind but between men of ill will possessed by super- and subhumans of ill will. (BEC 456)

Conflict must not be viewed as a superficial strife between plastically moldable worldviews, for "if the UNESCO lingua franca [were] enough to define all inhabitants of the planet, peace would already reign" (BEC 457). We cannot persuade the "others" to join our rationalist club, because "they have reason to believe that they themselves belong to the best clubs already and cannot fathom why others—when invited—refuse to join" (BEC 457). More generally, "the assumptions of naturalism have been shown—most recently and thoroughly by Philippe Descola—to be unshared by vast numbers of humans" (BEC 458). Rather than belittle all these dissenters as irrational dupes who need to be brought as quickly as possible to Western science and parliamentary democracy, Latour recommends a *constructivist* path: not in the sense of a "social constructionism" that would treat nature as independent and unconstructed, but in the sense of a theory that treats nature and culture as both constructed through due process. "It is possible—and from a Western (from my Burgundian) point of view, desirable—that, in the distant future, we come to live within a common world defined as naturalism defines it. But to behave as if the settlement were already in place and as though it requires no negotiation to achieve it is a sure trigger to further warfare" (BEC 458). Even this hypothetical future naturalism seems mostly rhetorical, given Latour's view that peace settlements require some compromise as to what objects exist. Moreover, rationalism is just another form of fundamentalism, which is itself a Western invention: "Naturalizers, those in the West who appeal to a Nature Out There, unconstructed and nonnegotiable, are now confronted by people saying the same of the Koran and *Shari'a*. And when one fundamentalism butts heads with another, no peace talks are possible because there is nothing to discuss" (BEC 461). Rather than trying to escape constructivism, we should simply learn "how to distinguish between good constructions and bad ... [for] there is no extant or extinct way of life that has not been passionately involved in making distinctions between good and bad fabrications" (BEC 459). This is our only possible path, since "the parliament in which a common world could be assembled has got to be constructed from scratch" (BEC 462).

LATOUR'S RESPONSE TO DE VRIES

Bruno Latour and the Dutch philosopher Gerard de Vries have long conducted a friendly but occasionally heated debate on political philosophy; their spirited exchange at Cerisy-la-Salle in 2007 is still fresh in my memory. De Vries once told me that his initial attraction to Latour's work was that Latour and his friends were among the few contemporary philosophers to display any sense of humor. In later years, de Vries did a great deal to solidify Latour's outstanding reputation as a philosopher in the Netherlands, the country where he is least likely to be pigeonholed as just a social scientist or a French postmodern relativist. In 2007, the same year as their debate in Cerisy, the two had an exchange of views in the pages of the journal *Social Studies of Science*.

For reasons of space we cannot analyze de Vries's article directly, but must confine ourselves to those criticisms that Latour himself takes to be most important, of which there are three:

1. "a contrast between a political theory that turns around the *subjects* of politics (whom [de Vries] amusingly calls 'mini-kings') and one that turns around its *objects*" (RGDV 811).
2. "a contrast between the official machinery of government and the multiple sites where political action might be seeping through without being recognized as such by political scientists [i.e., subpolitics]" (RGDV 811).
3. "[de Vries's] contrast ... between two ways of doing [science studies], one that takes political philosophy 'off the shelf' and another that would study the complex and entangled practices of politics as well as of the sciences symmetrically" (RGDV 811).

Latour makes three points of his own in response, though they do not correspond with those of de Vries in one-for-one fashion:

1. The political contribution of science studies to politics has been the reformulation of politics in cosmopolitical terms.
2. Despite de Vries's call for a return to Aristotle, the pragmatists are of greater contemporary relevance, "providing ... that the notion of *issue* is brought to the fore" (RGDV 811).
3. Finally, Latour tries to show "how the different meanings of the adjective 'political' could be redescribed as successive *moments* in the trajectory of an issue" (RGDV 811–812).

For the most part, Latour concedes de Vries's point about the failure of science studies to follow political networks in as much detail as scientific ones:

[W]e [in science studies] were so busy renewing some of the features of scientific practice that we took off the shelf whatever political theory we had. The result is that politics was expanded to the point of becoming coextensive to contemporary societies [as a whole] insofar as these include fragments of science and pieces of technology. Since by now "everything is political," the adjective "political" suffers the same fate as the adjective "social": in being extended everywhere, they have both become meaningless. (RGDV 812)

Latour admits that the time has come to pay more attention to how the political is constituted: "The tropism toward 'social explanation' probably accounts for part of this imbalance: in the 'knowledge slash power' composite, 'knowledge' triggered much more suspicion than 'power,' which (we wrongly thought) had been scrutinized enough" (RGDV 812). Indeed, actor-network theory has had a great deal to say about the social construction of scientific facts, but so far has not said much about the inverse phenomenon, which we might call "the shaping of political fictions by reality itself." One can easily imagine a Bruno Latour born in 1977 rather than 1947, annoyed with the force-fed social constructionist dogmas of a later educational system, orienting his career instead toward the real nonhuman forces that help "construct" what falsely seem to be arbitrary customs and values.

Latour reminds us that science studies was initially attacked from opposite directions—often an excellent sign that a new theory is misunderstood from all sides. On the one hand Latour and his friends "were accused of polluting the pure realm of knowledge by showing plays of power at work even in the remotest recesses of the laboratories" (RGDV 812). On the other, "we were accused by more politically minded social reformers of having 'depoliticized' the domain of 'concerned scientists' because we seemed to forget the weight of 'real domination'" (RGDV 812). What the two groups of critics shared in common was that they

> expected to find in the science studies literature the traditional characters that were supposed to occupy the political stage—citizens, assemblies of "mini-kings," ideologies, deliberations, votes, elections; the traditional *sites* of political events—street demonstrations, parliaments, executive rooms, command and control headquarters; and the traditional *passions* we spontaneously associate with the political: indignation, anger, back room deals, violence, and so on. What they found instead were white-coated technicians, corporate room chief executive officers,

mathematicians scribbling at the blackboard, patent lawyers, surveyors, innovators, entrepreneurs and experts of all sorts, all of whom were carrying out their activities in sites totally unrelated to the loci of political action and through means that were absolutely different from the maintenance or the subversion of law and order. A vaccine, an incandescent lamp, an equation, a pollution standard, a building, a blood screening procedure: those were the new means through which politics were being carried out. (RGDV 812–813)

Far from being a defect of science studies, Latour holds that "the discovery of this hidden continent" remains "its great breakthrough" (RGDV 813). Henceforth, "politics is something entirely different from what political scientists believe: it is the building of the cosmos in which everyone lives, the progressive composition of the common world. What is common to this vast transformation is that politics is now defined as the agonizing sorting out of conflicting *cosmograms*" (RGDV 813). Yet Latour concedes that de Vries is right to say that "this new wine was put, at first, into old bottles. The initial reaction of STS [Science, Technology, and Society] scholars was not to undermine the age-old definitions of politics but to see how to bring science into politics" (RGDV 813). Either traditional political notions were improbably expanded into the sphere of inanimate actors, or scientists were brought into negotiation with the non-specialist public. "The shortcomings of those two moves," Latour insists, "is that they equally retain the definition of politics taught in political science departments" (RGDV 814). But "what if the definition of politics were to be reshaped as deeply as the definition of science has by STS? Not simply expanded or shrunk but entirely *redistributed?*" (RGDV 814).

It is here that Latour makes his move towards pragmatism:

> In contrast to de Vries, I do not believe that returning to Aristotle is helpful … [instead,] let's turn to the pragmatists and especially to John Dewey. Following Noortje Marres' reinterpretation of Dewey, de Vries redefines politics as neither a type of procedure nor a domain of life. Politics is not some essence; it is something that moves; it is something that has a trajectory. (RGDV 814)

This is enough, Latour holds, to distinguish his own pragmatism "from the rather enucleated version of pragmatism proposed by Richard Rorty and Hilary Putnam" (RGDV 814). The key contribution of pragmatism is to redefine "political" from a professional specialty to a type of situation:

"pragmatism proposes that we focus on the objects of concern and then, so as to handle them, produce the instruments and equipment necessary to grasp the questions they have raised and in which we are hopelessly entangled" (RGDV 814). Latour says that rather than "object," a more accurate term can be found in Dewey's long-winded phrase "unexpected and unattended consequences of collective actions" (RGDV 814). He adds that this is the same thing as Marres's wording "issues and their trajectories" or Lippmann's slogan "problem of the public" (RGDV 814). Latour closes the thought with grand claims for the pragmatist approach: "Here is a Copernican revolution of radical proportions: to finally make politics turn around topics that generate a public around them instead of trying to define politics *in the absence* of any issue, as a question of procedure, authority, sovereignty, right, and representativity" (RGDV 814). And finally:

> Whatever the term one wishes to use—object, thing, gathering, concern—the key move is to make all definitions of politics turn around the issues instead of having the issues enter into a ready-made political sphere to be dealt with. First define how things turn the public into a problem, and only then try to render more precise what is political, which procedures should be put into place, how the various assemblies can reach closure, and so on. Such is the hard-headed *Dingpolitik* of STS as opposed to the human-centred *Realpolitik*. (RGDV 815)

We now need to ask *how* politics turns around issues. Here Latour makes use of a striking metaphor from astronomy: "In the same way as stars in astronomy are only stages in a series of transformations that astronomers have learned to map, issues offer up many different aspects depending on where they are in their life histories" (RGDV 815). My first time hearing Latour in person was at Northwestern University in April 1998, when he presented materials that would soon appear in *Politics of Nature*. One of Latour's passing remarks that day captured my imagination to an especial degree: public hygiene (water, sewage, street cleaning) was once a political issue but is now an accepted part of urban management that no political party would dispute; perhaps the same will happen one day with environmentalism. What intrigued me so much was the idea that an issue might mutate over time from overtly political into something more closely resembling infrastructure management, and perhaps the reverse could happen as well. In responding to de Vries nearly a decade later, Latour expands his 1998 remark from Northwestern into an even richer fivefold lifespan of political issues, much like the life stages of a star:

- The first stage, Political-1, refers to "new associations between humans and nonhumans" (RGDV 816), as in the Dutch biomedical tests cited by de Vries, which raised previously unsuspected political issues surrounding blood screening for pregnant women. Latour says that science studies deserves credit for drawing our attention to the political character of these associations "by resurrecting in effect one of Marx's definitions of materialism" (RGDV 816).
- Political-2 is the pragmatist sense of the term as just described, as in "Lippmann and Dewey's beautiful argument that the public is always a *problem*" (RGDV 816). In the case covered by de Vries, "the blood screening test has consequences that entangle many unanticipated actors without biologists and physicians having developed any instruments" to follow them (RGDV 816). While many pregnant women younger than the high-risk age group also wished to take the test, in the eyes of the Dutch government the spread of such tests had the effect of framing pregnancy as a medical disorder rather than a normal life event. An interested public suddenly materialized around this unprecedented problem.
- Poltical-3 concerns sovereignty in the usual sense, and is "much closer to the hard core of political theory, from Machiavelli to Schmitt" (RGDV 816). In de Vries's example, the Dutch cabinet tried and failed to intervene in the issue of blood screening for pregnant women, but despite its failure, "at least it had taken upon itself to make this issue bear upon the great question of Dutch sovereignty" (RGDV 816). As Latour adds, "here the blood screening test became part of what I have called the Political Circle: Can the whole be simultaneously what gives the Law and what receives the Law so as to produce autonomy and freedom?" We encounter this figure of the "political circle" quite vividly in the coming chapter. As Latour now puts it: "Just as not all stars have to end up as black holes or as red dwarfs, not all issues have to become political-3. But when they are in that stage, they look indeed very different from all the others" (RGDV 816).
- The stage called Political-4 is "when fully conscious citizens, endowed with the ability to speak, to calculate, to compromise and to discuss together, meet in order to 'solve problems' that have been raised by science and technology" (RGDV 817). Latour accuses

de Vries of wrongly "making fun" of this sort of politics, while conceding his point that it would be ridiculous to reduce all politics to this stage as some hope to do. In any case, "this Habermasian moment is not an absurd way of dealing with issues; it's simply what happens when issues have stopped being political-3 or -2, and have been metabolized to the point when they can be absorbed by the normal tradition of deliberative democracy" (RGDV 817). This may be more appropriate at some times than others: "Global warming is certainly not in this stage—nor is the case of extra-solar planets—but innumerable issues are perfectly amenable as problems to be solved by one of the many procedures that have been invented to produce the consensus of rationally minded citizens" (RGDV 817).

• Political-5 refers to issues that have "become part of the daily routine of administration and management" (RGDV 817). For example, "the silent working of the sewage systems in Paris has stopped being political, as have vaccinations against smallpox or tuberculosis. It is now in the hands of vast and silent bureaucracies that rarely make the headlines" (RGDV 817). But Michel Foucault is someone who did study this level of politics with especial intensity: "all those institutions appear on the surface to be absolutely apolitical, and yet in their silent, ordinary, fully routinized ways they are perversely the most important aspects of what we mean by living together—even though no one raises hell about them and they hardly stir congressmen out of their parliamentary somnolence" (RGDV 817).

Latour ends with the proposal that we use Stengers's word "cosmopolitics" to refer to *all five* stages in the life cycle of an issue. He adds the noteworthy remark that Politics-1 and Politics-5 "are taken as totally 'apolitical' for everyone but historians of science, feminist scholars and various science students" (RGDV 818). But there is also no reason for everything to become political for everyone: "*Not* having to participate should remain the ideal and is of course the most widely distributed response to calls for action" (RGDV 819). And again: "There is no cognitive, mental and affective equipment requiring all of us to be constantly implicated, involved or engaged with the working of the Paris sewage system, the search for weapons of mass destruction in Iraq, the development of stem cell research in California, global warming, peer-to-peer software, new accounting procedures for European companies, and so on" (RGDV 819). Nor would it even be wise to treat them politically in the customary sense of the term: "There is no sense in saying that global warming,

DNA probes, river pollution, new planetary systems, the building of a fusion research demonstrator, and so on, will all go through the same street demonstrations, the same parliamentary debates and the same governmental shuttles" (RGDV 819). These sentiments ("God protect me from politics whenever possible") cleanly separate Latour from many other present-day devotees of Schmitt, who are interested in the ominous German thinker precisely because of his apparent efforts to *repoliticize* much that has been taken off the political table.

This passage on the five stages of political life is the only one known to me where Latour attempts a *chronology* of one of his later fourteen modes of existence (each with its own three-letter abbreviation, as we shall see). As far as I am aware, he never attempts it for any mode but politics. It is interesting to contemplate whether such modes as religion [REL], law [LAW], and organization [ORG] also follow trajectories along a life cycle. But Latour does not pursue the issue, and seems to prefer discussing the modes in *topological* rather than chronological terms: politics is always the circle, while law and even science are referred to as *chains*. We now turn to the political circle, which serves as the gateway to the political philosophy of the late Latour: a phase still underway, and presumably still holding further surprises in store.

4

Late Latour: Politics as a Mode

With the public emergence of Latour's work on the different modes of existence, we have undeniably reached a new phase in his thinking, even though he had secretly been hard at work on the project since the late 1980s. Latour recounts the long history of these labors in his pleasant overview "Biography of an Investigation: On a Book About Modes of Existence," an intriguing essay that nonetheless tells us little about the specifically *political* ramifications of the AIME project. Whereas the first part of Latour's career employed a deliberately flat ontology in which all natural, human, artificial, simple, composite, and imaginary entities were equally linked together in networks, the new project reverses this flatness and tries to account for the incommensurability of various modes of being, each with its own criteria of truth. Law [LAW], religion [REL], and politics [POL] are three of the most recognizable modes, each of them governed by standards that cannot be applied to the others. Alongside these familiar modes from human life are the seemingly full-blown metaphysical modes such as reproduction [REP], reference [REF], and habit [HAB]. We also find the three modes entitled organization [ORG], attachment [ATT], and morality [MOR], the particles left behind when economics is smashed in the accelerator of Latour's mind.

Despite his now definitive shift to the modes-of-existence project, Latour sometimes writes and speaks in the idiom of his older system, much as when Coca-Cola continued to offer Coke Classic on the shelf alongside New Coke. The distinct old and new voices of Latour may co-exist for some time to come. Yet this presents no problem, since they are perfectly compatible: after all, networks remain in Latour's new system as a mode called networks [NET]. It is also rather easy to tell the early/middle philosophy from the late one. Whenever Latour emphasizes that we must dissolve the modernist opposition between nature and culture and throw all entities into a single witches' cauldron, we can be sure that we are drinking Latour Classic. But if instead we hear him distinguishing carefully between science with its referential mode and various other modes such as religion, law, and politics, we can be sure that we are drinking a bottle of New Latour.

TALKING POLITICS

Accepting the Siegfried Unseld Prize in Frankfurt in September 2008, Latour recalls that "beginning [at] Easter 1987, I started in earnest the first project about comparing regimes of enunciation (what I now call *An Inquiry into Modes of Existence*), even though I have not published a line about it ever since—until today that is" (COP 603). While this claim is mostly true, Latour in Frankfurt seems to be forgetting his fascinating earlier publications on the modes project, one of them perfectly suited to our topic: the neglected 2003 article "What if we *Talked* Politics a Little?"

Even the abstract of this piece gets straight to the point: "The political circle is reconstituted [in this article] and thus also the reasons why a 'transparent' or 'rational' political speech act destroys the very conditions of group formation" (TPL 143). Latour goes on to speculate that the widespread disillusionment with politics today is based on a misunderstanding, "as if, in recent years, we had begun to expect it to provide a form of fidelity, exactitude, or truth that is totally impossible" (TPL 143). The implication is that rationalism has tried to apply globally a model of truth-as-correspondence that is simply inapplicable to the political sphere. As a result, politics looks to the Moderns like nothing worth celebrating:

> Political expression is always *disappointing;* that is where we must start. In terms of the transfer of exact undistorted information on the social or natural world, we could say that it always seems to be totally inadequate: truisms, clichés, handshakes, half-truths, half-lies, windy words, repetitions mostly, *ad nauseam.* That is the ordinary, banal, daily, limp tautological character of this form of discourse that shocks the brilliant, the upright, the fast, the organized, the lively, the informed, the great, the decided. When one says that someone or something is "political," one signals above all this fundamental disappointment ... The expression "that's political" means first and foremost "it doesn't move straight," "it doesn't move fast"; it always implies that "if only we didn't have this load, we'd achieve our goal more *directly.*" (TPL 145)

There is now a genuine danger that our contempt for the political mode of existence will lead us to forget its true nature: "Could it be possible to *forget* politics? Far from being a universal competency of the 'political animal,' might it not be a form of life so fragile that we could document its progressive appearance and disappearance?" (TPL 143). The disappearance of the political mode would not even be unprecedented: "Perhaps, we are going to get to the point where talking in this [political] way will seem as incomprehensible as uttering religious statements" (TPL 152).

By politics, Latour is not referring merely to "conversations on explicitly political topics, such as parliamentary elections, corruption among elected representatives or laws that need to be passed … nor to all the ingredients of politics as an institution, as defined in the corridors of political science departments, that is, international relations, constitutional law, power struggles, etc" (TPL 144). The reason is that politics is *everywhere*. This does not mean that politics is once again ontologized to the point that "everything is political," the permanent risk run by the early and middle Latour. Instead, Latour wants to treat politics not as an explicit type of content, but as a specific *manner* of dealing with things. This political manner can be found in any place, though not necessarily at every time: "One can be a member of Parliament and not talk in a political way. Conversely, one can be at home with one's family, in an office, at work, and start talking *politically* about some issue or other even if none of one's words have any apparent link with the political sphere" (TPL 145). Politics can appear anywhere, but at any given moment might exist nowhere.

Everyone seems to dream of a rational politics that would consist "of information, transparency, exactitude, rectitude, and *faithful* representation. That is the dream of honest thinking, of non-deformation, of immediacy, of the absence of any mediator" (TPL 145–146). It is the dream of what Latour sarcastically terms "double-click" communication. Yet such transparency is merely a dream even for science, let alone for politics: "Demanding that scientists tell the truth *directly*, with no laboratory, no instruments, no equipment, no processing of data, no writing of articles, no conferences or debates, at once, extemporaneously, naked, for all to see, without stammering [or] babbling, would be senseless" (TPL 147). If any theme is typically Latourian, it is the idea that there is only mediation, never mere intermediaries through which entities could communicate without translation or distortion. Here Latour turns toward the major theme of his system of modes of existence:

Each enunciation regime [i.e., each mode of existence] elaborates its own criteria of truth and lies, its own definitions of felicity and infelicity. Saying that political discourse is "twisted" has a very different meaning, depending on whether one has chosen the curve or the straight line as an ideal for all utterances. Straight lines are useful for drawing a square, but they are hardly so when we wish to outline an ellipse. (TPL 146)

Why, we might ask, does politics fail to provide us with direct access to truth? Latour would respond with impatience: "A stupid question deserves a stupid answer. One could just as well complain about the poor quality of a modem that was incapable of percolating coffee ordered on the internet" (TPL 147). But there is really no problem between politics and truth: "Political discourse appears to be untruthful only in contrast with other forms of truth. In and for itself it discriminates truth from falsehood with stupefying precision. It is not indifferent to truth, as it is so unjustly accused of being; it simply differs from all the other regimes in its judgment of truth" (TPL 147).

This leads us to ask how politics can claim to judge truth, if it is not a matter of transparent access to a reality that could straighten out the crookedness of mediocre politicians. Latour's answer is clear enough. Politics "aims to *allow to exist* that which would not exist without it: the public as a temporarily defined totality. Either some means has been provided to trace a group into existence, and the talk has been truthful; or no group has been traced, and it is in vain that people have talked" (TPL 148). Philosophers usually tell us that a statement is true if it corresponds to a true state of affairs outside the mind in the world. But this criterion could not possibly work for political statements such as the following: "'I understand you,' 'We're one big family,' 'We won't tolerate this any more,' or 'Our firm must conquer a bigger market share'... 'All together, all together, all!'" (TPL 148). Such statements do not succeed or fail through some reference to an external state of affairs, but to "an entirely new phenomenon: the *resumption* or *suspension* of the continuous work of definition and materialization of the group that this talk intends to trace" (TPL 148). And now comes the final lesson: "Anything that extends [the group] is true; anything that interrupts it is false" (TPL 148). This explains Latour's frustration with the repeated failure-without-consequence of the unfalsifiable radicals of the Left. As Latour puts it in an interview with a Turkish periodical:

the will of total subversion is still there in some circles, but has now become even more immensely satisfying because it is also connected with the certainty of failure while maintaining the absolute comfort of being morally superior ... And this goes a long way toward explaining why the minority parties of the ultra-left are still able to intimidate all of the other movements: you are the best and the brightest, you will fail; failure will never be counted against you, only against those who failed to be as radical as you. (DBD)

Failure in politics signals untruth, not a superior truth that is simply too good for our corrupt world. Here we have Latour's definitive rejection of the "beautiful soul" in politics, which links him with Foucault's refreshing demand that activism must have genuine practical effects. Alienation is nothing but a failure on the part of the alienated.

As we have seen, Latour holds that politics can and should arise just about anywhere:

For *any aggregate*, a process of redefinition is needed, one that requires curved talk to trace, or temporarily to retrace, its outline. There is no group without (re)grouping, no regrouping without mobilizing talk. A family, an individual, a firm, a laboratory, a workshop, a planet, an organization, an institution: none have less need for this [political] regime than a state or a nation, a rotary club, a jazz band or a gang of hooligans. For each aggregate to be shaped and reshaped, a particular, appropriate dose of politics is needed. (TPL 149)

If we limited politics to discussions of voting, governance, and revolution, this would ignore the need of even the apparently "non-political" aggregates mentioned above to retrace themselves in existence. This brings us to the key idea of Latour's article: his *topological* definition of the political already touched upon in *Politics of Nature*. Unlike science and the law, which Latour normally describes as consisting of *chains* of mediators, politics is envisioned as a *circle*: "What exactly is [the political circle] about? About transforming the *several into one*, initially through a process of representation ... and subsequently through a process of retransformation of the *one into several*, [which] is often called the wielding of power but that I more bluntly call obedience" (TPL 149). The purpose of viewing politics this way is "to consider simultaneously the two parts of political science, too often disjoint: (a) how to obtain a representation? and (b) how to wield power? In fact it amounts to the same question asked twice but at different points in the same circular movement" (TPL 149). The reader may find it helpful to replace the word "representation" (too laden with everyday governmental associations) with "mediation." The ruling power *cannot* faithfully represent the ruled, since the latter does not always know what it wants in the first place. Latour is fond of Steve Jobs's offhand remark that Apple used no focus groups or market research for its products, since "a lot of times, people don't know what they want until you show it to them."[1] Reciprocally and by the same token the ruled *cannot* faithfully obey the ruling power, since all orders must be locally translated and can rarely be followed to the letter, as Latour made clear in *The Pasteurization of France* when expressing admiration for Tolstoy's *War and Peace*. This is the political circle, in which the ruler inevitably betrays the ruled and the ruled betrays the ruler in turn, through a series of translations or remixes of what one seems to tell the other.

The political circle is presented in a diagram (TPL 150), one that is not necessarily easier to understand than the prose of the text itself. The dream of political philosophy has always been *autonomy*, in which "there is no order received ... that is not also produced by those who receive it" (TPL 150). In other words,

> from the classical point of view I am *auto*-nomous (as opposed to *hetero*-nomous) when the law (*nomos*) is both what I produce through the expression of my will and what I conform to through the manifestation of my docility. As soon as this coincidence is broken, I leave the state of freedom and enter into that of dissidence, revolt, dissatisfaction or domination. (TPL 150)

Latour now interjects a doubt into this classical picture, since the remarkable thing is that this movement "should be totally impracticable. The movement of autonomy is impossible by construction since in it the multitude becomes a unit—representation—before the unit becomes a multitude again—obedience. This transmutation is at first sight even more improbable than that of the dogma of the transubstantiation of the host" (TPL 150). The problem Latour sees with the circle of autonomy is that if it were able to work as transparently as advertised, it would be useless:

> [Assume] we demanded that politicians ... "talk truthfully" by "repeating exactly" what their electors say "without betraying [or] manipulating them." What would happen? The several would remain the several and the multitude the multitude, so that the same thing would

simply be said twice (faithfully for information and therefore *falsely* for politics)… By demanding transparency, rectitude, and fidelity, we are asking for the circle no longer to be a circle but a straight line so that the same can remain precisely the same in the most perfect (and mortal) similitude. In practice, this amounts to calling for the end of politics and consequently the end of autonomy, despite it being so highly valued, for if the multitude never knows how to become one, there will never be a *gain* of representation … A choice must be made between authenticity, pursued in its most extreme consequences, and the difficult work of freedom which demands a particular form of "lie," or at least of curve. (TPL 151–152)

Nor is straight talk possible when it comes to obedience. For, "imagine politicians making the claim of being 'faithfully obeyed.' This time it is the passage from the one to the several that would be impracticable. The order given would be required to be exactly, directly and faithfully transported with no betrayal, deformation, bias or translation!" (TPL 152). Anyone generally familiar with Latour's writings will see why this is impossible. There is no transport without transformation, no way to move facts, goods, wishes, or commands from one place to another without coming to grips with the constraints of the new situation.

A critic from the camp of Truth Politics might now object that Latour is admitting that politics is nothing but lies and deception, a glittering or brutal form of sophistry. Latour responds that "we have to be careful here so as not to draw the hasty conclusion that it is enough to be devious in order to utter political talk accurately" (TPL 153). The point is not to lie or deviate, but to succeed in closing the political circle: forming a new and temporary collective, translating its wishes into unforeseen form, then awaiting the possibly surprising results of its unforeseen manner of obedience. If we were to say simply that "politicians must lie,"

that would be too easy. The Prince of Twisted Words would simply have replaced the White Knight of Transparency. Dissimulation, opportunism, populism, corruption, wrangling, and the art of compromise and *combinazioni* are not enough in themselves to guarantee the continuation of the circle. One can walk skew, think curved, cut across, be sly, without necessarily drawing the political circle … "Curved minds" are clearly distinct from one another, even if they are all an object of ridicule for "straight minds." (TPL 153)

But not only would political straight talk lead to a situation of motionless tautology. More than that, the road to this dismal outcome would be lined with a multitude of crimes:

> [W]ith the best intentions in the world, those who have wanted to rationalize politics (and God knows that history has not been stingy in that respect!) have managed to do nothing more than generate monstrosities infinitely more serious than those they wanted to eliminate. The Sophists may have been expelled, but they were replaced by various types of "commissars"—to put it bluntly. (TPL 156)

Another way of viewing the problem is that neither Truth Politics nor Power Politics is able to acknowledge any form of transcendence that lies beyond its range of mastery. We would be left with either knowable political truth or knowable political force, both of them simple tyrannies of whoever purports to have either right or might. Latour claims that his political circle provides us with a "mini-transcendence of political talk" (TPL 156). It is not hard to interpret the sense of the prefix "mini-." Latour cannot recognize any transcendence of independent things-in-themselves. Not only would this turn his ontology of relations and translations into a series of simple lies: it would also open the door to the epistemology police and others who claim to have *access* to those things-in-themselves. Instead, transcendence for Latour can only be obtained *politically*, meaning that it must be confronted by a collective engaged with the challenge of actants not yet incorporated into the collective. Transcendence can only be "mini-" because it refers to no otherworldly plane of realities, but only to actants already concretely in the world and simply not yet assimilated by the polity.

Truth Politics of the Left tends to view politics in terms of domination, and treats political talk as mere ideology designed to obscure the ugly realities of oppressive power. Needless to say, Latour does not adhere to such an outlook. If we were to begin our political philosophy with a well-defined map of classes or interest groups, "we would find ourselves with agents with set shapes who would be the exclusive owners of their words; they would be totally identical to their interests, wills, identities, and opinions" (TPL 159). And if this were the case, then "any work of composition [would appear] only as an intolerable compromise, even a dishonest one, [that] would break, shatter or annihilate wills, opinions, interests, and identities" (TPL 159). Furthermore, if we took as our principle that we must listen transparently to all interests, opinions, and wills, "we would never manage to close the circle—neither one way nor the other—since multiplicities would triumph, doggedly stubborn in their irreducible difference" (TPL 159). In short, "the only way of making the circle advance, of 'cooking' or 'knitting' politics, of producing (re)groupings, consists in never ever starting with *established* opinions, wills, identities and interests. It is up to political talk alone to introduce, re-establish, and adjust them" (TPL 159).

Public life, Latour holds, is always being rebrewed and never consists of the same fixed ingredients. Collectives are temporarily composed, and shift their identity as one issue after another arises. "It would be extremely dangerous to count on the natural inertia of politics, for if we suspend the 'forced' movement of the circle, even just for one day, the interests, identities, affiliations and wills each resume their own course and scatter like a flight of sparrows" (TPL 161). The present collective is fragile, not a scene of impregnable domination. As Latour sees it, "critical" politics too often lacks the patience to carefully reassemble, transform, and delegate the work of collectives: "It is so much more comfortable to stop at the stage of unarticulated complaints, of hatred for the elite, or ... to stay in one's office draped in a legitimacy that no longer needs to be put to the test" (TPL 161). Nonetheless, "neither the grumble, nor the complaint, nor the hatred, nor the legitimacy, nor the law, nor the order have any meaning unless we set out again to square the circle" (TPL 161). We need to preserve the key, tone, or "spin" of political statements: "By talking of 'relations of domination' we think we are talking politics, but since these power relations move *in a straight line*, like double-click information, and not in a curved line, by translation, we are not talking about them politically" (TPL 161–162). Indignation is not yet politics, and too often the indignant "have lost the tone that would enable them to sound political, the audacity to go around the circle again by representing the totality differently" (TPL 162). We must now consider how the political circle fits with the other modes of existence identified by Latour.

POLITICS AMONG THE MODES OF EXISTENCE

The publication of *An Inquiry into Modes of Existence* (2012 in French, 2013 in English) was the culmination of a quarter-century of mostly clandestine work by Latour on his new system. Hereafter, we shall refer to the book simply as *Modes*. I have often joked that while many philosophers have early and late phases, Latour is surely the first to have passed through both phases simultaneously. As we have seen, the signature intellectual maneuver of Bruno Latour up till now has been to flatten all entities onto a single plane. No longer did we have separate taxonomical domains of Nature and Culture, but only a unified plane of *actors* or *actants*, where everything's claim to reality hinged on whether or not it had an *effect* on something else. For this reason just about anything had to be counted as an actor: quarks, asteroids, horses, unicorns, square circles, Popeye, and present-day bald kings of France. For Latour all of these entities were equally real, but not equally *strong*: quarks simply had more or stronger allies testifying to their existence than did Popeye or unicorns. Reality was granted freely and equally to anything that had an effect, but strength came in various magnitudes ranging from feeble to mighty.

The new gesture of Latour's *Modes* is to deny that this flattening picture of the world can be maintained in unmodified form. A few dozen pages into the book, he indulges in a charming bit of self-satire, telling the imaginary story of an ethnologist who first discovers actor-network theory and later encounters its limits. Though at first she applies the methods of ANT (actor-network theory) with great fruitfulness, "to her great confusion, as she studies segments from Law, Science, The Economy, or Religion she begins to feel that she is saying almost the same thing about all of them: namely, that they are 'composed in a heterogeneous fashion of unexpected elements revealed by the investigation'" (AIME 35). And again: "To be sure, she is indeed moving, like her informants, from one surprise to another, but, somewhat to her surprise, this stops being surprising, in a way, as each element becomes surprising in the same way" (AIME 35). Though Latour criticizes the seeming monotony of his earlier method, there is still a freshness to actor-network theory that belies any weary claim that it has become boring. What Latour really faces here is not the trouble of a boring old social science method, but the same problem that confronts every ontology. Namely, once we have identified the most skeletal features belonging to everything that exists, how do we then account for the differences between the various *zones* of reality, or between all the numerous kinds of beings? If philosophy begins as a theory of ultimate reality, it must aspire to say something about non-ultimate reality as well. Latour has always renounced any pre-cooked divisions or commonsensical taxonomies, such as the emblematic modern rift between humans and world. For Latour as for all philosophers, this creates pressure to provide a new theory of how the world is cut apart into partially autonomous segments. The *Modes* project is his effort to rise to this perennial challenge of philosophy.

Latour's early unified field theory of actants has considerable virtues that must be retained. And in fact, actor-network theory *is* retained in the new project as a mode of existence called networks [NET]. It remains true that everything is equally an actant, and as Latour sees it, we must continue to focus on the actions of actants rather than rushing to stamp them with prejudiced words such as "natural," "artificial," "human," or "inanimate." None of this changes in *Modes*, and in that sense Latour no more passes through a radical *Kehre* or "turn" than does Martin Heidegger himself. Yet Latour is also aware that different types of reality require different standards of truth. The sciences apparently aim at an *adaequatio intellectus et rei*, a correspondence in which the mind makes accurate copies of things in the real world. But we have seen that Latour does not even recognize adequation as a valid model for science, let alone for politics [POL], which is clearly no straightforward exercise of revealing the truth and demanding that society bow down slavishly before it. Perhaps even more obvious is the case of law [LAW], in which judge's decisions often bring no closure even for victorious appellants, and in which facts are "taken to be true" rather than established directly as the definitive truth. There is also religion [REL], the object of modern scorn in a way not true of law or even politics. Religion admittedly cannot prove the existence of God outside the mind along the same paths that science uses to establish the existence or non-existence of the Higgs boson. For many rationalists, this means that religion has simply become a laughingstock; for Latour, it means instead that the type of veridiction belonging to science has wrongly acquired a monopoly on standards of truth. *Modes* aims to draw up a table of categories and to show how "category mistakes" (in Gilbert Ryle's sense) result whenever we mistake one mode of existence for another. All of these categories are different modes of existence. They resemble the parallel but disconnected networks found in today's urban infrastructure: gas, water, sewage, electric, fiber optic, telephone, cable television, ATMs, and underground trains. No one would expect to have flowers literally delivered over the telephone line, or gas through the tunnels of the Metro. Likewise, we should not expect to have "correspondence with the outside world" delivered via the networks of politics, religion, or law. This does not make these spheres of activity useless or inferior, any more than the Metro or telephone lines are "useless" or "inferior" for not providing us with drinking water. The modes can also be thought of as musical keys: if a statement is heard in the wrong key, a category mistake occurs. Latour gives these modes the name of prepositions [PRE], since they literally pre-position actors in a specific *kind* of network, not just in a global flat ontology where all actors are equally real.

The published version of *Modes* claims to identify fifteen modes in all, and suggests that they are not *a priori* categories of the understanding but pertain solely to the Moderns. The project is admirable in its ambition, and often breathtaking in its insights. But at the outset, three critical remarks are in order:

1. One of the modes, double click [DC], is not really a mode, and seems to be added to the table to create an artificial symmetry. A metaphor drawn from our recent world of computer mouse and track pad, double click refers to the belief that information can be obtained directly, without mediation. As such, it has more in common with category mistakes than with the other modes, and is the obvious black sheep on Latour's ultimate fifteen-fold list (AIME 488–489). The problem with the forced symmetry of five groups of three is that it obscures the overarching role of two of the fourteen modes that are more global than the others: network [NET] and preposition [PRE]. In fact, it is more helpful to think of Latour's new system as twelve modes grouped into four triads that result from prepositions cutting up the global network of the early/middle Latour into distinct regions, so that the addition of preposition and network brings the total number of modes to fourteen.

2. The subtitle of *Modes* is *An Anthropology of the Moderns*. There is no contradiction here for Latour, author of *We Have Never Been Modern*, since he is speaking of those who *think* themselves to have been modern. Modernity is a Western invention, and hence the modes in his book make no claim to speak of human history as a whole. Yet the book never delimits its precise geographical or temporal scope. Do Russia and Turkey belong to the Moderns? Did Japan join the list at some point? Do the United States and Canada deploy the same modes of existence as Europe? None of these questions are addressed. Nor do I recall even a single calendar date in the book, though the reader might have wished to know when and how some of the modes began in historical time. While these omissions can easily be excused as not belonging to the intended scope of the book, they do leave room for wondering whether some of the modes are not *a priori* ontological categories, despite Latour's claim to be doing nothing more than developing an anthropology of the moderns.

3. At least one of the modes, reproduction [REP], is undeniably a full-blown ontological category. What Latour means by [REP] is that entities do not automatically remain in existence, but must do the work of reproducing themselves from one instant to the next. This is a rather pointed ontological claim, one that unites Latour with Whitehead, the occasionalist philosophers of the seventeenth century, and ultimately the Ash'arite theologians of early Islamic Iraq, for all of whom there was a continuous re-creation of the universe from one moment to the next. But this notion would be an utter absurdity for Bergson, who thought it ridiculous that time could be composed of isolated instants. It would be rejected by Deleuze, the recent master thinker of becoming. It would even be refused by Aristotle, who in the *Physics* argued that time is a continuum that is not actually but only *potentially* divisible into instants. In short, [REP] is in no way a universal anthropological category of the moderns, but rather a point of lively metaphysical dispute among ancient, medieval, and modern philosophers alike. It represents not a basic structure of modern or Western civilization, but a blunt metaphysical decision by Bruno Latour against an alternative theory in which continuous becoming is prior to individual states. This is why Latour and Whitehead have nothing to do with Bergson and Deleuze, despite the misguided attempts of many gifted commentators (Stengers and Steven Shaviro come to mind) to unify the Deleuzian and Whiteheadian schools under the failed general rubric of "process philosophy."

We now return to our main topic, politics. We have seen that both the early and middle Latour run the constant risk of *ontologizing* the political. This is true both in the jaunty Machiavellian asides of the pre-1991 writings and in the more fragile liberal "parliament of things" that culminates in *Politics of Nature*. In both cases "politics" tends to become a name for reality as a whole, with all the accompanying virtues and vices that belong to any such ontologizing method. In *Modes* this is no longer the case. Now, for the first time in Latour's career, politics becomes a limited and specific zone of reality. Politics [POL] is discussed in Chapters 5, 12, 13, 14, 15, and 16 of *Modes*, all of which we briefly consider here. Chapter 5 undertakes a renewed discussion of the major themes of *Politics of Nature*: the disaster that results from mixing politics with any adequating reference [REF] to nature, and the "circular" or loop-like structure of politics covered most precisely in "What if We *Talked* Politics A Little?" Chapter 12 is devoted to politics in its own right. Chapter 13 distinguishes politics from law, while Chapter 14 draws a distinction between politics and organization [ORG], a mode that covers roughly the same terrain as sociology, but in Tarde's rather than Durkheim's sense: a sociology of associations between all things, not a sociology of human Society with a capital S. In Chapter 15 Latour warns us not to confuse politics and organization, and in Chapter 16 he hints surprisingly at moral foundations for politics and each of the other modes.

We proceed in order, beginning with Chapter 5. Here Latour continues his campaign against straight talk and double click. Chains of inference do not proceed in the supposed geometrical manner, as if free of cost and devoid of mediation: "What is striking, rather, in the establishment of chains of reference, is the continual invention of modes of writing, types of visualizations, convocations of experts, setups of instruments, new notations that permit the cascades of transformations we have noted above" (AIME 127). Straight talk too easily makes "poets, rhetoricians, common people, tradesmen, soothsayers, priests, doctors, wise men, in short, everyone" seem guilty of "*crooked talk*; they become double-dealers, liars, manipulators." More generally, "if the range of what [rationalists] call the 'irrational' is so vast, it is because the rationalists adopt a definition of 'rational' that is far too unreasonable and too polemical" (AIME 128). Here once again, we see Latour's preference for the Sophists over a rationalized version of Socrates:

> But who speaks better? Who is more sensitive to the requirements of this veridiction? The one who learns to speak "crooked" in an angry crowd, looking for what it wants, or the one who claims to speak straight, perhaps, but leaves the crowd to its disorderly agitation? In the agora, at least, the answer is clear. And yet isn't it strange that we continue to abhor the Sophists and heap praise on the hemlock drinker? (AIME 135–136)

Against Socrates, who disastrously insisted on straight talk while being tried in Athens, Latour warns us in a marginal note against any "dangerous amalgam between knowledge and politics" (AIME 128).

The next appearance in the book of the political mode [POL] is in Chapter 12, which is devoted entirely to the theme. The moderns want to rationalize politics: "They want it to be straightforward, flat, clean; they want it to tell the truth according to the type of veridiction that they think they can ask of the Evil Genius, Double Click ... This began with Socrates and has never stopped, through Hobbes and Rousseau, Marx and Hayek, to Habermas" (AIME 333). This long movement develops a political epistemology, which "was a rival of religion before it took religion's place, through a sort of moral rationalism, by claiming to reign over all metalanguage in the name of the 'scientific view of the world'" (AIME 329). As a result, "it is acknowledged that the political world is not, cannot be, cannot ever become, must not become the kingdom of any veridiction whatsoever. The case is closed: to go into politics, to take courses in political communication, to participate in an electoral campaign would be to *suspend* all requirements of truth" (AIME 331). It is not surprising when Latour objects that this is an exaggeration. He now pivots from his critique of epistemological Truth Politics to a critique of the opposite vice: Power Politics as represented by Machiavelli, one of the heroes of his early period. In doing so, he draws a fascinating analogy with the way people also exaggerate the unreality of another mode of existence, *fiction*. As Latour puts it:

> We find the same problem [with politics] as with fiction [FIC], which people have sought to reduce too quickly to the suspension of all requirements of objectivity and truth. No longer able to see by what thread one could follow the reason of the political, they began to overestimate unreason, and to brandish lies, skill, power struggles, violence, no longer as defects but as qualities, the only ones that would remain to that form of life. Such is the temptation of Machiavellianism. Now, if people misunderstand the political mode by requiring transparency and information from it, they misunderstand it just as much by propagating the belief that it has to abandon *all* rationality. (AIME 335–336)

For Latour, the middle course between Truth Politics and Power Politics might be called Object Politics, which he names instead both *Dingpolitik* (politics of things) and object-oriented politics.[2] As he puts it in the initial headings before Chapter 12: "An object-oriented politics allows us to discern the squaring of the political Circle, provided that we distinguish between speaking about politics and speaking politically" (AIME 327). Only the Circle is able to bring mediation into politics, and hence only the Circle can be displaced by the "mini-transcendent" issues it encounters along the way. Latour makes his case in several fine passages. For example: "If politics has to be 'crooked,' this is first of all because it encounters stakes that oblige it to turn away, to bend, to shift positions. Its path is curved because on each occasion it turns around questions, issues, stakes, things—in the sense of *res publica*, the public *thing*—whose surprising consequences leave those who would rather hear nothing about them all mixed up" (AIME 337). And furthermore: "in the forceful slogan proposed by Noortje Marres: 'No issue, no politics!' It is thus above all because politics is always object-oriented—to borrow a term from information science—that it always seems to elude us" (AIME 337). The reference to Marres indicates that we are now moving in the orbit of the American journalist and political thinker Walter Lippmann, since it was Marres who first acquainted Latour with Lippmann and his notion of the phantom public. As Latour puts it: "It is for just this reason—Walter Lippmann may be the only person who really got it—that one can respect the ontological dignity of the political mode only by grasping it in the form of a phantom public to be invoked and convoked" (AIME 352). We meet Lippmann again in Chapter 7, but it should already be clear that Latour takes Lippmann and Dewey to be the exemplary mentors of an object-oriented politics.

Latour now speaks more poignantly of the political circle than ever before:

> it is a Circle; it is impossible to trace; it must be traced, however, and once it has been traced it disappears; and we have to start all over again at once ... it is so contrary to our rigidities, our other certainties, our other values—it *hurts* so much, it so threatens to do bad things we don't want rather than the good things we would like to do. (AIME 338)

Moreover, the repetitive character of politics is unavoidable: "Like religion [REL] and law [LAW], political discourse [POL] engages the entire collective, but in an even more particular way: one has to pass from one situation to another and then come back and start everything, *everything*, all over again in a different form" (AIME 338). Or stated differently: "What is most magnificent in the political, what makes those who discover its movement shed tears of admiration, is that one has to *constantly start over*" (AIME 341). This also provides us the clue as to how politics can go wrong:

> the principal infelicity condition of the political is to have its course *interrupted*, the relay broken off. "That's not going anywhere." "That's pointless." "That won't do any good." "They're forgetting about us." "They don't give a damn about us." "Nobody's doing a thing about it." Or, in a more scholarly fashion, "We are not represented." "We are not obeyed." In other words, something rings false in each example taken separately precisely because it is *taken separately*. (AIME 341)

But even when it remains uninterrupted, there is always something perilous about the political circle, since

> nothing in this movement ensures its duration; here is the source of all
> its hardness, all its terrible exigency, since it can at any moment grow
> larger by multiplying inclusions, or shrink by multiplying exclusions.
> Everything depends on its renewal, on the courage of those who, all
> along the chain, agree to behave in such a way that their behavior *leads*
> to the next part of the curve. (AIME 342)

Latour notes that "when this happens, a *political culture* begins to take shape and gradually makes the maintenance, renewal, and expansion of the Circle less and less painful" (AIME 343). And yet, "things can also turn in the other direction: they can literally 'take a turn for the worse,' 'turn out badly'" (AIME 343).

Before leaving Chapter 12, we should also note an important appearance by Carl Schmitt, to whom we will turn our attention soon enough. One of Schmitt's central themes is the "state of exception," a sheer struggle with the enemy for survival that cannot be arbitrated by any transcendent standard. Far from seeing this as a lamentable lapse into irrational power struggle, Schmitt views this state of exception as the very essence of the political. Despite Latour's admiration for Schmitt (shared by many on the political Left), he rejects the notion of a state of exception that would appear only in monumental historic crises resolved by dictatorial figures. Latour opposes this notion by spreading out the "exceptional" moments over the whole of political life. As he puts it:

> It will have become clear by now that everywhere there are only *little*
> transcendences. This definition of the curve also has the advantage of
> keeping the state of exception from needing an "exceptional man" who
> would "be decisive" because he would be "above the law." Schmitt's
> error lay in his belief that it is only on high, among the powerful and on
> rare occasions, that the political mode has to look for exceptions. Look
> at the Circle: it is *exceptional at all points*, above and below, on the right
> and on the left, since it *never goes straight* and, in addition, it must always
> *start over* especially if it is to spread. (AIME 347–348)

In fact, Latour had already aired a similar claim in a footnote buried in his 2003 article on the political mode. There we read as follows:

It is interesting to notice that those who talk of sovereignty so much like Schmitt are unable to see that political talk requires a curve in every single [one] of its points, so they concentrate in one single point the oddity of political transubstantiation. In effect they confuse the curvature of the political circle with the "state of exception," as if putting in Zeus's hands the full power of thunder and lightning. (TPL 163, note 10)

Though Chapter 13 is devoted to law [LAW] as a mode of existence, politics makes several key appearances here as well. Indeed, politics and law are both assigned to the triad of modes called "quasi-subjects." As Latour puts it:

> At the end of Part Two, we proposed to regroup the beings of technology [TEC], fiction [FIC], and reference [REF] under a single heading, that of quasi objects … This is why it would be quite useful to continue to nurture our little classification scheme by putting politics [POL], law [LAW], and religion [REL] together in a single group, that of quasi subjects. (AIME 371–372; sentence order reversed)

Incidentally, the other modes of existence are grouped according to precisely the same criteria. There are three modes that *ignore* the distinction between quasi-subjects and quasi-objects, acting everywhere with impunity, and these are the most blatantly metaphysical in flavor: reproduction [REP], metamorphosis [MET], and habit [HAB]. There are three other modes said to link quasi-subjects with quasi-objects: attachment [ATT], organization [ORG], and morality [MOR]. That would appear to leave three other modes thrown into a miscellaneous basket, though we have seen that double click [DC] is really a category mistake rather than a genuine mode. Meanwhile network [NET] and preposition [PRE] have a higher status than the other twelve modes, since it is their very intersection that produces the others (AIME 488–489). For a full account of the various modes of existence, the reader is referred to my forthcoming book *Prince of Modes: Bruno Latour's Later Philosophy*.

In passing, we should note at least two potential problems with how the modes are organized. First, the highly symmetrical structure of triads grouped with respect to the quasi-subject/quasi-object distinction casts grave doubt on any claim that *Modes* is merely an empirical history or anthropology of the West. This is not to say that overarching structures have no place in anthropology: the contrary is proven not only by Claude Lévi-Strauss in his classic *Structural Anthropology*, but more recently by

Latour's friend Philippe Descola in *Beyond Nature and Culture*, with its intriguing fourfold classification of animist, naturalist, totemist, and analogist societies. But these are the exceptions that prove the rule, since Lévi-Strauss is widely interpreted in philosophical terms, Latour increasingly so, and Descola has an ardent readership among French philosophy students that could eventually make him the Lévi-Strauss of some unknown future Derrida. The case of Descola is especially instructive, since even though it took him years of painstaking fieldwork to develop his anthropology, the underlying mechanism of his fourfold structure cannot have been generated by historical contingency. For Descola holds that there are only four *possible* ontologies, all of them resulting from binary decisions on two central questions: (1) Do other beings have the same interiors as we do? and (2) Do other beings have the same physicalities that we do? Naturalism, the ontological standpoint of the West and most urban civilization, holds that other beings have the same sorts of bodies that we do but different inner lives. Animism flips these decisions by saying that we have similar interiorities to other beings but dissimilar physicalities. Totemism claims that we are similar to other beings both within and without, while analogism holds the reverse: we are dissimilar to other beings in both respects.[3] Though the philosopher Latour carefully subtitles his book *An Anthropology of the Moderns*, the anthropologist Descola might well have used the subtitle *An Ontology of All Cultures*, since he shows no philosophical modesty about his own central dualism:

> As we shall see, this distinction between a level of interiority and one of physicality is not simply an ethnocentric projection of the Western opposition drawn between the mind and the body. Rather, it is a distinction that all the civilizations about which we have learned something from ethnography and history have, in their own fashions, objectivized. (p.116)

As concerns Latour, the point is as follows. Given that his modes are grouped symmetrically according to the duality of quasi-subjects and quasi-objects, it is hard to see how any more could be added (or even subtracted, if not for the specter of "forgetting" that haunts religion and politics). If Latour's list of modes really holds good only for the modern West, it would need to be explained how other cultures could orbit different stars than Latour's chosen pair.

The second problem with the list of modes is precisely its use of "quasi-subject" and "quasi-object" as the central operators. When Latour's ontology of actants effaced the difference between nature and culture, it also seemed to eliminate the modern notion that human beings must comprise a full half of any situation. Latour's ontology holds that actants are defined by their relations with other actants, not that they exist only in correlation with a human observer, as in the "correlationism" attacked by Quentin Meillassoux. Given Latour's global relationism between all actants of every kind, there is no obvious reason why *people* should be entitled to meddle in half of the modes of existence. At times Latour seems to use the phrase "humans and nonhumans" merely as a catch-all term to ensure that nothing is left out, but at other times (as in the present case) the distinction continues to linger in Latour's philosophy as a primary dualism, as if the legacy of Descartes had not fully been shaken off.

Elsewhere in Chapter 13, Latour repeats his prior discussions of the political Circle, now rechristened as the mode of politics [POL]. But he adds something more, the notion that [POL] joins all modes except law [LAW] in not preserving its own traces:

In fact, all the modes identified up to now have this distinctive feature: they *pass*, they move forward, they launch into the search for their means of subsistence. Each one does it differently, to be sure, but they have in common the fact that they never *go back* to the conditions under which they started. Even the political Circle [POL], while it always has to start over, disappears, as we have seen, as soon as it is interrupted, without leaving any traces but the slight crease of habit … In other words, the other modes [besides law] *do not archive* their successive shiftings or translations. They leave wakes behind, of course; they begin again, each making use of the preceding ones, but they do not *go back* to *preserve* the traces of their movements. The predecessors disappear once the successors have taken over. This what they do: they pass; they are passes. (AIME 368–369)

Earlier in the book, Latour had explained that his key term "passes" is meant in the sense of football or basketball passes. One political state always passes to another, and since the collective is constantly transformed from one to the next, no return to an earlier time is possible. We now skip ahead four pages: "This is why politics can never be based on a preexisting society, and still less on a 'state of nature' in which bands of half-naked humans end up coming together. The exploration of successive alterations takes us in the opposite direction from this implausible scenography" (AIME 373).

Chapter 14 proceeds in remarkable fashion, identifying three new modes by pointing to three distinct failings of economics, which claims to be the master discourse of our time. Economics, rather, is "a contrast drawn together by *three modes of existence* that the history of the Moderns has blended for reasons [that the ethnologist] is going to have to untangle. It is this interweaving that explains why she has to resist the temptation of believing either in The Economy or its critique" (AIME 385). Given Latour's claim that the Left too often misreads political questions as economic ones, we should give a brief summary of how Latour decomposes economics into three distinct modes. He does this by trying to demonstrate three gaps between economics and reality.

The first gap is between hot reality and cold calculation. Latour's beautiful passage on this gap deserves to be quoted at length:

> A first gap. You observe goods that are starting to move around all over the planet: poor devils who drown while crossing oceans to earn their bread; giant enterprises that appear from one day to the next or that disappear into red ink; entire nations that become rich or poor; markets that close or open; monstrous demonstrations that disperse over improvised barricades in clouds of teargas; radical innovations that suddenly make whole sectors of industry obsolete, or that spread like a dust cloud; sudden fashions that draw millions of passionate clients or that, just as suddenly, pile up shopworn stocks that nobody wants any longer … and the immense *mobilization* of things and people; they say it is driven only by the simple transfer of *indisputable necessities*.
>
> Everything here is hot, violent, active, rhythmic, contradictory, rapid, discontinuous, pounded out—but these immense boiling cauldrons are described to you as the ice-cold, rational, coherent, and continuous manifestations of the calculation of interests alone. (AIME 386)

The philosophy of mind often speaks of hypothetical "zombies," beings that would show all outward signs of an inner life while actually having no conscious experience whatsoever.[4] By analogy we might imagine "economic zombies" who would move about the earth making decisions based on rational self-interest, while taking not the least pleasure or pain in any of their actions. What Latour seems to suggest in the passage above is that economics is effectively describing economic zombies rather than humans. Economics misses our passionate attachments to various people, enterprises, and things even as these are successively buffeted by market forces. In a word, economics misses the mode of attachment [ATT].

A second gap is found between the apparently high stakes of economics and the air of silent determinism that surrounds it. In Latour's own words:

A second gap. In The Economy, the question, [the ethnologist] is told quite gravely, consists in dividing up rare goods, in parceling out scarce materials, benefits, or goods, or, on the contrary, in making the largest number profit from a horn of plenty debited from one resource or another. As everyone repeats, with imperturbable seriousness, these are the most important questions we can address in common, because they concern the whole world, all humans and all things, henceforth engaged in the same flows of mobilization, in the same history, and in the same common destiny … And in recent times, they tell her even more energetically, these questions have become all the more constraining since a scarcity more unexpected and more fundamental than all the others has been discovered: we don't have enough planets! We would need two, three, four, five, six, to satisfy all the humans, and we only have one, our own, the Earth, Gaia.

[The ethnologist] wonders what procedures they will adopt to bring off such feats of decision, division, and distribution, and what instruments, what protocols, what assurances, what verifications, what scruples they will deploy. She is already directing her gaze toward the noisy assemblies where such common matters are going to be violently debated. And there, what is she told? *Nothing* and *no one* decides: "It suffices to calculate." The very place where everything must be decided and discussed, since these are matters of life and death for everyone and everything, appears to be a public square *emptied* of all its protagonists. (AIME 386–387)

Here a new sort of economic zombie appears: a deterministic stoic who identifies the economy with fate itself, as if it were a divine power beyond all human intervention. What this new zombie fails to register is the vast number of scruples that limit the economy from the outset. We might easily force children into slave labor, gouge resalable kidneys from the homeless, sweet-talk the elderly into ludicrous swindles, exploit the market for ivory and tiger skins, and auction off Gaia on eBay, if not for the mode of morality [MOR].

The third and final gap lies between the apparently mammoth organizational infrastructure needed to maintain the economy, and the fact that we can never really pin this infrastructure down. As Latour puts it:

A third gap ... [The ethnologist] sets out to approach enterprises, organizations qualified under the law as "corporate bodies." She extends her hand and what does she find? Almost nothing solid or durable. A sequence, an accumulation, endless layers of successive disorganizations: people come and go, they transport all sorts of documents, complain, meet, separate, grumble, protest, meet again, organize again, disperse, reconnect, all this in constant disorder; there is no way she could ever define the borders of these entities that keep on expanding or contracting like accordions. The investigator was hoping to get away from stories of invisible phantoms; she finds only new phantoms, just as invisible.

And if she complains to her informants that they have taken her for a ride, they reply with the same unfathomable confidence: "Ah, it's because *behind* all that agitation you haven't yet detected the assured presence of the real sources of organization: Society, the State, the Market, Capitalism, the only great beings that actually hold up all this jumble ..." And, of course, when she begins to investigate such assemblages, the gap reappears, but this time multiplied: more corridors, more offices, more flowcharts, other meetings, other documents, other inconsistencies, other arrangements, but still not the slightest transcendence. No great being has taken charge of this ordinary confusion. Nothing stands out. Nothing provides cover. Nothing decides. Nothing reassures. It is immanent everywhere, and everywhere illogical, incoherent, caught up at the last minute, started over on the fly. (AIME 387–388)

The third economic zombie revealed here might be described as a "Lacanian zombie," since it tacitly assumes that some hyper-competent Big Other is keeping the world organized from behind the scenes.[5] In reifying the market as an independent and hyper-alert super-entity, economics misses the on-the-fly character of the mode of existence called organization [ORG], in which humans jump daily between multiple different scripts, sometimes feeling above them and other times beneath them.

It is interesting to note that of the three post-economic modes, [ATT], [MOR], and [ORG], it is [ORG] that will be least surprising to readers of the early and middle Latour. After all, one of the long-time staples of actor-network theory is the notion that whether we analyze a Cabinet meeting of the government, a corporate boardroom, a middle-class household, a religious summit, or a waterfront drug deal, we generally encounter the same number of people and hear the same sorts of conversations. There is no master level of macroscopic authority where everything is magically held together. By contrast, [ATT] and certainly [MOR] feel like newer additions to Latour's philosophy. The best previous example of passionate attachment in Latour's prior career was probably in the technological detective thriller *Aramis* (subtitle: *The Love of Technology*) in which the proposed Aramis automated Metro system for Paris died unloved, as if by an army of economic zombies. As for morality, it was subjected to a great deal of scorn in Latour's dashing early Machiavellian days. It was then given a major role in *Politics of Nature*, but in a way that had the feel of a concession about it, and only after a belittling reference to its formerly weak state: "In the old framework, the moralists cut rather a sorry figure, since the world was full of amoral nature and society was full of immoral violence" (PN 160).

[ORG] turns out to be just as precarious as [POL] itself. Latour describes the risk as follows:

> Organization *can never* work: the scripts always define dispersed beings; they always achieve their outcomes in staggered fashion: one can only try to *take them up again* through other scripts that add to the ambient dis/reorganization … From this standpoint, the organizing act is just as constantly interrupted as the movement of the political Circle [POL], or the attachment of law [LAW], or the renewal of religious presence [REL], or the mere survival of a body [REP]. Sameness can never nourish these strange beasts. They require otherness. (AIME 394)

Despite this similar fragility of numerous modes, in Chapter 15 we are urged not to confuse [ORG] (or the matter of sociology) with [POL] (or the matter of politics). Latour gently critiques the Moderns for succumbing to this "temptation to mix [ORG] with politics" (AIME 415). While it is certainly true that both [ORG] and [POL] give us the sense of being in a group larger than ourselves, Latour glosses their difference in the following rather subtle manner:

> [I]t was a mistake to define the social tautologically, and an even greater mistake to seek to extend it to all the modes. Scripts do not present themselves as tautologies … unless we forget the slight temporal *gap* thanks to which we never find ourselves "above" or "below" a given scenario at exactly the same time or with exactly the same capacities. Unfortunately, the notion of tautology completely misses this sinuosity, which is so particular to scripts. And even if it managed to follow that mode of extension, it would still not be able to serve as a yardstick for

politics, religion, law, or psyches … Once again, we observe the tendency
of each mode to propose a hegemonic metalanguage for speaking about
all the others; a quite innocent tendency, but one from which this inquiry
aims to protect us. (AIME 416)

If this distinction between [POL] and [ORG] seems somewhat elusive,
there may be an easier way to crack the nut. We need only recall the
different position of these two modes in Latour's fifteen-fold chart.
Whereas [POL] belongs to the mode of quasi-subjects, [ORG] belongs
to those which link quasi-subjects with quasi-objects. This immediately
suggests that for all the concern [POL] shows for the "mini-transcendence" lying beyond it, [POL] still has a more solipsistic tendency than
[ORG]. As far back as Chapter 5, Latour wrote as follows: "In this mode
of existence [POL] there is something sui generis, in the literal sense of
'self-engendering,' something the Greeks called *autophuos*, and that we
are going to have to learn to treat with as much respect and skill as we
grant to chains of reference" (AIME 135). Now, Latour's use of the term
autophuos immediately suggests another technical term of Greek origin: I
speak of *autopoiesis*, a notion promoted by the Chilean biologists Humberto
Maturana and Francisco Varela and further developed by the German
sociologist Niklas Luhmann.[6] The idea, first born from considerations of
immunology, is that the cell is a homeostatic system with the sole aim
of keeping its internal parameters stable. For this reason it has no direct
access to its environment, but only understands that environment in its
own terms. So far Latour has not entered into dialogue with this parallel
school of *autopoiesis*, and to my knowledge he has had nothing but harsh
words for Luhmann and his influence on German sociology, viewing
Luhmann's theory as too biologistic in character.[7] It is easy to understand
why Latour would reject any biological model of society, since this would
amount to interpreting organization as a unified organism rather than as
the scattered and haphazard assemblage that it is. This in turn would run
the risk of returning to Durkheim's model of a pre-given organic Society
with a capital S: "The sociology of 'the social' (as opposed to the sociology
of associations) may have been right to see the social as one of the major
phenomena of the human sciences." Two things in this brief passage are
telling: (1) the hesitant concession that sociology *may* have been right to
grant importance to the social; and (2) the invocation of the "sociology of
associations," which refers in large part to Durkheim's failed rival Tarde.
For Latour, society cannot be treated as an organism because it is always
an improvised collage built of numerous human and nonhuman elements.

Cut off from nothing, [ORG] barely maintains its identity as actors come and go and many scripts fail badly. By contrast, we have seen that [POL] is *autophuos* or self-engendering. This suggests that even if Latour must categorically reject Luhmann's use of a biological model for *society*, he might well accept it for *politics*. In Latour's own words: "the political body is a phantom, yes, but it is not an ectoplasm like the phantom of Society. Greek and Latin must not be confused here: autophuos is a mode of existence; Society sui generis is not" (AIME 416–417).

We now arrive at the closing chapter of *Modes*, Chapter 16, where Latour touches briefly on the relation of politics to morality. The early Latour would probably have scoffed at any such relation, given his initial view of moralists as beautiful souls who cannot get the political job done as well as Hannibal, with his powerful mixture of strategy and cruelty. The middle Latour then shifted views, placing moralists side-by-side with scientists as important detectors of entities previously excluded from the collective. But the late Latour of *Modes* goes even further, claiming (whether whimsically or not) that morality lies at the basis of his entire project. First, there is a stirring mention of the relation between [POL] and [MOR], beyond all Machiavellianism: "How could we deny that, in the renewal and abandonment of the Political Circle, there is one of the most important sources of what is called morality [POL]? It is hard to overlook the difference between political courage and political cowardice" (AIME 453). Yet Latour's morality is not that of the beautiful soul, who forever remains above it all. It is the morality of those who take sides and who also act:

> It does not suffice to be simply troubled, vaguely uneasy: we have to *commit* to a new movement of exploration in order to verify the *overall quality* of all the links ... Some even find in the religious mode's requirement of salvation and in its end times a pretext for ending all exploration, even for denying the very necessity of any compromise ... "What's the point in being moral, since I'm saved?" In taking this position, one is betraying religion as much as morality. (AIME 460)

We now come to Latour's claim that morality underlies the whole of the *Modes* project: a surprise ending indeed from an author who began his career visibly more sympathetic to the power players of success than to the beautiful moralizers of failure. Latour imagines a sarcastic reader wondering if morality is being served at the end of the book in the manner of a gratuitous helping of dessert. He responds as follows:

Before ironizing about our inquiry, the reader will perhaps acknowledge that I have been "moralizing" from the outset, in the sense that I have brought out the felicity and infelicity conditions for *each mode*. Every instauration implies a "value judgment," the most discriminating judgment possible. Consequently, the "moral question" is not being brought into this inquiry *after* all the questions "of fact" have been dealt with. It has been addressed from the start. There is not a single mode that is not capable of distinguishing truth from falsity, good from evil *in its own way*. (AIME 452)

Although morality and values are mentioned here in the same breath, we should note that they actually occupy opposite sides of the spectrum for Latour. This was most clear in *Politics of Nature*, where Max Weber's fact/value distinction (transmuted rather than discarded in Latour's book) assigned "fact" to the outside of the collective and "value" to the inside. But while we might have expected Latour to line up moralists in the "values" camp, he actually performs the opposite maneuver, pairing moralists with scientists on a mission to look outside for excluded entities. If values are commonly associated with relativism, Latour links morality with a kind of *realism*. For morality with its scruples is what prevents the self-engendering collective from mistaking itself for the universe as a whole. If the politics of the early Latour left no room for any sort of transcendence, his increasing interest over the years in "mini-transcendence" culminates in what he now claims is a moral foundation for the cosmos. It is morality alone that provides the basis for felicity or infelicity in how the various modes are deployed.

5

"Usefully Pilloried": Latour's Left Flank

In the Introduction to this book, I suggested that the familiar distinction between the political Left and Right is crossed by an even more determinative rift between Truth Politics and Power Politics. Both truth and power are Latour's enemies, since both short-circuit politics by trying to silence their enemies once and for all, whether by proofs or by force. We also saw that these two kinds of politics come in both Left and Right flavors. Since the time of the French Revolution, the Left has sought to change the existing order in more or less fundamental ways, while the Right has stressed that change entails a high risk of disorder. Though Left and Right cannot be correlated either with truth and power or the reverse, all four brands of politics are modern in origin, and therefore Latour cannot accept any of them. From a Latourian standpoint, the problem shared by Truth Politics and Power Politics is that both prematurely answer the political question rather than letting politics grow in its natural environment of uncertainty and ignorance. Truth Politicians are too quick to dismiss the claims of those who are wrong, and Power Politicians too quick to belittle the demands of those who are weak. Latour gives us no equivalent critique of the political Left and Right, but we are not forbidden to speculate as to how he might do so.

Latour does reject *revolution* as a political model, but this is less a critique of the Left than of Truth Politics. After all, Latour would have just as little interest in the concept of a right-wing revolution, and he dislikes the notion of revolutions in science no less than in politics. The problem Latour has with revolution is not its proposed redistribution of wealth and power, but its claim to do so in an extra-political manner based on appeals to knowledge or natural right. To an equal degree Latour would reject the political model of an authoritarian system that severed its links with knowledge, but this is less a critique of the Right than of Power Politics. For it is also possible to imagine an authoritarian *relativist* government that enforced sheer multiculturalist perspectivism and banned all definitive claims to truth, and even easier to imagine a theory of science that would turn science into nothing but power plays while reacting angrily to any truth claims by scientists. Latour's problem with relativism is not with the diverse perspectives it allows on the world, but with its claim to do so internally with no reference to anything other than a free-floating language game. In short, while Latour makes very clear why he rejects both Truth Politics and Power Politics, he never explicitly innovates on the question of Left versus Right. And insofar as this distinction continues to dominate our political identification of individuals and groups, Latour has remained a politically elusive figure. In the final chapter of the present book, I speculate on how a Latourian might innovate past the Left/Right distinction in politics, which is just as bound up with the modern dichotomy between nature and culture as is the war between truth and power.

Yet we need not wait for the concluding discussion to consider the difference of Latour from certain characteristic Left and Right positions. While we have not yet seen a full-fledged engagement with Latour from the Left, several preliminary samples of such engagement have already been published. The most substantial of these can be found in Benjamin Noys's 2012 book *The Persistence of the Negative*. By comparison, Sande Cohen's 1997 article "Science Studies and Language Suppression" is already too dated thanks to its high postmodernist tone, which at times becomes almost comically opaque. The final two sentences of Cohen's piece is an almost perfect exemplar of the whole:

> Despite many of its brilliant insights into modern historicism and other social formations, [*We Have Never Been Modern*] finally strikes me as yet another project in the mimesis of *demand*, of order-words, here science studies as laying out a model in the desire for satisfaction (synthesis), a model which suppresses intellectual skepticism. [Paul] de Man's notion, that epistemic suppression requires the violence of language directed against epistemology, delivered by aesthetic formations of grammar and logic, seems confirmed.[1]

Rather than spend much time pondering what "the mimesis of demand" is supposed to mean, we move along quickly. I am hardly more fond of Mark Elam's 1999 critique "Living Dangerously with Bruno Latour in a Hybrid World," though it is certainly better written than Cohen's piece. After beginning with the claim that Latour succeeds only by "telling stories," as if he were merely a rhetorical snake charmer with little interest in argument,

Elam skips ahead to a rhetorically grandstanding claim of his own. Latour, as Elam has it, "shows no appreciation for the work of prominent feminist scholars who have shown equal dedication to the task of rereading and rewriting the history of modern ontology."[2] Never mind that Latour's works are peppered with notices of genuine intellectual debt to such women as Donna Haraway, Noortje Marres, Isabelle Stengers, and Shirley Strum—Elam is completely preoccupied with the absence of footnotes to Luce Irigaray. Under these circumstances, a fair-minded author might have written as follows: "though the Latour/Irigaray link admittedly might not seem obvious at first glance, I will show that there is much to be learned from such an untested comparison." Instead, Elam chooses to portray this missing dialogue as if it were a grave signal of patriarchal oppression on Latour's part, though of course no reciprocal mention is made of Irigaray's failure to discuss Latour. In Elam's own words:

> By continuing to leave women's otherness unrepresentable in his repre-
> sentations of our non-modernity, Latour is guilty from a feminist point
> of view of breaking a complicity between masculinity and rationality,
> only to affirm his support for a new and potentially more powerful
> connivance between masculinity and the construction and regulation
> of hybrid networks. (p.5)

Yet Latour's "guilt" and the "powerful connivance" between networks and masculinity are merely insinuated in Elam's article, with its general atmosphere of incriminating innuendo at the expense of argumentative vigor. Latour is an important figure who deserves better enemies than this. And while the analysis by Noys is by no means free of crude psychologizing and arch point scoring, he at least has a well-informed estimate of Latour's philosophical aims.

Before turning directly to Noys, we note the following obvious point: while Marx's critique of capital is intellectually central to today's political Left, it is of hardly any interest to Latour at all. As he sees it, "Capital" cannot be reified as a freestanding structure any more than "Society" as defined by Durkheim. What comes first is a flat plane of motley actants, and any supposed structure or context linking them must be demonstrated from a grass-roots level rather than presupposed. As early as *Irreductions* in 1984, we read the following words:

It has often been said that "capitalism" was a radical novelty, an unheard-of rupture, a "deterritorialization" pushed to the ultimate extreme. As always, the Difference is mystification. Like God, capitalism does not exist. There are no equivalents; these have to be made, and they are expensive, and do not last very long. We can, at best, make extended networks. Capitalism is marginal even today ... My homage to Fernand Braudel ... who does not hide this fact and shows how long-distance control may be achieved through tenuous networks. (PF 173)

The reference to Braudel is noteworthy. For not only does that eminent French historian conduct a rather Latourian-looking investigation into the history of capitalism as it emerged from local and regional markets, he has even had a certain appeal on the Left as an alternative to Marx.[3] As the prominent Deleuzean Leftist Manuel DeLanda put it during his conversation with Timur Si-Qin:

> against historical materialism we need a new vision of history without teleology, one which avoids a periodization into internally homogenous eras: feudalism, capitalism, socialism (or the Age of Agriculture, the Age of Industry, the Age of Information). There were never such Ages or Eras. Braudel, for example, shows how in the 14th century the areas of Europe that would become France and Spain did have manors run by feudal lords, but the city-states in northern Italy and northern Germany (the Hanseatic league), as well as Flemish and Dutch towns, were already modern in many respects. Thus, we need to rethink our philosophy of history in the face of historical evidence.[4]

DeLanda thus shows himself open to reinventing the political Left on a new basis: one that is attentive both to the importance of local actors and to a robust philosophical realism freed from the ultimately idealist (even if supposedly "materialist") legacy of Marx. This remains untrue for most of the intellectual Left. Here the basic picture of the world is one of a free, transcendent human subject oppressed by the alienating otherness of capital, fetishes, objects, ideology, or society. Given that the whole of Latour's philosophical advance consists in demolishing any such human/ nonhuman dualism at its root, it is little wonder that he is increasingly unpopular on the Left.

This apparent incompatiblity of Latour's philosophy with radical Leftist politics often trumps everything else for those who might otherwise be sympathetic to actor-network theory. The philosopher Tom Eyers is a good example of this. Originally somewhat favorable towards Latour,[5]

Eyers by 2011 seems deeply persuaded by Noys's critique. As Eyers puts it in his interesting review of *The Persistence of the Negative*:

> We can also thank Noys for his entertainingly brisk and forthright denunciation of Bruno Latour, a sociologist whose work has proved especially influential in the fields of social anthropology and the sociology of science, but whose "flat ontology" of human and non-human "actants" mitigates against an understanding of radical change. Noys puts it well, if polemically, when he writes that Latour's "commitment to ontological equality, figured as the positivity of all objects, lacks the ability to grasp capitalism's logic of real abstraction" ... Even more, Noys accuses Latour of harboring anti-left politics, a bias that is said to infect perhaps his central philosophical contention, namely that modernism's separation of nature from culture fails to capture the inherently "hybrid" nature of things, of their incessant networking and association. Latour's explicit target is the very concept of oppositional, and in particular Marxist, critique, which can only proceed by drawing lines of separation and contestation, in precisely the movement of critical abstraction I mention above ... [Noys's] attacks on Latour ... seem well made. There is a richness to Latour's ethnographic reflections on the work of scientists in the field that Noys ignores, but the philosophical and political underpinnings of "flat ontology" are usefully pilloried here.[6]

Eyers makes two explicit charges against Latour in the passage above, both of them very much visible in Noys's book:

(a) Latour's flat ontology mitigates against radical change. To some extent this is true, though it is difficult to see why an ontology should be thrown out solely because we are displeased by its possible consequences. Eyers's implication seems to be that we must retain a *non-flat* ontology for the exclusive purpose of safeguarding radical change. This suggests an unwillingness by Eyers (and Noys himself) to question whether extant models of radical change are philosophically defensible or politically sufficient.

(b) Latour harbors an anti-left political bias that "infects" his critique of the modern separation between nature and culture. This is another knife that cuts both ways. For as long as we persist in charges of personal bias, the accusation is easily reversible. We might say this, for instance: "Eyers and Noys harbor a pro-left political bias that infects their refusal to accept Latour's devastating critique of the modern separation between nature and culture." No progress can be made along this path. If we speak in this way, it is simply a matter of entertaining those who happen to agree with us already. And furthermore, it is not clear why we should be more suspicious of the purity of Bruno Latour's motives than those of Tom Eyers and Benjamin Noys. But Eyers's review is a brief one, without the scope to develop his views on Latour in any detail. It is different with Noys himself, who devotes the entirety of Chapter 3 of his *The Persistence of the Negative* to Latour, taking the trouble to engage with his ideas at a length that is still unusual among Latour's detractors on the Left.

BENJAMIN NOYS'S CRITIQUE OF LATOUR

The purpose of Noys's book is to offer a broad critique of various "affirmationist" authors, a critique that lumps Latour together with Deleuze, Derrida, and others. This broader project need not concern us here, since we are interested only in Noys's critique of Latour. Noys begins with the facts, stating accurately that "[Latour's] work is not rooted in the anti-hegemonic struggles of the 1970s and, in fact, he evinces considerable political skepticism with regard to the Marxist or revolutionary tradition."[7] Noys also refers to Latour's "refusal to engage in political activity or theory (at least from the 'Left' as usually identified)." The fact that Latour "[self-identifies] as a patient anthropological or sociological tracker of networks" seems to entail "the rejection of any radical or revolutionary model of change" and "dictates a new political gradualism." Noys's claim that "Latour makes explicit the implicitly conservative political effects of affirmationism" echoes Brassier's shot-in-the-dark assault on Latour as a "neo-liberal."[8]

But here Noys accidentally conflates two different issues. The rejection of radical or revolutionary models by no means entails political gradualism, though Noys can certainly be forgiven for sensing an air of gradualism in Latour's writings. It is crucial to note that Latour rejects radical or revolutionary models in politics for the same reason he rejects them in science and elsewhere: namely, most self-proclaimed revolutions proceed by way of a modernist claim to strip away the corrupt accidents of cultural accretion and replace them with some appeal to nature or truth. For instance, what allows Badiou and Žižek to behave as old-guard communist revolutionaries in their political theories is their claim to *know* that we are all actually or potentially "subjects" and therefore all simply equal, as Badiou holds in celebrating "the communist invariant" at the root of all politics. Yet Latour's rejection of revolutionary purification need not entail gradualism, since sudden and significant change, even cataclysmic change, can occur without the modern attempt to separate nature and culture. We need only recall Latour's history of Louis Pasteur, which denied Pasteur's "revolutionary" credentials as a bringer of light to the ignorant but certainly did not deny the epochal shift induced by Pasteurian medicine, which had nothing the least bit "conservative" or "gradual" about it. Latour the Catholic presumably has little regard for the "revolutionary" force of the Protestant Reformation, but that does not prevent his making a half-joking reference to "St. Luther" (AIME 44) in honor of the great historical change brought about by this Protestant "saint." Noys might still object that none of these examples distinguish Latour's political philosophy from mere liberal gradualism. Yet at the time of publishing *The Persistence of the Negative* in 2012, Noys would have seen neither Latour's assault on economics towards the end of *An Inquiry into Modes of Existence*, nor his call for Schmittian warfare against climate skeptics in the 2013 Gifford Lectures. Indeed, there is some evidence that Latour's politics are becoming more vociferous in connection with climate change and his critique of the capitalist *Homo oeconomicus*, even though he can never be a "revolutionary" in the ontologically purifying sense of the term that underpins much of the modern Left.

Latour's hostility to revolution in the modernist purifying sense is perfectly clear from another passage in the interview in the Turkish journal cited above, which Noys himself quotes:

> To change the Body Politic and to end up with a mere representative government, this is now considered as a rather disgusting limitation of the possibility of demiurgic action on matter. More is possible: a total revolution. [Bernard] Yack shows how this extraordinary metamorphosis of the notion goes from Rousseau, then to Kant, Hegel, Marx and then Nietzsche. He could have continued this argument all the way to the disciples of Negri or even to the militants fighting violently for a new Caliphate: the revolution is either total or nothing. (DBD)

Noys takes evident pleasure in his willingness "to act the amateur psychoanalyst"[9] with Latour, portraying him as a sort of fearful bourgeois whose repressed "real target ... is Marxism" (p.81). At this point Noys becomes somewhat more intemperate in his portrayal of Latour. He takes a passing dig at Latour's reference to the "disciples" of Negri as if it were a weasel word ("note the careful distancing maneouvre") and goes on to call it a "slightly ironic charge" given the reformist note struck at the end of Negri and Michael Hardt's *Empire*. But whatever the contents of *Empire*, it is odd for Noys to hand reformist credentials to Negri, whose political track record is sufficiently hardcore that Latour seems perfectly justified in calling him a "total revolutionary" (any summary of Negri's career in the 1970s should be sufficient to prove the point). Yet perhaps more interesting is the passage already cited in which Latour points to a kind of dishonesty on the Left:

> [T]he notion of total Revolution has been transmogrified yet again in a psychopathology of great interest: the will of total subversion is still there in some circles, but has now become even more immensely satisfying because it is also connected with the certainty of failure while maintaining the absolute comfort of being morally superior ... And this goes a long way toward explaining why the minority parties of the ultra-left are still able to intimidate all of the other movements: you are the best and the brightest, you will fail; failure will never be counted against you, only against those who failed to be as radical as you. (DBD)

Latour concludes the interview with the claim that "if there is one thing the Left needs less than the plague, it is this remnant of the past: the specter of revolution, this valley of dust and whitened bones. Can we stop imitating the past to take the future, at last, into account?" (DBD). In any case, Latour is by no means a free-market "neo-liberal," the lazy person's polemical term of choice in early twenty-first century political thought.[10] Noys correctly states that "what stands at the core of [Latour's] thought is a new constructivism that can account for, and dissolve, the distinction between social and natural."[11] He rejects critique "by assimilating it to a principle of division that constantly tries to establish a pure point of sure knowledge against a sea of myth, ideology, or false consciousness." What concerns Noys about Latour is that his "crisis is not the crisis of capitalism, but the crisis of the modern project—or, as Latour prefers, the modern constitution" (p.82). Ironically, Latour joins Badiou in treating 1989 as the pivotal year in recent history, though for Latour it marks the end of modernism while for Badiou 1989 provides an "opportunity to re-invent the modern project in a fidelity to the twentieth-century's passion for the real" (p.83). This overlap with Badiou is interesting for another reason, since Latour will later be scolded by Noys for a "triumphalist substitution of the crisis of 1989 for Serres's crisis of Hiroshima" (p.93), even though Hiroshima is not prominent on Badiou's own list of "events," and even though Latour writes rather movingly of Serres's commitment to Hiroshima in a passage that Noys himself has read (he quotes from the essay in which it occurs) but chooses not to cite (EWC 92). Furthermore, it is unclear why Noys thinks that Serres's horror at Hiroshima and other disturbing events during his wartime youth amount to a *de facto* endorsement of modernist critique despite Serres's continually vehement rejection of such critique.

Noys correctly notes Latour's commitment to a "flat ontology" or irreductive theory in which all entities are treated as real as long as they have an effect on something else: hence the term "actors" or "actants" at the heart of Latour's theory. "This recourse to a flat and concrete ontology is the means by which Latour hopes to cure materialism of its idealistic tendency to posit one particular form of matter as superior to any other" (p.84). Yet Noys thinks he detects a sneaky hypocrisy in this method, since "while all entities should be equally real some are less real than others, and these just happen to be entities associated with a critical left politics; no irreduction allowed for the supposed reductionists." Noys's claim seems to be that Latour loads the dice, proclaiming fairness to all even while excluding those he dislikes, with "critical left politics" singled out in advance for special maltreatment. But this misses the point of the theory of irreduction. Latour's claim is not that all *philosophical positions* are equal, but that all *actors* are equal. That is to say, Latour makes an ontological decision that reductionism is best avoided by attending only to a basic feature shared by everything that is real: the fact that everything that exists "modifies, transforms, perturbs, or creates" some other actor (PH 122). Though I argued in *Prince of Networks* that Latour is wrong to use actions and effects as the basic criteria of reality, there is no question that he offers this theory in a spirit of providing the broadest possible definition for everything that in some way exists. Contrast this with mainstream materialism, which begins with the prior dogmatic decision that what *truly* exists is nothing but particles of material stuff occupying positions in a Cartesian space-time grid. Even if one disclaims this crude version of materialism and adds numerous qualifying subtleties, the assertion that only one type of entity truly exists at the basis of the world replaces the real with an *abstract theory* of the real. Latour argues this point convincingly enough in his memorable 2007 essay "Can We Get Our Materialism Back, Please?" The principle of irreduction requires that entities be treated as equally real, though not equally *strong*, insofar as they have some effect on something else. By no means does it require that a reductionist materialism opposed to flatness has equal rights with flatness itself. Noys is free to oppose flat ontology with a more convincing theory, if he can, but is not free to accuse Latour of hypocrisy in the matter of irreduction.

Noys's next criticism is that "Latour coquettes with the Marxists" even while disdaining their liberatory power (p.85). The argument for this runs as follows: "Writing with Michel Callon, Latour turns the screw further by using Marxism against Marxism, claiming that it runs the risk of reifying capitalism whereas there are only ever 'capitalisms.'" Noys views this as an uncomfortable contradiction for Latour, who joins Callon in accounting for capitalism as a "formatting regime," and in the same moment supposedly denying its existence. This is cut from the same cloth as Noys's sarcastic remark that Latour seems to be saying , "revolutionary violence is impossible ... *so don't do it!*" (p.94). Noys even has the effrontery to depict Latour's claim as fearfully reminiscent of the incest taboo (p.94), just pages after accusing *Latour* of "stylistic smugness" (p.91). Yet there is no contradiction in urging readers to avoid pursuing the impossible. There is no inconsistency, for example, when Latour both speaks of a modern era and denies that it was ever really modern, since in doing so he merely says that the moderns *conceived* of themselves as purifying nature from culture without ever actually doing so. The same holds for revolutionary violence: obviously Robespierre, Saint-Just, and Lenin all attempted to conduct revolutionary violence, and all had a certain degree of success in doing so. Latour would simply add that such revolutionary gestures did not do what they thought they were doing: they did not purify society by sweeping away the long accretion of cultural strata in the name of a universal egalitarian principle, but simply rearranged actors on the chessboard in the same manner that non-revolutionary leaders do. Latour argues against revolutionary violence simply because it cannot do what it thinks it is doing, and this is by no means a contradictory claim.

It is also true, as Noys states, that "for Latour and Callon capitalism is an eminently vulnerable regime, always subject to being generated by local effects and so capable of disruption. In this way Latour has his cake and eats it: outflanking Marxism by accusing it of reification and inattention to the detail of capital, and retaining an attenuated critique of capital that has a disavowed reliance on Marxism" (p.85). But here it is Noys who begs the question, by first assuming that only Marxism is allowed to criticize capitalism, then going on to accuse all other critics of being nothing more than copycats and flirts. It is hard to see any "disavowed reliance" on Marxism in Callon and Latour's claim that what we call capitalism was never very strong in the first place. Indeed, it is hard to imagine a less

Marxist notion than that of a *feeble* capitalism, which Marxists view instead as an insatiable dragon. If merely mentioning the feebleness of capitalism is enough to "outflank" or "coquette with" Marxism, then its position was not very vigorous in the first place.

Noys goes on to complain that Latour shows the supposed "nonexistence" of capitalism only by setting impossibly high hurdles to prove its existence. "What Latour cannot countenance is that being immanent to capital does not mean being completely determined by it, but instead dictates the need to struggle on that terrain if one should want to overturn it—what is classically called 'class struggle'" (p.86). A related passage by Noys runs as follows:

> This treatment of capitalism as a fantasy of total domination at work in the heads of its critics and supporters is achieved by posing a ridiculously high standard for what would constitute capitalism. Latour himself abstracts or refines capitalism by arguing that it can only exist if it were to fulfill its own internal obligation: "that an *absolute* equivalence has been achieved." In this way he ignores the actual definition of capitalism by Marx as the formal operation of accumulation, structured through real abstractions, that would confront "absolute equivalence" as its own limit—and that is therefore riven by contradiction. (p.87)

While this poses as a sophisticated Marxist rejoinder to Latourian word tricks, it is really just a misunderstanding of Latour's ontology. That is to say, Latour's claim is not that capitalism does not exist insofar as it never appears in pure form, any more than he opposes Durkheimian sociology by saying that society never appears in "pure form" insofar as we also find inanimate objects such as rocks, trees, and streams. In short, the error of modernism is not to think that it has *already succeeded* in purifying everything (did even the most rabid modernist ever think the job was finished?), but to view purification as its *ongoing task*. In political terms, Latour's complaint is not that Marxism holds that people are "completely determined" by capital, but rather that Marxism views the continuing struggle between capital and its other ("class struggle") as the basic structural dualism into which everything else is shoehorned from the start.

Despite these deficiencies in his critique, Noys to my knowledge has so far made a more serious effort to engage Latour than anyone else on the Left. For this reason, we should end the discussion by noting two points where Noys may be correct. The first is his nagging sense, shared by many critics and friends alike, that Latour leaves too little room for political standards higher than power struggle itself. As Noys puts it: "Adopting the pragmatic desire to convince as the standard again reproduces the equation of what is successful with what is right. In his qualified defence of sophistry [in *Pandora's Hope*] Latour denies this involves the equation of might with right, but instead argues that it permits an opening of democratic debate through a questioning of the authority of knowledge" (p.91). On the question of sophistry, Noys is gentler than he might have been. As I argued in *Prince of Networks*, Latour is wrong to view Socrates as a member of the "epistemology police," which leads him in turn to the additional error of embracing the Sophists in order to oppose Socrates' supposed authoritarian knowledge claims. As for the equation of might and right, Noys is also correct to worry about this element in Latour's thinking. Perhaps every philosophical standpoint is born with an original excess that it must struggle to master throughout the rest of its career. Spinoza's global deity/nature leaves him ill-equipped to handle individual entities, however loud the claims of his disciples to the contrary. Husserl's phenomenological starting point leaves him relatively helpless in clarifying the physical world, and later he must engage in increasingly far-fetched efforts to address this deficiency. Heidegger's valorization of concealed being over visible beings leaves him stranded in contempt for everyday entities, and ultimately requires the gnomic complexities of the fourfold to begin to recover them. In the case of Latour's initially Hobbesian political philosophy, the original danger is the closing off of all forms of political transcendence, all courts of appeal beyond the Leviathan itself. As we have seen, this has consequences for Latour's intellectual development. Yet it also seems to me that Noys fails to appreciate the reason for Latour's hope of "questioning the authority of knowledge": namely, the fact that knowledge claims are a terrible basis for politics, something that much of the present-day Left does not take seriously enough.

Yet there is a related point where Noys (and other adherents of the Left) may still be right. Noys argues that "[Latour's] anxiety concerning the effects of violence is not simply general, but turns on the problem of *revolutionary* violence. What revolutionary violence proposes is a macro-level change, violence directed against the limits of the micro-scale changes of networks in favor of the change of the 'network' itself" (p.93). The complaint is not without merit. I have already defended Latour's critique of modernist revolution, which makes an untenable claim to purify the obstructions of culture and history and rebuild society in the name of an adequate idea. In this sense, there is no real "macro-level" for Latour, just larger and smaller micro-levels. Nonetheless, there is a danger inherent in Latour's position that after fending off modern revolutionary claims, he leaves *insufficient* room for sub-revolutionary change that would still be significant or even cataclysmic. One need not adhere to a modernist nature/culture split to call for a slave rebellion, to be outraged that Wall Street emerged largely unscathed following the 2008 economic meltdown, to hold that the Kennedy assassination or the crash of certain passenger aircraft resulted from shadowy military conspiracies, or to claim that the developed West enjoys an artificially high standard of living at the expense of the rest of the world. All are typically stirring claims of the Left, and all might be able to survive Latour's proposed end of nature/culture purification. But if it remains to be seen whether Latour's political philosophy is capable of calling for truth and justice in this non-absolute sense, it *also* remains to be seen whether the Left is willing to uncouple itself from a rationalist version of the nature/culture divide, and from its now widespread epistemological view that human politics is the transcendental condition of access to reality.

HEKMAN AND OTHERS ON LATOUR AND FOUCAULT

The most widely referenced figure in the humanities and social sciences in our time is surely Michel Foucault. With the assistance of Google Scholar, we can even quantify the magnitude of Foucault's influence. As of this writing (June 2014), the ubiquitous Jacques Derrida has a remarkable 148,000 recorded citations of his work. While this figure is impressive enough, Foucault has a jaw-dropping 481,000, a testament to the more immediate employability of his ideas across an even wider range of disciplines than Derrida's. Foucault is worth mentioning here due to recent whispers that Latour himself might one day rival Foucault as the nearly universal referent in the humanities and social sciences. After all, the intellectual methods of Latour make a good fit with nearly any subject matter. They offer a more detailed (if controversial) treatment of the natural sciences than Foucault's own. And surely Latour tells us more about inanimate actors than Foucault, whose purported concern with "materiality" is really just a concern for how the nonhuman world shapes the human subject through history. Though Latour is currently still more of a niche figure than Foucault (whom nearly everyone has read) the tools he gives us are sufficiently flexible that it is no longer foolish to wonder if Latour might eventually replace Foucault as the standard referent of all work that presents itself as cutting-edge.

Let's briefly consider the intellectual relationship between the respective positions of Foucault and Latour. Perhaps the most detailed treatment of this relationship so far is Susan Hekman's 2009 article "We Have Never Been Postmodern," which comes down largely on the side of Foucault. Also useful is a 2011 article by the Finnish scholars Olli Pyyhtinen and Sakari Tamminen, whose title ("We Have Never Only Been Human") is yet another play on that of Latour's most famous book. Another helpful piece is an earlier 2001 article by Gavin Kendall and Mike Michael. As for Latour's own view on the matter, while he has never made a full frontal response to Foucault, it is perhaps in *Paris: Invisible City* that Latour (with co-author Emilie Hermant) gives the most vivid indication of where he differs from Foucault. For despite Latour's positive remarks about Foucault in print, which tend to become even more positive in private conversation, it is hard to escape the sense that Latour has no wish to follow in Foucault's footsteps. Consider the following remarks about "power" from *Irreductions* in 1984:

> The philosophers and sociologists of power flatter the masters they claim to criticize. They explain the masters' actions in terms of the might of power, though this power is efficacious only as a result of complicities, connivances, compromises, and mixtures which are not explained by power. The notion of "power" is the dormitive virtue of the poppy which induces somnolence in the critics at just the moment when powerless princes ally themselves with others who are equally weak in order to become strong. (PF 175)

However one tries to finesse Foucault's definition of "power," it is hard to imagine a sense of the term that would pass muster with Latour. But let's consider Hekman's alternative view of the matter.

Hekman quite reasonably takes *We Have Never Been Modern* to be Latour's most representative work. While the key claim of that book was the untenability of the modernist split between nature on one side and culture on the other, Hekman is not especially impressed by this claim. "This in itself is not controversial," as she somewhat hastily puts it. For "in one sense what Latour is arguing here is not new. Critiques of modernism and the dichotomies on which it rests can be found in much nineteenth and twentieth century thought. Hegel, Nietzsche, and Heidegger, among others, offered approaches to the material/discursive dichotomy that challenged modernism."[12] In short, for Hekman the Latourian critique of modernity is relatively old hat, and is of interest only through its provocative challenge to the form of the dichotomy most dominant in recent times: the linguistic turn. "The importance of Latour's challenge … is its timeliness. He is addressing a problem—the linguistic turn in contemporary thought—that is unique to late twentieth century and early twenty-first century thought" (p.436). Though the linguistic turn actually needs to be dated to well before the late twentieth century, Hekman's point is clear enough: the linguistic turn is still very much our contemporary intellectual horizon. What makes her most uneasy about this turn is its sacrifice of grand political narratives. Unlike many authors sympathetic to recent French theory, Hekman is willing to concede that Derrida is partially blinded by his linguistic allegiances: "The nature of this problem and its effect on political theory is most evident in the work of the quintessential postmodernist: Jacques Derrida. Derrida's concern is exclusively with language—its 'difference,' its deconstruction, the play of language in writing and speech, the death of man." And while he may seem to venture beyond such linguistic themes in his various writings on ethics and politics (not to mention religion), "nowhere in any of these discussions is there any reference to the real, material consequences of these political concepts or to the political world that they inhabit. True to his deconstructive theory, Derrida's text does not venture beyond the linguistic."

Yet unlike Derrida, or so Hekman asserts, Foucault is not guilty of remaining trapped in one pole of the modern nature/culture split. With an apparently Latourian flourish, Hekman notes that "moving to the language side of the language/reality dichotomy does not deconstruct dichotomy but, rather, perpetuates it. What we need is a theory that can incorporate the insights of the linguistic turn without losing the material … Articulating a theory that describes the intra-action (Karen Barad's term) of language and reality is a formidable task" (p.438). And yet, "Latour is wrong about one thinker who is not only classified as a postmodern, but has come to be identified as the quintessential postmodern: Michel Foucault." Under Hekman's reading, Foucault, "far from emphasizing discourse to the exclusion of the material or 'reality' is always acutely aware of the interaction between discourse and reality." This sets the table for the remainder of Hekman's article, which in my view overrates Foucault's originality while underestimating that of Latour.

Before looking to the details of what Hekman says about Foucault and Latour, we should note three troublesome features in the passages just cited. First, Hekman defends Foucault by saying that he does not reduce the world to the "discourse" pole, but is "always acutely aware of the interaction between discourse and reality" (p.438). This is already a crucial misunderstanding of Latour's *We Have Never Been Modern*. The point of that book was not that the nature/culture dualism should be replaced by their constant interchange, but that both poles are useless from the start. This is why Latour dumps both nature and culture in favor of the unified notion of "actants," a concept that both encompasses and cuts across the modern nature/culture dyad. Everything is real for Latour insofar as it *acts*, not insofar as we can plausibly identify it as either natural or cultural. The fact that Latour sometimes slips back into echoes of the modernist dualism (as in his unfortunate recourse to "quasi-objects" and "quasi-subjects" in *An Inquiry into Modes of Existence*) does not change the general spirit of his critique. The point is not to mix nature and culture any more than it is to take one of them as primary; both nature and culture are invalid classifications of entities from the start. Second, the recourse to Barad's theory of intra-action is dubious in this context. The intellectual starting point for Barad's investigations in *Meeting the Universe Halfway* is Niels Bohr's theory of complementarity, which does not challenge the dichotomy of mind and world but simply fuses the two poles together permanently. While this may be what Barad and Hekman want, it is not Latour's own intention. In particular, Barad's term "intra-action" is employed as a substitute for the usual word "interaction" precisely because Barad does not agree that mind and reality are separate terms in the first place. This is why agents act "intra-" in a place where they are always already pre-unified. Barad has no notion at all of simply discarding mind and reality as two separate poles, which is the whole point of Latour's critique of modernism. Third and finally, we should not ignore the following phrase in Hekman's remarks: "far from emphasizing discourse to the exclusion of the material or 'reality.'" While "material" and "reality" seem to be utilized by Hekman as synonyms (already a bad idea), only "reality" is surrounded with quotation marks, as if Hekman were comfortable with the usual associations of "material" but wished to distance herself from the usual sense of "real" as something lying altogether outside human engagement. This latter point not only fits well with Hekman's support for Barad's model of intra-activity, but is also a point where she and Latour largely agree. The main difference is that while Hekman explicitly regards the world as resulting from an interplay between two specific entities known as "reality" and "discourse," Latour's position allows in principle for interactions between "reality" and "reality" with no "discourse" to be found on the scene: as when a speed bump damages a car's suspension even if it has rolled downhill without a driver or even an eyewitness.

Along with Foucault, Deleuze is another hero of the contemporary philosophical Left. But in Hekman's view, "Deleuze leaves us [politically] in an ill-defined limbo" (p.439). Such leading Deleuzeans as Claire Colebrook, William Connolly, and Michael Hardt are praised by Hekman but still judged to be lacking, since "Foucault provides a much better understanding of how a politics beyond both modernism and linguistic construction-ism would be structured" (p.440). Still retaining the dualism critiqued by Latour, and merely fusing its opposite terms together, Hekman salutes Foucault for "[describing] a world in which nature and culture interact in complex ways. He wants to privilege neither the linguistic nor the material but, rather, integrate them in an interactive continuum." Foucault is praised for greater concreteness than Deleuze: "His descriptions of prisons, hospitals, asylums, practices of sexuality and many other elements of contemporary life give us a concrete sense of what our politics should be. In short, he gives us something to do." The difference between the discursive and the material in Foucault is also glossed by Hekman as "the intimate relation between discourse and practice." Now that the "material" has been identified with "praxis," we gain some insight into just how anthropocentric Hekman's Foucault remains—which is not to say that her reading is inaccurate. While Hekman agrees with the classic Dreyfus/Rabinow interpretation that "Foucault is always interested not just in discourse, but in discursive *practices*, how discourses are used, and what role they play in society" (p.442), she is chagrined by their conclusion that interpretation is always arbitrary for Foucault. She dismisses this view as a well-worn cliché, and as "the standard interpretation not only of Foucault but of postmodernism in general." But Hekman has already conceded the point about Derrida having an exclusively linguistic universe. How does she absolve Foucault of the same charge? Oddly, she does so not by proclaiming that the "material" has independent reality, but by again insisting that "Foucault's method always presupposes that the material and the conceptual are inseparable." What is most material for Foucault is "power," and Hekman admits that "Foucault is obsessed with power. He saw power everywhere." We shall see that this is simultaneously Foucault's most and least Latourian side.

It is well known that one aspect of Foucault's history of power, also known as "the intricate interweaving of discourse and practice," is the history of the police and of surveillance more generally, which "spread to schools, barracks, hospitals and other institutions" (p.444). Moreover, "surveillance produces discipline, and discipline is of bodies ... What emerges through the disciplinary practices that Foucault describes is something he calls bio-power ... the technique for achieving the subjugation of bodies and the control of populations" (p.445). Finally, we must recognize that "power is not a possession, but a multifarious series of relations" (p.446). Sexuality is hardly alone for Foucault in being "a historical construct" (p.447), meaning that Foucault's vaunted "materialism" is really nothing more than a historicism of the human subject. And again, "the discursive and the non-discursive merge into the event, the practice" (p.449) After citing Dreyfus and Rabinow's view that Foucault was "seduced by discourse and, giving discourse priority, essentially ignored the material," Hekman makes a defense of Foucault that is hardly compelling: "[Foucault's] focus, clearly, is on discourse. But in focusing on discourse, Foucault never loses sight of the connection between the discursive and the non-discursive." Yet we have already seen that Hekman takes the "non-discursive" or the "material" in the all-too-human sense of praxis and history.

In short, the reason Hekman thinks it unfair to say that Foucault ignores the material is that he takes great pains to *dissolve* the material into the human. Supposedly, this dissolution of the material proves that he does not ignore it! Though in vain, Hekman protests that words "do not constitute ... being but, rather ... disclose it. And, importantly, [Foucault] never questions that the material reality is there to *be* disclosed. Our concepts apprehend that reality in very different ways but, for Foucault, there is always something there—the ontological continuum, being or its modes—to be disclosed" (p.450). This is Hekman's first mention of ontology or being, and given her identification of the material with the practical/historical, we have no reason to expect her "being" to have anything but a human face. If this seems unlikely, just consider Hekman's gloss of "disclosure" as meaning that "objects exist under the positive conditions of a complex group of relations—economic, social, and so on" (p.451). There is no indication that "and so on" would include anything other than the known topics of the social sciences; Hekman's "relations" seem to be solely human relations. She finds it significant that "in his early life Foucault flirted with Marxism" (p.452), and proclaims in closing that "perhaps what we need at this juncture is a return to Marx" (p.453). But we can hardly help noting that what lingers in Foucault's work is "an element of Marx's concern with the material" (p.452), and not, judging from Hekman's terminological choices, with the *real*. The point is not a minor one, but hints at the strangely *idealist* version of Marx that has grown increasingly popular in cultural studies circles. Hekman has already described the "material" as made up of social and economic relations, not of anything other than such relations. Yet this is hardly the view of Marx himself. Despite recent attempts to view Marx as subsuming everything beneath social relations and viewing the non-relational remainder as an illusion of "commodity fetishism," Marx leaves plenty of room for a non-commodified reality outside the human sphere. He tells us himself, in the opening pages of *Das Kapital*, that air, water, and virgin forests are not commodities, and neither are objects produced in communal tribes nor corn-rents delivered by peasants to feudal lords. When Hekman ends her article with the prediction that Foucault "will guide intellectual thought, and political theory, for decades to come" (p.453), she seems to imagine a political thought entirely occupied with the mutual shaping of nature and culture (and nature only in the very weak sense of non-discursive practice), and with a system of social and economic relations that will define reality as a whole.

While it is true that Latour at certain stages also seems to view the world as a landscape made up of nothing but power, there are several features that differentiate Latour from Foucault. First, Latour obviously has a more robust sense of the role of inanimate entities than does Foucault, which is precisely the reason that some researchers are now turning from Foucault to Latour. In Foucault it often seems as if the only role of the "material" is to shape some new historical form of the human subject. While it is true that Latour only rarely considers object-object relations explicitly, he does supplement Hobbesian baboons and humans with non-animal mediators. Another key point of difference is Latour's less dismal view of power than Foucault's, in a way that goes beyond differences of temperament or general stylistic mood. Foucault's basically gloomy view of power, of the disciplinary practices of biopolitics, betrays the ultimately Rousseauian orientation of his thought. Hekman herself quotes Foucault as saying that everything is *dangerous* even if everything is not bad, and the reason for the danger is that the primary role of power is to shape, tame, and control. But Latour, a close cousin of Hobbes with little of Rousseau about him, tends to see the negotiations of power in a positive light: as a risky and fragile gambit, not as the insidious biopolitics of paranoid ruling institutions.

If this is not sufficient to convince readers that Latour and Foucault are not working in the same vein, we need only turn to the Latour/Hermant *Paris: Invisible City*. Not only is it difficult to imagine a less Foucauldian book than this one, it is even hard to read it as anything but an explicit satire on Foucault. Consider the numerous delicious passages of the following sort:

Megalomaniacs confuse the map and the territory and think they can dominate all of Paris because they do, indeed, have all of Paris before their eyes. Paranoiacs confuse the territory and the map and think they are dominated, observed, watched, just because a blind person absent-mindedly looks at some obscure signs in a four-by-eight metre room in a secret place. (PIC 28)

Or again:

From the Prime Minister's window, at Matignan? We'd simply see a well-tended garden and not France, even though he governs it. From the balcony of the Mairie de Paris, at the Hôtel de Ville? An empty and cold square, cluttered with ugly fountains; nothing that gives life to this metropolis. Does that mean that Paris is invisible? "Move on, there's nothing to see." Well yes, let's do just that, let's move and then, suddenly, Paris will begin to be visible. (PIC 29)

Foucault would justifiably read the following words of Latour as a sardonic remark on his legacy: "No bird's eye view could, at a single glance, capture the multiplicity of these places which all add up to make the whole Paris. There are no more panopticons than panoramas; only richly colored dioramas with multiple connections, criss-crossing wires under roads and pavements, along tunnels in the metro, on the roofs of sewers" (PIC 32). And then there is this crowning bit of mockery, as Latour and Hermant approach the office of a senior official of the national police:

Going through the series of sentry posts that led us to the office of Mr. Henry, a member of a hierarchically organized corps of 17,000 people, had we perhaps reached the supreme panopticon, the thousand-eyed peacock, capable of encompassing all of Paris and of justifying the worst restrictions on those—Cain and Abel alike—who know that no tomb is deep enough to hide from the centralizing Napoleonic French state? (PIC 51–52)

We are hardly surprised when Latour answers in the negative: there is no panopticon, indeed no central power anywhere at all. Nor does Latour have much time for the method that pretends to discover this non-existent panopticon: namely, critique, [which] whether high-brow or popular, cumbersome or miniaturized, costly or cheap, brave or facile, sees nothing but lies everywhere. It still longs for a full, wholesome reality and finds only strands, paths or channels that it doesn't know how to follow, objects that it can't see how to fathom, stumbling at each step on the same abysmal distance between words and things, past and present. (PIC 94)

Let's turn now to the 2011 article of Olli Pyyhtinen and Sakari Tamminen, who are not wrong when they say that "the oeuvres of [Foucault and Latour] have not been compared in a systematic fashion in the secondary literature,"[13] since even Hekman's article is less a comparative account than a defense of Foucault from possible Latourian accusations. Pyyhtinen and Tamminen correctly identify the main point of difference between the two thinkers: "[W]hile Foucault focused exclusively on games of truth where the object of knowledge is man, Latour's concerns are not confined to the boundaries of the human sciences. Instead, he characteristically studied the 'hard sciences' by focusing on laboratories, microbes, technology and the like" (p.136). Yet there is also an obvious agreement between the two authors in the sense that rather than viewing humans as a timeless essence, "both [Foucault and Latour] view humans as compounds of relations" (p.137). Pyyhtinen and Tamminen are less convincing in their additional claim (made in part against my own book *Prince of Networks*) that "notwith-standing their relationism, neither Foucault nor Latour holds that relations would exhaust the whole of the real. We argue that for both Foucault and Latour it is the outside of associations that ultimately provides the resources for every action and also for every compound of the human." This sets the bar much too low, since only a full-blown Berkeleyan idealist would ever explicitly *deny* an outside world beyond whatever is now directly accessible to us. Indeed, the Finnish authors immediately concede the point by adding that "both [Foucault and Latour] also fail to do this [outside] justice." Though Foucault offers "life" as a source of resistance (in *The History of Sexuality*) and Latour offers a formless "plasma" to the same end (in *Reassembling the Social*), "neither Foucault nor Latour succeeds in providing a detailed and comprehensive account of life/plasma itself and of its share in network relations" (p.145).

Another piece on the Foucault-Latour relation worth considering is an even earlier article (from 2001) by Gavin Kendall and Mike Michael.[14] Midway through their piece, the authors utter what might sound at first like the proclamation of Latour as the next major French thinker:

So far, the answer to the question "What comes after Foucault?" would appear to be "Latour." Latour enables us to develop a couple of gaps in a Foucaultian programme, in particular enabling us to think seriously about technology (in case we had imagined that Foucault's "technologies of the self" were enough) and to think seriously about the hybrid character of subjectivity, enabling us to escape from an inappropriate emphasis on the pure human or the pure social.

This assessment relies on the somewhat forced distinction between Latourian "technologies" and Foucauldian "techniques" that makes up the core of the authors' argument. Yet the distinction leads to possibly interesting results. As the authors put it, "Latour stresses systematicity—the tying together of actors through the movement of intermediaries which must be more or less routinized if a network is to be successfully put together and operate durably." Stated differently, "Latour's thought ... dwells on the 'technological' (the systematic, routinized, enframing) rather than the technical (the singular, the discrete, the *ad hoc*)," whereas Foucault by contrast supposedly dwells on the latter triad of the technical. Kendall and Michael hold that this gives Foucault an important theoretical resource that is missing from Latour: "For Foucault then, *soi* [self] has an irreducible fluidity (*multiplicité*) that is the 'object' of discipline, knowledge, govern-mentality, and so forth. It is always on the verge of escaping the techniques and technologies which are deployed in knowledge/power networks—of becoming 'deterritorialised,' as Deleuze and Guattari put it." In contrast to such fluidity, which is essentially ungraspable, "the role that Latour unravels is only too graspable: it ends up being a mere cipher for the network as a whole—it is wholly determined." And now comes the article's final punch:

> It is probably not too difficult to guess where we are going next. Imagine the power and flexibility of an analysis that puts Latour's emphasis on heterogeneous networks together with Foucault's insistence on the historically conditioned emergence of such networks. Where Latour's networks sometimes appear to emerge fully formed, Foucault can help us see how they were slowly, painstakingly and accidentally put together; where Foucault stresses the human social world as the dynamic mechanism behind new social arrangements, Latour can help us see how the world stretches far beyond the human or the social.

On the downside, the authors get two things wrong about Latour. The first is the notion that networks are filled with "intermediaries" that fit neatly into one another. In fact, Latour's system is one of nothing but incompletely formed *mediators*. Latour's use of the opposed terms mediators/intermediaries is not a taxonomy used to describe two different sorts of entities existing in the world, but a polemical device designed to show that, strictly speaking, there is *no such thing* as an intermediary. Even if something *looks* like a mere transparent vehicle for conveying the forces of another actor, this is a merely apparent result of a mediation that took much labor to create. The supposed intermediary—say, a reliable bicycle messenger or telephone line—is actually a mediator with individual quirks that can cause surprise or disruption at any given moment. In this sense, the authors exaggerate the systematicity of Latour's outlook, which always takes account of the possible recalcitrance or subversiveness of even the most trivial actors. Yet Kendall and Michael's instincts are correct when they detect an excessive holism in Latour's position, which (as I argued in *Prince of Networks*) is too relationist to allow for change to be truly possible. Whether Deleuze and Foucault offer superior resources to explain such change, as the authors hold, can be left here as an open question. But at least they are aware that Latour's relationist approach is incompatible with a model of change and fluidity, and in this respect they deftly avoid the widespread error of assuming that the phrase "process philosophy" is sufficient to unify the Whiteheadian tradition to which Latour belongs (which is based on the utter relational determinacy of objects at any given moment) with the Bergsono-Deleuzean tradition (for which such determinacy never exists).

The second point where the authors misunderstand Latour is more egregious, though also less important. When they say that Latour's networks appear to emerge fully formed whereas Foucault does painstaking historical work, I have to wonder if we are reading the same Latour— the Latour who expends so much effort to tell the story of how Pasteur spread his influence, or how the Aramis metro system in Paris ultimately failed. Foucault never fails to boast about how much time he spends in the archives, but it is by no means clear that Foucault is a better storyteller or even a more conscientious archivist than Latour. If there is a weakness in Latour's position, it is not that his actors emerge fully formed, but that their history ends in the present. His relational conception of actors makes him much better at describing things that have already occurred than at considering things that might still occur. Nor does Latour's relational model of actors provide sufficient resources for treating counterfactual cases that *might* have occurred if only the actors had been placed in different sets of relations. After all, this would be a somewhat nonsensical notion for Latour, since for him an actor *is* nothing more than its relations.

What Pyyhtinen/Tamminen and Kendall/Michael both get more right than Hekman is the fact that Latour is not just pirating "materialist" insights already available in Foucault. Instead, Latour is breaking fresh ground with his appeal to inanimate entities, and this may one day establish him as Foucault's successor. Both authors seem to remain trapped in the perplexities of relationist ontology, though whether Foucault has greater resources to escape relationism than Latour (as Kendall and Michael hold) is not entirely clear. I for one am skeptical on this point since, as Hekman concedes, Foucault's "material" domain itself consists of social relations. Though Kendall and Michael think that "the self" is what allows Foucault to escape relationism, this would merely ratify human beings as uniquely free entities, while other entities (lacking "selves") would remain trapped in a relational whole. In this way, Latour's powerful critique of the nature/culture divide would be lost. We would return to the modern conception of a purely robotic, mechanistic nature subverted only by a purely human indeterminacy.

6

"An Interesting Reactionary": Latour's Right Flank

The contemporary political philosopher Chantal Mouffe writes about a major twentieth-century intellectual as follows: "In spite of his moral flaws, he is an important ... thinker whose work it would be a great mistake to dismiss merely because of his support for Hitler in 1933."[1] The person she is describing is not Martin Heidegger, but Carl Schmitt, whose wartime behavior under Hitler was seemingly even worse than Heidegger's own. While Heidegger was merely banned from university teaching under the French Occupation authorities, Schmitt was actually imprisoned by the Americans, a discrepancy that owes more to an actual distinction between the deeds of the two men than to any difference in the respective rigors of French and American military justice. Whatever the reason for Schmitt's greater immunity than Heidegger's to recurrent scandal over the decades, Mouffe is right to say that Schmitt "[is now widely recognized] as one of the great political and legal theorists of [the twentieth] century ... His amazing erudition and the breadth of his reflections—which always fascinated those who encountered him—help to explain his impact on so many different fields." But there is a more timely reason for Schmitt's recent surge in popularity: especially on the Left, where no one would expect the stock of a Nazi author to rise. As Mouffe puts it, "Schmitt's thought serves as a warning against the dangers of a triumphant liberalism" (p.2), which was even more triumphant when she published these words in 1999 than is the case today. The nature of Schmitt's warning is clear enough. In Mouffe's own words: "[H]umanitarian rhetoric has today displaced political stakes and, with the collapse of communism, Western liberals imagine that antagonisms have been eradicated. Having reached the stage of 'reflexive modernity,' ethics can replace politics ... Alas, Schmitt's insistence on the ineradicable dimension of conflictuality inherent in 'the political,' and on the political 'exterior' of law, reveal all this to be wishful thinking."

Schmitt's most famous idea is that politics emerges only with the distinction between friend and enemy, a distinction that he claims is as central to politics as those between good and evil in morality, or beautiful and ugly in aesthetics.[2] As he puts it in *The Concept of the Political*:

> The political enemy need not be morally evil or aesthetically ugly; he need not appear as an economic competitor, and it may even be advantageous to engage with him in business transactions. But he is, nevertheless, the other, the stranger; and it is sufficient for his nature that he is, in an especially intense way, existentially something different and alien, so that in the extreme case conflicts with him are possible. These can neither be decided by a previously determined general norm nor by the judgment of a disinterested and therefore neutral third party. (p.27)

It is easy to see what would interest Latour about such a thinker. With his view that political conflict ultimately lies beyond all "impartial" or "rational" arbitration, Schmitt precedes Latour in decisively rejecting what we have called Truth Politics. Political struggle is not just a lamentable pre-rational incident that might be remedied by the creation of transparent ideal speech situations. Pessimism about human affairs (such as Schmitt's) is most often associated with the political Right, and that may be the reason for Latour's 2008 statement at the London School of Economics that "reactionary thinkers are more interesting than the progressive ones ... in that you learn more about politics from people like Machiavelli and [Carl] Schmitt than from Rousseau" (PW 96). The problem with progressive thinkers, it seems, is their wish to replace politics with science, morality, commerce, law, justice, truth, or some other mode of reality.

The present chapter is organized as follows. In the first section we consider the most basic aspects of Schmitt's political philosophy and what they mean for Bruno Latour. For reasons of space we limit ourselves to Schmitt's short treatise *The Concept of the Political* rather than considering one of the more monumental works of this prolific author, such as his *Constitutional Theory*. In the second section, we note the strange resemblance between Right and Left versions of Truth Politics in considering the somewhat similar rejections of Schmitt by the arch-conservative Leo Strauss and the contemporary communist philosopher Slavoj Žižek. In the third section, again for reasons of space, we limit ourselves to Mouffe's critique of Schmitt, which is more germane to Latour's own concerns than equally prominent treatments of Schmitt by Giorgio Agamben in *Homo*

Sacer and Jacques Derrida in "Force of Law," works that are therefore not considered in the present book.

SCHMITT AND LATOUR

Though Schmitt's treatise *The Concept of the Political* is divided into eight sections, it can be read as containing just two central ideas. Sections 1 through 6 are a passionate rejection of Truth Politics in favor of the political conceived as an existential struggle against the enemy. This need not require that we depict the enemy as immoral or monstrous, though it may involve physically killing him in order to preserve our own way of life. Sections 7 and 8 are a rejection of leftist or liberal progressivism in favor of the right-wing intuition that human beings are not fundamentally improvable. In terms of the four basic positions described in this book so far, Schmitt belongs with Hobbes among the right-wing orientation of Power Politics: both deny that politics can appeal to any standards beyond politics itself, and both are innately distrustful of the human character. This would be sufficient for Latour to classify both Hobbes and Schmitt as "interesting reactionaries." While Truth Politicians of a left-wing stripe uphold an optimistic and egalitarian notion of the political sphere and its possibly glorious future, even if considerable bloodshed may be needed to reach it, they tend to replace what Schmitt calls the political with either scientific or moral operations: "the proletariat must inevitably prevail due to the contradictions inherent in capitalism"; "society is responsible for corrupting the natural goodness of human beings." But for Latour as for Schmitt, the political first appears only when claims to knowledge are absent, and only when the prospects of peace take account of the mutual ill will between us and our enemies rather than leaning on rationalist appeals to our shared common nature.

We now turn directly to Schmitt, beginning with the first sentence of the text: "The concept of the state presupposes the concept of the political" (p.19). By no means does this imply a lowly status for the state. Quite the contrary:

> In its literal sense and in its historical appearance the state is a specific entity of a people. Vis-à-vis the many conceivable kinds of entities, it is in the decisive case the ultimate authority ... All characteristics of this image of entity and people receive their meaning from the further

distinctive trait of the political and become incomprehensible when the nature of the political is misunderstood. (pp.19–20)

One such misunderstanding, according to Schmitt, is the liberal replacement of politics with a potpourri of economics and morality. Yet Schmitt holds that "democracy must do away with all the typical distinctions and depoliticizations characteristic of the liberal nineteenth century" (p.23). It is Hegel, he says, who exposed the flaws of liberal depoliticization by offering

> the first polemically political definition of the bourgeois. The bourgeois is an individual who does not want to leave the apolitical riskless private sphere. He rests in the possession of his private property, and under the justification of his possessive individualism he acts as an individual against the totality. He is a man who finds his compensation for his political nullity in the fruits of freedom and enrichment and above all in the total security of its use. Consequently he wants to be spared bravery and exempted from the danger of a violent death. (pp.62–63)

These words might easily have been written by Marx or Lenin rather than Hegel or Schmitt, which gives us further insight into the otherwise surprising appeal of the Nazi Schmitt to contemporary Leftists. Yet Schmitt's conception of the political is sufficiently grim that the bourgeois temptation of security might sound rather appealing by contrast.

Schmitt's key political antithesis is that between friend and enemy, who engage in a purely immanent struggle without any higher court of appeal. The struggle with the enemy is existential strife occurring under exceptional conditions in a manner that cannot invoke shared standards of justice or morality to settle the dispute. As a present-day example, consider the burgeoning dispute over the waters of the Nile between Egypt on the one side and Sudan and Ethiopia on the other. Both sides claim moral or at least legal superiority in the dispute. Egypt possesses a treaty giving it the right to a specific percentage of Nile water, while Sudan and Ethiopia counter that this treaty was forcibly signed during the era of British Imperialism and thus is no longer binding. When Egypt notes that the Nile is its sole source of water while Sudan and Ethiopia also have rain, these latter countries reply that Egypt is wasting too much Nile water through inefficient irrigation practices. Who is right in this dispute, and who is wrong? There is much to be said for both sides of the conflict. But let us imagine hypothetically that all the nations of the world came to side with

Sudan and Ethiopia against Egypt in this dispute. Even under this scenario, it remains quite conceivable that sunbaked Egypt, with its booming population, might still go to war to secure its water supplies by bombing any dam on the Nile constructed by Ethiopia or Sudan. For Schmitt this would not be primarily an "immoral" or "illegal" act opposed by all the nations of the world, but a maneuver of existential necessity by Egypt against the enemy that wants to deprive it of sufficient water and hence of its way of life. Reciprocally, if Sudan or Ethiopia were to construct a dam only to find it bombed by Egypt, they might see themselves as locked in existential struggle with an enemy who destroys their most expensive and beneficial public infrastructure projects. For Schmitt there is simply no higher court of appeal to settle such a dispute, which ultimately might need to be settled by armed conflict. As he puts it, "only the actual participants can correctly recognize, understand, and judge the concrete situation and settle the extreme case of conflict. Each participant is in a position to judge whether the adversary intends to negate his opponent's way of life and therefore must be repulsed or fought in order to preserve one's form of existence" (p.27).

While the various powers in a possible Nile Water War might portray one another as evil or immoral aggressors, whether to stir up martial fervor in the populace or from a sincere belief in the justice of their cause, Schmitt contends that this is not really the point. What is truly important is the mere fact of existential strife without higher standards of arbitration. Such struggle is not incompatible with a certain grudging respect or admiration for the enemy. For instance, I well remember a conversation I once had at a Cairo house party with one of the leading Egyptian generals of the October 1973 war against Israel. What surprised me most was the general's professional admiration for Israel's Ariel Sharon, generally depicted in the Arab press as an inhuman butcher due to various historical events in the Sinai and the Beirut suburbs. Carl Schmitt would not have been surprised by such admiration, however, since for Schmitt it is a key principle that the enemy can be respected, rather than morally despised or targeted for utter annihilation. What Schmitt really deplores are notions such as Woodrow Wilson's idealistic call for a "war to end all wars." As Schmitt sees it,

> such a war is necessarily unusually intense and inhuman because, by transcending the limits of the political framework, it simultaneously degrades the enemy into moral and other categories and is forced to make of him a monster that must not only be defeated but also utterly

destroyed. In other words, he is an enemy who no longer must be compelled to retreat into his borders only. (p.36)

The moral approach to war, Schmitt contends, is a distraction with dangerous side effects. Though during recent years there has been renewed talk of "just war" theory, for Schmitt this concept is a complete waste of time: "it would be senseless to wage war for purely religious, purely moral, purely juristic, or purely economic motives ... A war need be neither something religious nor something morally good nor something lucrative. War today is in all likelihood none of these." Instead, "the inherently objective nature and autonomy of the political becomes evident by virtue of its being able to treat, distinguish, and comprehend the friend-enemy antithesis independently of other antitheses" (p.27).

The contemporary human being generally belongs to many different associations: "he is a member of a religious institution, nation, labor union, family, sports club, and many other associations" (p.41). Thus, the political state might seem to be just one form of human association among others. Yet for Schmitt the state is unique, since it alone can potentially dispose of the lives of its members.

> The state as the decisive political entity possesses an enormous power: the possibility of waging war and thereby publicly disposing of the lives of men. The *jus belli* contains such a disposition. It implies a double possibility: the right to demand from its own members the readiness to die and unhesitatingly to kill enemies ... By virtue of this power over the physical life of men, the political community transcends all other associations of societies. (pp.46, 47)

But by its very nature, this power must be used only in situations of existential danger, not merely for the material aggrandizement of the state. As Schmitt puts it, "to demand seriously of human beings that they kill others and prepare to die themselves so that trade and industry may flourish for the survivors or that the purchasing power of grandchildren may grow is sinister and crazy" (p.48). And again: "If such physical destruction of human life is not motivated by an existential threat to one's own way of life, then it cannot be justified. Just as little can war be justified by political or ethical norms ... That justice does not belong to the essence of war has generally been recognized since [Hugo] Grotius" (p.49). Here again, Schmitt drives home the nature of armed combat between enemies:

For to the enemy concept belongs the ever present possibility of combat ... The essence of a weapon is that it is a means of physically killing human beings ... [Combat] does not mean competition, nor does it mean pure intellectual controversy nor symbolic wrestlings in which, after all, every human being is somehow always involved ... The friend, enemy, and combat-concepts receive their real meaning precisely because they refer to the real possibility of physical killing. War follows from enmity. War is the existential negation of the enemy. (pp.32–33)

The pacifist renunciation of war cannot stop warfare any more than the abandonment of aesthetic or economic production would stop it. As Schmitt grimly remarks: "If a people no longer possesses the energy or the will to maintain itself in the sphere of politics, [politics] will not thereby vanish from the world. Only a weak people will disappear" (p.53). By cutting off politics from all moral or legal considerations, Schmitt rejects every form of Truth Politics in favor of a politics grounded in the notion of possible existential strife with the foreigner. By suggesting that the political is a completely different sort of thing from morality or law, he is walking right up the alley of the late Latour, the author of *Modes*.

But not only does Schmitt make an extended case against Truth Politics in favor of what we have called a Power Politics without external standards or referents. He also has something to tell us about the other political axis of modernity, the even better-known distinction between Left and Right. Schmitt begins Section 7 as follows:

One could test all theories of nature and state and political ideas according to their anthropology and thereby classify these as to whether they consciously or unconsciously presuppose man to be by nature evil or by nature good. The distinction is to be taken here in a rather summary fashion and not in any specifically moral or specifically ethical sense. The problematic or unproblematic conception of man is decisive for the presupposition of every further political consideration, the answer to the question whether man is a dangerous being or not, a risky or a harmless creature. (p.58)

This is as clear a description of the foundations of the political Left and Right as one could hope for. For the Left, to cite Rousseau's words, "man is born free, and everywhere he is in chains."[3] But for the Right, as Machiavelli puts it, "one can generally say this about men: they are ungrateful, fickle, simulators and deceivers, avoiders of danger, and greedy for gain."[4] Naturally, we need not pin this argument to any specific conception of good or evil, since Schmitt reminds us that "evil may appear as corruption, weakness, cowardice, stupidity, or also as brutality, sensuality, vitality, irrationality, and so on. Goodness may appear in corresponding variations [such] as reasonableness, perfectibility, the capacity of being manipulated, of being taught, peaceful, and so forth."[5]

Schmitt continues the thought: "I have pointed out several times that the antagonism between the so-called authoritarian and anarchist theories can be traced to these formulas [of good and evil humans]" (p.60). Moreover, "a part of the theories and postulates which presuppose man to be good is liberal." Although liberals are obviously not anarchists, they do hold that "society determines its own order and that state and government are subordinate and must be distrustingly controlled and bound to precise limits" (pp.60–61). Citing Thomas Paine, Schmitt summarizes the liberal view as holding that "society is the result of our reasonably regulated needs, government is the result of our wickedness" (p.61). And here once again we encounter Schmitt's primary complaint against liberalism:

> Bourgeois liberalism was never radical in a political sense … Its neutralizations, depoliticizations, and declarations of freedom have … a certain political meaning … But this is neither a political theory nor a political idea … [Liberalism] has produced a doctrine of the separation and balance of powers, i.e., a system of checks and controls of state and government. This cannot be characterized as either a theory of state or a basic political principle. (p.61)

Against all anarchist, socialist, or liberal theories which hold that humans were born for the good, if only they were not oppressed by out-of-control institutions, Schmitt airs a more sobering view. Namely, "what remains is the remarkable and, for many, certainly disquieting diagnosis that all genuine political theories presuppose man to be evil, i.e., by no means an unproblematic but a dangerous and dynamic being." By contrast, the anarchist method (like the liberal one) holds "that only individuals who consider man to be evil are evil. Those who consider him to be good, namely the anarchists, are then entitled to some sort of superiority or control over the evil ones" (p.64). And yet, all of our moral and political disciplines can function only insofar as they recognize the bad or the evil to be genuine possibilities of human beings, rather than just the transient side effect of bad societies or institutions:

A theologian ceases to be a theologian when he no longer considers man to be sinful or in need of redemption and no longer distinguishes between the chosen and the nonchosen. The moralist presupposes a freedom of choice between good and evil. Because the sphere of the political is in the final analysis determined by the real possibility of enmity, political conceptions and ideas cannot very well start with an anthropological optimism. (p.64)

The mention of theologians here does not entail that Schmitt holds a favorable view of the mixing of theology and politics: "The methodical connection of theological and political presuppositions is clear. But theological interference generally confuses political concepts because it shifts the distinction usually into moral theology" (p.65). Admittedly, this is a point of some dispute in the scholarship on Schmitt. In the words of Jean-François Kervégan: "On the one hand, there are those who believe the central element in Schmitt's thought to be a religious, even a theological one ... On the other hand, we have those for whom the most original and most powerful of Schmitt's work is based on legal-political matters."[6] We cannot settle the debate here, but for our purposes the Schmitt under discussion is the one who wrote that "theological interference generally confuses political concepts because it shifts the distinction usually into moral theology."

The genuine political philosophers, according to Schmitt, "are always aware of the concrete possibility of an enemy. Their realism can frighten men in need of security ... As long as man is well off or willing to put up with things, he prefers the illusion of an undisturbed calm and does not endure pessimists."[7] A good antidote to such squeamishness can always be found, Schmitt believes, in the clear-headed greatness of Thomas Hobbes: "For Hobbes, truly a powerful and systematic political thinker, the pessimistic conception of man is the elementary presupposition of a specific system of political thought. He also recognized that the conviction of each side that it possesses the truth, the good, and the just bring about the worst enemies, finally the war of all against all" (p.65). This is reminiscent of Latour's warnings, cited above, about the cosmopolitan optimism of Ulrich Beck. Schmitt continues:

Hobbes has drawn [the] simple conclusions of political thought without confusion and more clearly than anyone else ... The rule of a higher order, according to Hobbes, is an empty phrase if it does not signify politically that certain men of this higher order rule over men of a lower order. The independence and completeness of political thought is here irrefutable. (p.67)

The example of Hobbes reminds us that "the high points of politics are simultaneously the moments in which the enemy is, in concrete clarity, recognized as the enemy." By contrast, "everywhere in political history, in foreign as well as domestic politics, the incapacity or unwillingness to make this distinction is a symptom of the political end" (p.68).

Since few political thinkers in our time are comfortable giving their full endorsement to the Nazi jurist Carl Schmitt, those who utilize his works are generally at pains to emphasize their points of difference with him. What, then, are Latour's disagreements with Schmitt? We already encountered one such criticism in a footnote to "What if we *Talked* Politics a Little," where we read as follows:

It is interesting to notice that those who talk of sovereignty so much like Schmitt are unable to see that political talk requires a curve in every single [one] of its points, so [instead] they concentrate in one single point the oddity of political transubstantiation. In effect they confuse the curvature of the political circle with the "state of exception," as if putting in Zeus's hands the full power of thunder and lightning. (TPL 163, note 10)

Later, in *Modes*, we find a rephrasing of the same point:

Schmitt's error lay in his belief that it is only on high, among the powerful and on rare occasions, that the political mode has to look for exceptions. Look at the Circle: it is *exceptional at all points*, above and below, on the right and on the left, since it *never goes straight* and, in addition, it must always *start over* especially if it is to spread. (AIME 347–348)

There is the additional difference that while Schmitt expels all transcendence from the question of the political, Latour has spent much of his later career arguing for the existence of "mini-transcendences" that prevent the political sphere from becoming a purely self-contained system.

But let's turn now to Latour's Gifford Lectures of February 2013, where Schmitt makes a rather obtrusive appearance. The topic of these lectures is Gaia: the earth considered as an organism, according to the well-known theory of James Lovelock. Latour's interest in Gaia comes from the fact that it is "the most *secular* figure of the Earth ever explored by political theory. It is because it is *not* already unified that it should be composed, thus becoming the only entity able to mobilize in a new way science, politics and theology" (GIFF 8). To repeat, Latour claims that Gaia *has not yet been composed*, since it has not yet managed to be fully integrated into the political collective, given that we are not yet acting as if we *truly* believed in the coming ecological catastrophe. The first point to note is that this is not how Lovelock himself would see it. Rather than saying that Gaia has not yet been composed insofar as we have not yet integrated it politically, Lovelock would presumably take a more standard scientific realist line on the question: Gaia has long since been composed, and it is now headed in a direction that is highly perilous for humans, whether we like it or not. I heard this with my own ears at a grim, nearly apocalyptic lecture by Lovelock at University College Dublin in April 2009. As he put it that night, the melting of the polar ice caps will ultimately lead to three lethal events: the death of algae and rain forests (both events destroying much of the earth's capacity to remove excess carbon dioxide) and finally the melting of the permafrost in Canada and Siberia (thereby releasing even more carbon dioxide from previously frozen biomass). One of the basic defects of the Latourian intellectual framework—and one of his surprising inheritances from Kant, who is not one of his heroes—is that it generally remains somewhat difficult to consider object-object relations (such as those between ice caps, algae, rainforests, and permafrost) without also considering the human means by which these entities became accessible. While this follows nicely from Latour's concept of science as mediation, it does make it rather difficult for him to distinguish the object of knowledge from the means by which it is known. Hence, from the fact that the existence of Gaia is still only half-heartedly believed even by those informed parties who know the evidence of the earth's degradation, Latour seems to conclude that *Gaia itself* has not yet been composed. He is certainly right to fight any *holistic* concept of Gaia: "It is because there is no engineer at work, no watchmaker—whether blind or not—that no *holistic* view of Gaia could be sustained" (GIFF 66). But for no convincing reason, Latour concludes from this lack of holism in Gaia that Gaia also lacks pre-established *unity*. He therefore surmises that it can achieve such unity only through a human-led process of composition: "If there is unity neither in nature nor in politics, it means that whatever universality we are looking for has to be *composed*" (GIFF 82). Latour holds that peace would be impossible not only if Gaia's features were already known, but even if Gaia already *existed* prior to being known: "it is precisely these peace conditions that are *not even going to be looked for* as long as we believe that the world has *already* been unified once and for all—by Nature, by Society or by God, it doesn't matter which" (GIFF 83).

But our real interest here is the relevance of Carl Schmitt to the Latourian conception of Gaia. In Edinburgh, Schmitt makes his first appearance in the fifth of the Gifford Lectures. As Latour puts it: "To understand why [the] state of war has been generalized, it is best to turn to the writer who has defined this situation as being one, as he calls it, of *exception*: the toxic and unavoidable Carl Schmitt, the main expositor of 'political theology'" (GIFF 101). As we have already seen, the enemy appears only with the disappearance of any higher court of appeal. "As long as there is a referee, an arbiter, a Providence, a Super-dispatcher … the thousands of inevitable struggles among fractious humans are nothing more than internal strife that can be solved through mere management or through *police operations*" (GIFF 101). In other words, "they can be *judged*, they can be *calculated*; they don't need to be decided" (GIFF 101–102). For "there is no war where management and accounting are sufficient; there is no war when conflict can be solved by sending in the police, when those who dissent agree that the State has the right to define the situation. War begins when there is no sovereign arbiter … such is the extreme '*state of exception*'" (GIFF 102).

This becomes especially relevant in an age of environmental crisis. The innate complexity of climate science is such that science can no longer play its accustomed role of a neutral arbiter able to silence all political disputes. Or in Latour's own words:

> The complex set of natural sciences that compose climatology will no longer be able to play the role of indisputable and final referee—not because of the spurious "controversy" over the anthropic origin of climate change, but because of the number of loops they have to establish, one after the other, to make us sensitive to Gaia's sensitivity. This is what I have called their post-natural, post-epistemological situation. Strangely enough, Nature, at least the sublunary Earth, has been placed into a "state of exception," that is, in a situation that obliges everyone to make decisions because of the "extremes" of life and death. (GIFF 102)

And here is where reactionary politics can possibly do us a good turn: "The great virtue of dangerous and reactionary thinkers like Schmitt is to force us to make a choice much starker than that of so many wishy-washy ecologists still swayed by unremitting hope" (GIFF 105). Latour continues:

Schmitt's choice is terribly clear: either you agree to tell foes from friends, and then you engage in politics, sharply defining borderlines of real enough wars ... or you shy away from waging wars and having enemies, but then you *do away with* politics, which means that you are giving yourself over to the protection of an all-encompassing State of Nature. (GIFF 105)

But we know that for Latour, no pre-existent nature exists, and hence there is no alternative to politics, which ultimately means no alternative to war. Though Latour plausibly assures us that he "is not a bellicose person" (GIFF 105), his assessment of our current impasse on the climate problem verges closely enough on the warlike. Since there is no unified nature, state, or science able to solve the problem for us, "what passes for common sense is simply criminal since [we] accept to place [our] safety and that of others in the care of an entity that does not exist" (GIFF 105). He now assesses the situation as follows: "It's a stark choice, I agree: either Nature extinguishes politics, or politics resuscitates nature—that is, finally agrees to face Gaia ... Without meeting such a challenge, there will only be police operations that would inevitably and miserably fail, but no plausible politics of nature" (GIFF 105). Stated more plainly, Latour is calling for Schmittian warfare against climate change skeptics. So much for the complaints that Latour is locked into a political gradualism! With this move, Latour even outstrips the political Left, with its basically human-centric politics unable to conceptualize the climate threat as anything but the inevitable side effect of a more encompassing *human* problem called Capitalism. In the sixth Gifford Lecture, Latour strikes an even more imperious note of Green Schmittianism, hoping to revive "what Schmitt, in his queer, toxic, and profound language had called *Raumordnungkrieg*, 'the wars for the ordering of space,' an expression, once purged from its association with twentieth century conflicts, that offers a radical definition of ecology, but an ecology able at last to carry on with politics with sufficient strength to limit the coming wars" (GIFF 135).

We now consider the similarities and differences between Latour and Schmitt. We have already encountered Latour's most explicit objection:

Schmitt's error lay in his belief that it is only on high, among the powerful and on rare occasions, that the political mode has to look for exceptions. Look at the Circle: it is *exceptional at all points*, above and below, on the right and on the left, since it *never goes straight* and, in addition, it must always *start over* especially if it is to spread (AIME 347–348).

For Schmitt, a sovereign intermittently decides the state of exception in which any appeal to an outside standard is suspended and existential struggle commences. For Latour, the state of exception is not confined to isolated instants of crisis, but occurs everywhere at all times, at least whenever the political circle is active. By claiming that the state of exception occurs constantly, Latour seems to allow for even less transcendence in politics than Schmitt does and may look like even more of a Power Politician. Yet we already know from *Politics of Nature* that for Latour the political is filled with invocations of *mini*-transcendence, since the collective must constantly be taking account of what lies outside it: including *moral* considerations of a sort that are entirely foreign to Schmitt's state of exception. The point is that Latour cuts off maxi-transcendence at all times while embedding mini-transcendence at every moment in the political circle, whereas for Schmitt we can always have recourse to maxi-transcendence (justice, morality ...) until the state of exception arises, at which point there is no longer any transcendence at all.

This more or less summarizes Latour's position with respect to Schmitt's on the question of truth vs. power. Though Latour's instincts as a political philosopher are basically compatible with the approaches of Hobbes and Schmitt, Latour does allow for more transcendence beyond sheer power struggle than his older models, even if in the watered-down form of a mini-transcendence of actors not yet integrated into our political collective. But what about the other political distinction, the more familiar one between Right and Left? We have already encountered Schmitt's view on this theme: "One could test all theories of nature and state and political ideas according to their anthropology and thereby classify these as to whether they consciously or unconsciously presuppose man to be by nature evil or by nature good" (p.58). If we recall the debate between Latour and Ulrich Beck, it might initially seem tempting to assign Latour to the Right and Beck to the Left. After all, against Beck's hopes for a universal cosmopolitan peace, Latour twice sides with Isabelle Stengers's version of political realism, first joining her in disdain for "the malady of tolerance" (BEC 454) and then agreeing that "peace settlements are not, as Stengers emphasizes, between men of good will who have left their gods (their narrow attachments) behind but between men of ill will possessed by super- and subhumans of ill will" (BEC 456). And further: "When men of good will assemble with their cigars at the Habermas Club to discuss an armistice for this or that conflict and they leave their gods on hooks in the cloakroom, I suspect that what is under way is not a peace conference at all" (BEC 456). On this basis, it might seem that Latour and Stengers "consciously or unconsciously presuppose man to be by nature evil," and thus side with the basic assumption of the political Right. But in fact, on this point Latour and Stengers are merely allying themselves with Power Politics against any Beckian or Habermasian notion that humans can put aside their selfish interests and come to agree on a binding set of universal norms. The same holds for Latour's claim, so similar to Schmitt's own, that political reactionaries are more interesting than progressives. This is not so much a claim on Latour's part that humans are dark and problematic. Instead, he is simply claiming that we lose sight of the political mode whenever we slip into thinking that political truth is already known or knowable, and that this truth could soon be implemented if not for the greed, ignorance, and selfish interests that happen to obstruct it. On this one important point, reactionaries know better.

When it comes to the Left/Right political divide, Latour is in fact somewhat difficult to place. In one sense he has realist instincts of a sort that are often associated with the Right. But in another sense he is not a conservative who clings to the world of the past, but constantly celebrates new hybrid formations that blur the lines between nature and culture or humans and machines. Indeed, if we take just the first part of Schmitt's formula ("One could test all theories of nature and state and political ideas according to their anthropology") we immediately see why it makes little sense to classify Latour according to the Left/Right schema at all. Despite Latour's great love for the discipline of anthropology, his is not an anthropology of the inherent good or evil of humans, but an "anthropology" of humans and non-humans woven into networks and lacking any inherently "problematic" or "unproblematic" character apart from those very networks. If we weigh Latour's political soul according to Schmitt's criterion of whether one's theory of humans is that they are good or that they are evil, it becomes clear that Latour has no real theory of human nature at all. Nor would it make much sense for him to have one, since the political sphere for Latour does not coincide with the human sphere. Stated differently, there is a sense in which the political Left and Right are humanistic political theories that have continued to hang around in an era when humans are losing their place at the ontological center of reality.

In Chapter 4, we briefly considered another difference between Schmitt and Latour that is worth revisiting here. Much of Schmitt's surprising appeal to today's political Left stems from his impatience with the far-reaching depoliticization carried out by bourgeois liberal democracy, which seeks peace and order by replacing political controversy with ethical issues and economic management. Yet this problem of depoliticization is not an aspect of Schmitt that seems to interest Latour, who takes the opposite tack at least twice in his exchange with Gerard de Vries: "*Not having to participate* should remain the ideal and is of course the most widely distributed response to calls for action" (RGDV 819). We quoted the following detailed passage as well: "There is no cognitive, mental and affective equipment requiring all of us to be constantly implicated, involved or engaged with the working of the Paris sewage system, the search for weapons of mass destruction in Iraq, the development of stem cell research in California, global warming, peer-to-peer software, new accounting procedures for European companies, and so on" (RGDV 819). Whereas Schmitt and the Left both tend to use "depoliticization" only as a swear word, Latour sees no problem with the fact that "Politics-5" contains all those issues that are now mastered and routinized and rarely opened up for political discussion by anyone but feminists, scholars of science studies, and Michel Foucault. Though Latour clearly respects the work of these black-box openers, he does not seem troubled by the fact that many political boxes remain forever unopened. In a passage already cited, "the silent working of the sewage systems in Paris has stopped being political, as have vaccinations against smallpox or tuberculosis. It is now in the hands of vast and silent bureaucracies that rarely make the headlines" (RGDV 817). If there is any issue that reveals Latour to be more Hobbesian than Schmittian, it is this one. While Schmitt wants to repoliticize human life, Hobbes is perfectly happy to depoliticize it, given the inherently grim character of political struggle as Hobbes sees it. As we see in the next section, this is why Leo Strauss (among others) regards Hobbes as the founder of liberalism, and also helps us to see why there is more sympathy with liberalism in Latour's writings than we would ever find in Schmitt's. If forced to choose between Hobbes and Schmitt, Latour would surely follow Hobbes.

SCHMITT ACCORDING TO LEO STRAUSS AND SLAVOJ ŽIŽEK

It is hard to imagine many contexts in which Leo Strauss and Slavoj Žižek could plausibly be mentioned in the same breath. In Strauss we have an arch-conservative German émigré who held somber court for decades at the University of Chicago with a small number of student initiates, some of them later becoming major participants in right-wing think tanks and American Presidential administrations. In Žižek, by contrast, we have one of today's most visible figures on the Left, a globetrotting jester and stimulating interpreter of German Idealist philosophy and Lacanian psychoanalysis. It is difficult to imagine a conversation taking place between the two, even if Strauss had not died a generation before Žižek's emergence as a significant public figure. But however great the disparity of their respective political positions, their views on Schmitt share an important point in common. Namely, both Strauss and Žižek confront Schmitt's decisionism with the demand for a politics grounded in knowledge.

Strauss wrote his critique of Schmitt in 1932, one year prior to Hitler's rise to power, which also means one year prior to both Schmitt and Heidegger joining the Nazi Party. Strauss writes in the same way that he believes so many great thinkers write: subtly concealing his main point with understatement or deliberately clumsy contradiction, while loudly placing false emphasis on a more visible but ultimately more mediocre argument. On the bright side, this is a signal that Strauss takes politics too seriously ever to use it as just an opportunity to claim the moral high ground over others. This makes Strauss another of those "interesting reactionaries" from whom one can often learn more about politics than from Locke, Rousseau, Jefferson, or Marx. On the dark side, Strauss often expends so much energy in detecting and constructing conspiratorial subtleties that the open-minded reader easily feels excluded from a discussion that seems to be aimed solely at the initiates of Strauss's "esoteric" oral teachings. Indeed, his followers often literally refuse to share documents that circulate semi-freely within Straussian circles. Furthermore, these intricate shows of conspiratorial secrecy too often protect Strauss's views from being considered and judged in the same way as everyone else's, since his admirers can always claim that his critics have read him superficially and hint at a supposed esoteric surplus in an oral Straussian tradition or *hadith* closely guarded from outside critics.

We now turn to Strauss's critical assessment of Schmitt, who is concerned with preserving the political against growing depoliticization. Liberalism seems to be the primary enemy from which Schmitt hopes to save the political. As Strauss puts it: "Depoliticization not only is the accidental or even necessary result of the modern development but is its original and authentic goal; the movement in which the modern spirit has gained its greatest efficacy, liberalism, is characterized precisely by the *negation* of the political."[8] Yet liberalism only *seems* to have killed the political, since it has really just replaced it with morality and economics: "Liberalism has thus killed not the political but only understanding of the political, the sincerity of the political" (p.100). Strauss seems to admire Schmitt's attitude of philosophical questioning, devoid of easy answers. This is especially evident in Schmitt's awareness that no good replacement has yet been found for liberalism. As Strauss wittily puts it, "for this awareness [Schmitt] stands wholly alone among the opponents of liberalism, who usually carry an elaborate unliberal doctrine in their back pocket" (p.101). In fact, "[Schmitt,] too, will be compelled to make use of elements of liberal thought in the presentation of his views. The tentativeness of Schmitt's statements results from that compulsion."

Unlike Latour, Strauss both supports the notion of a state of nature and salutes Schmitt for restoring this concept to its full glory. As Strauss puts it: "Whether culture is understood as nurture of nature or as a fight with nature depends on how nature is understood: as exemplary order or as disorder to be eliminated. But however culture is understood, 'culture' is certainly the culture of nature" (pp.104–105). He continues: "The term for natural social relations understood in this manner is *status naturalis* [state of nature]. One can therefore say: the foundation of culture is the *status naturalis*" (p.105). And furthermore:

> Hobbes describes the *status naturalis* as the *status belli* [state of war], simply, although it must be borne in mind that 'the nature of war consisteth not in actual fighting, but in the known *disposition* thereto' (*Leviathan* XIII). In Schmitt's terminology this statement means that the status naturalis is the genuinely *political* status ... It follows that the political that Schmitt brings to bear as fundamental is the 'state of nature' that underlies every culture; Schmitt restores the Hobbesian state of nature to a place of honor. (p.105)

Yet Strauss is even more interesting when he points to the *differences* between Schmitt and Hobbes. For example: "the state of nature is defined by Schmitt in a fundamentally different fashion than it is by Hobbes. For Hobbes, it is the state of war of individuals; for Schmitt, it is the state of war of groups" (p.106). There is also the strange fact that whereas Hobbes is concerned to *end* the horrific state of nature through the absolute power of the Leviathan, Schmitt wants to *return* us to the state of nature, at least on the international level. In Hobbes, the "state of war of all against all is supposed to motivate the abandonment of the state of nature. To this negation of the state of nature or of the political, Schmitt opposes the position of the political." And this leads to another difference, concerning the amount of loyalty the individual owes to the state, with Schmitt apparently taking a more hardcore position. For whereas "according to Schmitt it belongs to the essence of the political group that it can 'demand ... from the members of its own group the *readiness to die*'... the justification of this claim is at least qualified by Hobbes: in battle he who deserts the ranks out of fear for his life acts 'only' dishonorably, but not unjustly (*Leviathan* XXI)." More generally, for Hobbes, "while man is otherwise obliged to unconditional obedience, he is under no obligation to risk his life; for death is the greatest evil. Hobbes does not shrink from the consequence and expressly denies the status of courage as a virtue (*De homine* 9)" (pp.106–107). Given this natural right of the individual in Hobbes, which appears to be absent from Schmitt, Strauss concludes that "Hobbes, to a much higher degree than Bacon ... is the author of the ideal of civilization. By this very fact he is the founder of liberalism" (p.107). Indeed, Strauss concludes his essay on Schmitt with the following words: "A radical critique of liberalism is thus possible only on the basis of an adequate understanding of Hobbes. To show what can be learned from Schmitt in order to achieve that urgent task was therefore the principal intention of our notes" (p.122).

Yet despite these crucial differences between Hobbes and Schmitt, Strauss tries to show that Schmitt is more caught up in liberalism than he is willing to admit. After quoting the aforementioned passage from Schmitt about the difference between political theories that view humans as fundamentally dangerous and those that see them as basically good or improvable, Strauss follows with a bit of ... vintage Strauss. To wit: "The train of thought just recounted is in all probability not Schmitt's last word, and it is certainly not the most profound thing that he has to say. It conceals a reflection that moves in an entirely different direction, a reflection that cannot be reconciled with the line of thought described above" (p.111). Namely, Strauss will try to claim that while Schmitt looks at first like a Power Politician who views the landscape entirely in terms of a friend/enemy antithesis, he actually lapses into the opposite position: that of a strange sort of dark liberal moralist. The problem, Strauss holds, is that Schmitt can only claim the dangerousness of humans as a "supposition." This leads Strauss to wield the sword of *knowledge* against Schmitt's resort to mere supposition: "if man's dangerousness is only supposed or believed in, not genuinely known, the opposite, too, can be regarded as possible, and the attempt to eliminate man's dangerousness ... can be put into practice." In other words, both Schmitt and his rivals in the opposite "humans are basically good" camp have nothing more to rest on than "an anthropological profession of faith."[9] As Strauss sees it, Schmitt's profession of faith rests on moral grounds: "Ultimately, Schmitt by no means repudiates this ideal [of the negation of the political] as utopian—he says, after all, that he does not know whether it cannot be realized—but he does abhor it. That Schmitt does not display his views in moralizing fashion but endeavors to conceal them only makes his polemic the more effective."[10] He then cites a passage in which Schmitt speaks deploringly of a world of sheer entertainment and amusement that might emerge after the end of the political. This indicates that Schmitt's defense of the political neither justifies itself nor stems from any definitive *knowledge* of an innately dangerous human character, but is grounded in a *moral* sense reminiscent of liberalism itself. Schmitt's concept of the political turns out to yield nothing more than an upside-down liberalism, one that prefers the morality of political dangerousness, of "the affirmation of power as the power that forms states, of *virtù* in Machiavelli's sense" (p.112).

Strauss now gives us the final twist of his argument against Schmitt's position. Even if Schmitt were capable of a commitment to the political for its own sake, devoid of any secret moral commitments, "being political means being oriented to the 'dire emergency.' Therefore the affirmation of the political as such is the affirmation of fighting as such, wholly irrespective of *what* is being fought *for*" (p.120). Schmitt's model political actor "does not have the *will* … to the avoidance of decision at all costs, but in fact is eager for decision; an eagerness for *any* decision *regardless of content*." Strauss's conclusion is almost comical in its Straussianism, despite being fully justified by his argument:

> He who affirms the political as such respects all who want to fight; he is just as *tolerant* as the liberals—but with the opposite intention; whereas the liberal respects and tolerates all "*honest*" convictions, so long as they merely acknowledge the legal order, *peace*, as sacrosanct, he who affirms the political as such respects and tolerates all "*serious*" convictions, that is, all decisions oriented to the real possibility of *war*. Thus the affirmation of the political as such proves to be a liberalism with the opposite polarity. (p.120)

Yet Strauss has in fact made a good argument to the effect that the liberal's peaceful tolerance of all peaceful views *and* Schmitt's bellicose tolerance of all bellicose views make the same mistake, insofar as they avoid the topic of *knowledge*. And here Strauss turns to his greatest intellectual heroes, Socrates and Plato: "Agreement and peace [for liberals] mean agreement and peace at all costs. In principle, however, it is always possible to reach agreement regarding the means to an end that is already fixed, whereas there is always quarreling over the ends themselves: we are always quarreling with ourselves only over the just and the good (Plato, *Euthyphro* 7B–D and *Phaedrus* 263A)" (pp.117–118). This is followed by perhaps the most candid expression of Strauss's own views anywhere in his essay on Schmitt:

> Agreement at all costs is possible only as agreement at the cost of the meaning of human life; for agreement at all costs is possible only if man has relinquished asking the question of what is right; and if man relinquishes that question, he relinquishes being a man. But if he seriously asks the question of what is right, the quarrel will be ignited ... the life-and-death quarrel: the political—the grouping into friends and enemies—owes its legitimation to the seriousness of the question of what is right. (p.118)

This passage works equally well against both a soft liberal conception of tolerance and the decisionism of Schmitt. To obtain Schmitt's position, we need only change the first half-sentence to read as follows: "*Disagreement* at all costs is possible only as *disagreement* at the cost of the meaning of human life." After all, we should not prematurely abandon discussion in favor of conflict any more than the reverse. By viewing politics in terms of friend and enemy, Schmitt perhaps unwittingly repeats one of the Sophists' definitions of justice as "helping one's friends and hurting one's enemies," which (as Socrates observes) assumes that one *knows* who one's true friends and enemies really are. Yet in Plato's dialogues we never actually meet a Socrates who claims to have knowledge of any sort. Thus, when Strauss plays the "knowledge" card against Schmitt's mere "anthropological profession of faith" in the badness of humans, we need not agree that Socrates stands side-by-side with Strauss. The fact that Strauss badly *desires* such a link with Socrates is emphasized by Tracy B. Strong's remark that

> the nature of Strauss's critique of Schmitt indicates that whatever [Strauss's] own critique of liberalism will be, it cannot be a simple reaffirmation of moral truths. Rather (and all too gnomically) 'IT IS TO UNDERSTAND SOCRATES,' as the highlighted words beginning the Introduction and chapters 3 and 4 of Strauss's *Natural Right and History* (a book overtly about liberalism and not Socrates) let us know.[11]

Sophistry is opposed by philosophy, not by knowledge, and this is because philosophy (unlike both sophistry and knowledge) means the profession of uncertainty and ignorance. In this respect Latour is closer to Socrates than Strauss is.

We turn now to the inimitable Slavoj Žižek. If Strauss critiques Schmitt by appealing to a Truth Politics of the Right, Žižek deploys a Truth Politics of a distinctly Leftist stripe. Much like Strauss, Žižek is bothered by Schmitt's tolerance for any decision no matter what its content might be. In Žižek's words: "The basic paradox of Carl Schmitt's political decisionism ... is that his very polemic against liberal-democratic formalism inexorably gets caught in the formalist trap."[12] Žižek insightfully adds that "this is the main feature of modern conservatism which sharply distinguishes it from every kind of traditionalism: modern conservatism, even more than liberalism, assumes the lesson of the dissolution of the traditional set of values and/or authorities—there is no longer any positive content which could be presupposed as the universally accepted frame of reference" (pp.18–19). Indeed, Žižek seems to view this gap between decision and content as the root of modernity as a whole, despite the hedging mood of his scare quotes: "What is 'modern' is the gap between the act of decision and its content ... The paradox ... is thus that the innermost possibility of modernism is asserted in the guise of its apparent opposite, the return to an unconditional authority which cannot be grounded in positive reasons" (p.20). For Žižek this can also be seen in the modern Calvinist God who saves through grace alone rather than due to any string of good deeds by the sinner, as well as in the modern Cartesian God who might decide unilaterally and without reason that $2 + 2 = 5$ (pp.20, 26). This leads Žižek on a typically long and hilarious digression, this time concerning tragedy and Freud's various models of the father, which cannot be considered here.

As Žižek has it, Schmitt's formalist trap is not the only problem with his decisionist politics. Another problem is that Schmitt "already displaces the *inherent* antagonism constitutive of the political on to the *external* relationship between Us and Them" (p.27). But while this is certainly true of Schmitt, it is hardly the most important question at hand. For even if we could somehow persuade Schmitt to shift his focus from inter-state strife to domestic antagonism among social classes, the key Schmittian problem would remain. Namely, does one social class fight another on the basis of some supposed political *truth*? Or does it do so only from the sheer decision that it must destroy the enemy class for pressing existential reasons? We already know Žižek's own answer to this question, since he is a purebred politician of truth, and his political ontology is spelled out in the following historical terms:

[P]olitics proper is a phenomenon which appeared for the first time in Ancient Greece when the members of *demos* (those with no firm determined place in the hierarchical social edifice) demanded a voice: against those in power, in social control, they protested the wrong they suffered, and wanted their voice to be heard, to be recognized as included in the public sphere. (p.27)

Žižek goes on to evoke a trio of present-day French allies on the Left (Alain Badiou, Étienne Balibar, and Jacques Rancière) all of them grounding politics in an equality of all human beings that all of these thinkers take to be self-evident. As Žižek puts it, "political conflict involves tension between the structured social body, where each part has its place, and the 'part of no-part', which unsettles this order on account of the empty principle of universality, of what Étienne Balibar calls *égaliberté*, of the principled equality of all men *qua* speaking beings" (pp.27–28). Note that the Schmittian and Latourian conception of politics, as a struggle between unproven positions, is hereby erased. In Žižek's political theory as in those of his allies, the universal resemblance of all humans is posited from the outset, while all other commitments to various gods, principles, cultures, and customs are tacitly portrayed as mere ideologies by comparison with our shared heritage as thinking subjects. If politics is struggle for Žižek, then it is simply a struggle against the ignorance and vested interests of those who occupy privileged positions by contrast with the neglected *demos*. Yet there are at least two problems with the notion that "politics proper" (as Žižek terms it) is equivalent to the demand of the *demos* to be heard. First, if we say that politics proper has as its sole topic "the principled equality of all men *qua* speaking beings," this offers nothing more than a lowest common denominator. If many of us would be willing to fight and die against oppressive elitist hordes contesting such a fair-minded principle, there are also a number of more *specific* things than Balibar's *égaliberté* for which we would give our lives. The point is that by appealing solely to our equality, Žižek seems to imply that humans are nothing more than politically interchangeable speaking and thinking beings, with our other features and commitments counting as merely peripheral, accidental, or ideological by comparison. To fight for one's particularity or for other sub-egalitarian aims could only appear unjust to a theory (such as Žižek's) that only definitions of the human being as a Cartesian or Lacanian *cogito* count as "politics proper." The second problem is that by identifying "politics proper" with the egalitarian cries of the oppressed *demos*, Žižek loses the ability to speak in political terms of situations of more limited importance.

The political maneuverings of a local school board, telecommunications policy in the European Union, or even the 2016 Republican Presidential nomination in the United States are all fascinating in their own way. Yet insofar as none of them touch directly on the *égaliberté* of equal speaking humans, they will all tend to look like subrevolutionary "governance" as opposed to "politics proper." But here we lose the valuable flexibility entailed by Latour's conception of a politics that can be found wherever the formation or retracing of any group is at stake.

Whereas Strauss opposed Schmitt's decisionism by appealing to the knowledge of Socrates and a handful of worthy peers capable of understanding him, Žižek opposes Schmitt with a truth belonging to a much broader human mass. If Strauss launches his Truth Politics by misreading philosophy as a form of elite and esoteric knowledge, Žižek inaugurates his own by misreading political philosophy as a banal stabilizing force: "something emerged in Ancient Greece under the name of demos demanding its rights, and from the very beginning (i.e., from Plato's *Republic*) to the recent revival of liberal 'political philosophy,' 'political philosophy' was an attempt to suspend the destabilizing potential of the political, to disavow and/or regulate it in one way or another" (p.29). Žižek goes so far as to psychologize those who pursue political philosophy, which "is thus, in all its different forms, a kind of 'defence-formation', and perhaps its typology could be established via the reference to the different modalities of defence against some traumatic experience in psychoanalysis." We should not be misled by the scare quotes around "defence-formation" and the qualification that "perhaps" political philosophy is merely the reaction to some psychic trauma. For this is clearly what Žižek really believes. The truth of the universal equality of humans is so evident to Žižek that he thinks only those with vested arrogant interests or psychological problems could possibly refuse to ground their politics (and not just their morality) in this very principle. In this sense Žižek's position can be viewed as simply a more hardcore revolutionary version of Ulrich Beck's, which Latour criticized for its cosmopolitan self-assurance that at bottom we are all alike, though in fact such settlements should be the *result* rather than the starting point of political discussion. From a Latourian standpoint, Žižek fails at politics insofar as he is simply not *philosophical* enough in his politics, not committed in the manner of diplomats to the possible uncertainty of his position. Consider Žižek's response to the plight of McDonald's when it offended the Hindu population of India by pre-frying French fries in beef fat:

[W]hen I asked my friends who were defending this measure, saying isn't it nice that McDonald's has to respect local traditions, my question was, but wait a minute, what about a simple fact, which may sound horrible, that it is not true that cows are really sacred and that, to put it in very vulgar terms, this is simply a stupid religious belief? Then they ask me, but aren't you just imposing the Western objective notion of truth? Here problems begin for me. I am not fetishizing Western objectivity; all I am saying is that we should not accept this kind of respect for the Other's ideological-religious fantasy as the ultimate horizon of ethics.[13]

But the question concerns the ultimate horizon of politics, not of ethics, and here Žižek seems to be confusing the two. For all its amusing candor, there are obvious problems with this passage. First, if Žižek were in charge of India operations for McDonald's, he could not possibly speak in this way, since it would result in a massive political-diplomatic failure and would therefore display colossal political misjudgment. Obviously, no skilled politician would ever make such a statement. This hardly matters to Žižek, of course, because he interprets both philosophy and politics as forms of knowledge, and believes that he happens to possess such knowledge—to be specific, a Lacanian conception of the subject joined to a "materialist" conception of the world (though Žižek's materialism is a strange one in which matter does not exist objectively outside the mind). Latour would say, correctly, that Žižek simply wants to *replace* both politics and philosophy with claims to knowledge. Both politics and philosophy will simply become ways of disabusing the ignorant of their naïve (or "stupid") belief in sacred cows, liberal democracy, or analytic philosophy. Strauss is equally convinced that the philosopher possesses knowledge capable of laying waste to the gullible beliefs of the masses. The difference is that Strauss is far more convinced of the *danger* of these gullible masses to philosophers, which entails that the masses must be handled prudently through the philosopher's deceptive conformity to their everyday views. We have seen that if Žižek were in charge of McDonald's in India, he would probably end up removed from his position or even lynched in the streets. If Leo Strauss were in charge, his public attitude would be precisely the opposite of Žižek's, and he might even pretend to be a Hindu. If Ulrich Beck were in charge, he would presumably take Hindu beliefs with a grain of salt while placing his hopes in our shared underlying rational agreement with Hindus. If Schmitt were in charge, he would respect India's belief in sacred cows but would also be prepared to crush that belief if the very existence of McDonald's were somehow threatened by it. But if Latour were in charge, he would not be so quick to assume the falsity of belief in sacred cows. His approach would be more patient, since he would realize (like the diplomat) that he is not even sure which of his own beliefs are essential and which are inessential. Žižek, by contrast, is already quite sure that all humans are equal *qua* speaking beings, and that this fact provides the true foundation for politics. Indians and Slovenians are both *res cogitans* or thinking beings; what a shame that Hindus cling to an unneeded "ideology" of sacred cows. But in this way, Žižek simply replaces politics with supposed knowledge, and the views of those who fail to live up to this knowledge are not to be taken into account.

Does this mean that Latour is simply a relativist? The problem with this question is that it only points to the pitfalls of relativism, while assuming that non-relativism comes without costs of its own. To escape relativism means to claim some manner of direct access to truth, and this results in the equally dangerous pitfall of *idealism*. For it is inherently idealistic to assume that reality can be adequately modeled in the form of some truth or other, which is precisely what Latour denies with his global theory of *translation*. Against Latour, we could certainly avoid relativism about human nature by saying that "at bottom, we are all just thinking and speaking beings, and all of our other differences are superficial or merely ideological." This is more or less what Žižek and Badiou tell us. It is the same maneuver as when Descartes uses the example of melting wax to argue that only extension counts as a primary quality of physical entities. The problem with such philosophical decisions is that they proclaim the end of all uncertainty or ignorance as to the character of humans or physical objects. By replacing this uncertainty with claims to scientific knowledge about humans or objects, it oversimplifies them in terms of certain sets of mastered knowable qualities. If any political struggle follows this moment of supposed enlightenment, it is simply the struggle to force the corrupt and the ignorant to shut up and cede power. The tendency of Latour's political theory, as of his metaphysics, is to convert knowledge into translation: into philosophy, or Socratic ignorance. But Strauss and Žižek evade the Socratic legacy for precisely the same reason: their claim that politics must be grounded in knowledge. Both are irrevocably committed to a form of Truth Politics.

SCHMITT ACCORDING TO CHANTAL MOUFFE

In the opening paragraphs of this chapter we already met Chantal Mouffe, the important Belgian political theorist who co-authored *Hegemony and*

Socialist Strategy with the late Ernesto Laclau. Their book was once praised by Žižek himself in the following words:

> It is the merit of Ernesto Laclau and Chantal Mouffe that they have, in *Hegemony and Socialist Strategy* ... developed a theory of the social field founded on ... an acknowledgment of an original 'trauma,' an impossible kernel which resists symbolization, totalization, symbolic integration ... They emphasize that we must not be 'radical' in the sense of aiming at a radical solution: we always live in an interspace and in borrowed time; every solution is provisional and temporary, a kind of postponing of a fundamental impossibility. The term 'radical democracy' is thus to be taken somehow paradoxically: it is precisely *not* 'radical' in the sense of pure, true democracy; its radical character implies, on the contrary, that we can save democracy only by *taking into account its own radical impossibility.*[14]

While words such as "trauma" and "kernel" seem to link Laclau and Mouffe's position with Žižek's own, Laclau and Mouffe are far less absolutist in their political claims than Žižek. Indeed, more than a few of Mouffe's sentences about Schmitt might have been written by Latour himself, and she is certainly not a Truth Politician in the manner of Žižek, Badiou, or Strauss.

Mouffe recommends a confrontation with Schmitt, even though this means "confronting some disturbing questions, usually avoided by liberals and democrats alike ... Indeed, I am convinced that a confrontation with his thought will allow us to acknowledge—and, therefore, be in a better position to try to negotiate—an important paradox inscribed in the very nature of liberal democracy."[15] Mouffe's use of these terms mirrors Schmitt's own. As she puts it:

> Schmitt asserts that there is an insuperable opposition between liberal individualism, with its moral discourse centered [in] the individual, and the democratic ideal, which is essentially political, and aims at creating an identity based on homogeneity. He claims that liberalism negates democracy and democracy negates liberalism, and that parliamentary democracy, since it consists in the articulation between democracy and liberalism, is therefore a non-viable regime. (p.40)

Mouffe then uses Schmitt's concepts to clarify present-day debates concerning "the boundaries of citizenship and the nature of a liberal-democratic consensus" (p.39). We pass over these interesting discussions and move directly to the conclusion of Mouffe's essay, a section intriguingly entitled "Schmitt's false dilemma." That false dilemma is as follows: "either there is unity of the people, and this requires expelling every antagonism outside the demos—the exterior it needs in order to establish its unity; or some forms of division inside the demos are considered legitimate, and this will lead inexorably to the kind of pluralism which negates political unity and the very existence of the political" (p.49).

Mouffe's response to this purported dilemma is not only simple and convincing, it could surely be endorsed by Latour himself. Namely, the problem with Schmitt's view is that he assumes that political unities are already given in advance. As Mouffe puts it: "The unity of the state must, for [Schmitt], be a concrete unity, already given and therefore stable. This is also true of the way he envisages the identity of the people: it also must exist as a given. Because of that, his distinction between 'us' and 'them' is not really politically constructed; it is merely a recognition of already-existing borders" (p.50). Mouffe continues with words that are as compatible with Dewey as with Latour. Rather than a simple "identity" of the people, Mouffe rightly speaks of its "multiple possible identities," and continues as follows: "such an identity of the people must be seen as the *result* of the political process of hegemonic articulation. Democratic politics does not consist in the moment when a fully constituted people exercises its rule. The moment of rule is indissociable from the very struggle about the definition of the people, about the constitution of its identity" (p.51). Like Schmitt, Mouffe sees politics as a conflict between "us" and "them," but (like Žižek) sees it as occurring within the *polis* itself rather than referring primarily to external strife between distinct political entities. And like Žižek, she recognizes an internal "conflictual field," though unlike Žižek (but very much like Latour) she holds that the conflict is not preordained as being between the deprived demos and the privileged rulers of a given political situation. Rather, the terms of this conflict are themselves always in dispute. To the extent that incompletely defined conflict belongs to the interior of a liberal-democratic political system,

> we can begin to realize … why such a regime requires pluralism. Without a plurality of competing forces which attempt to define the common good, and aim at fixing the identity of the community, the political articulation of the demos could not take place. We would be either in the aggregation of interests, or of a process of deliberation which

eliminates the moment of decision. That is—as Schmitt pointed out—in the field of economics or ethics, but not in the field of politics. (p.51)

All of this sounds perfectly compatible with Latour, as does Mouffe's deep suspicion of rationalist Truth Politics of the Habermasian variety (pp.45–46). What, then, is the major difference between Latour's political theory and that of Mouffe? The difference between Latour and Mouffe, like the difference between Latour and pretty much any other intellectual neighbor, stems from Latour's greater concern to incorporate nonhuman entities into his theory. This is the issue to which we now turn as the central topic of Chapter 7.

7

"A Copernican Revolution": Lippmann, Dewey, and Object-Oriented Politics

The moment has arrived to speak of the importance of John Dewey and Walter Lippmann for Latour's recent political thought. Dewey hardly needs an introduction, since he is widely known as one of the most influential American philosophers of all time, and as someone with a lasting influence on the public life of the United States more generally. Lippmann is no longer as well known to academics outside political science, though in his prime he was a formidable author and journalist of international acclaim. We recall the following words from Latour in his 2007 exchange with Gerard de Vries:

> In contrast to [de Vries], I do not believe that returning to Aristotle is helpful ... instead of Aristotle, let's turn to the pragmatists and especially John Dewey ... [who], taking his cue from Walter Lippmann, [spoke of] "the problem of the public." Here is a Copernican Revolution of radical proportions: to finally make publics turn around topics that generate a public around them instead of trying to define politics *in the absence* of any issue. (RGDV 814–815)

It is no accident that Dewey and Lippmann should come up in this exchange. Latour and de Vries had recently served as co-directors of the 2005 University of Amsterdam doctoral thesis of one Noortje Marres, currently Senior Lecturer in Sociology at Goldsmiths, University of London.[1] In Chapter 2 of her dissertation, Marres dealt at some length with the Lippmann-Dewey debate in a way that clearly left a mark on Latour.[2] We find Marres cited in several of Latour's most interesting remarks on political philosophy. For instance, we read as follows in his response to de Vries: "Following Noortje Marres' reinterpretation of

Dewey, de Vries redefines politics as neither a type of procedure nor a domain of life. Politics is not some essence; it is something that moves; it is something that has a trajectory" (RGDV 814). On the same page, Latour treats Marres's phrase "issues and their trajectories" as the equivalent of Lippmann's slogan "problem of the public" (RGDV 814). And we are already familiar with the following 2008 remark by Latour at the London School of Economics:

> Can I add one more thing? Because usually it's true, I mean this is a common thing in political philosophy, that reactionary thinkers are more interesting than the progressive ones [*Laughter*] in that you learn more about politics from people like Machiavelli and [Carl] Schmitt than from Rousseau. And the exceptions are extremely rare, like [Walter] Lippmann (an example I owe to Noortje [Marres]). (PW 96)

In *Modes*, in a series of closely related passages, Latour links both Marres and Lippmann to the politics of things. Here is his reference to Marres: "in the forceful slogan proposed by Noortje Marres: 'No issue, no politics!' It is thus above all because politics is always object-oriented—to borrow a term from information science—that it always seems to elude us" (AIME 337). And here is his reference to Lippmann: "It is for just this reason—Walter Lippmann may be the only person who really got it—that one can respect the ontological dignity of the political mode only by grasping it in the form of a phantom public to be invoked and convoked" (AIME 352). And here is where he speaks of things: "If politics has to be 'crooked' … its path is curved because on each occasion it turns around questions, issues, stakes, things—in the sense of *res publica*, the public *thing*—whose surprising consequences leave those who would rather hear nothing about them all mixed up" (AIME 337). But in some ways, the political turn to things was stated even more explicitly in the exchange with de Vries. As Latour put it there:

> Whatever the term one wishes to use—object, thing, gathering, concern—the key move is to make all definitions of politics turn around the issues instead of having the issues enter into a ready-made political sphere to be dealt with. First define how things turn the public into a problem, and only then try to render more precise what is political, which procedures should be put into place, how the various assemblies can reach closure, and so on. Such is the hard-headed *Dingpolitik* of STS as opposed to the human-centred *Realpolitik*. (RGDV 815)

With the turn to *Dingpolitik*, we approach the state of the art in Latourian political philosophy. Latour escapes the dualism of Truth Politics and Power Politics by noting our basic political ignorance. But what are we ignorant *about?* We are ignorant about whatever issues or things arise in the republic, and it is precisely this ignorance about things that transforms the public. And further, Latour escapes the dualism of Left and Right by having no particular interest in the question of whether humans are basically improvable or unimprovable, since he is not especially interested in the topic of human nature at all. The ultimate fate of humans will result not from some durable inner nature, or from our basic equality or inequality with one another, but from our *attachments* to various things. Strum and Latour were able to outflank Hobbes quite early on by embedding nonhuman actors in the political sphere. More than 30 years later, what remains most characteristic of Latour as a political thinker is the unusually significant role he grants to objects or things. Let's turn now to Latour's 2005 essay contrasting *Dingpolitik* with *Realpolitik*, and follow it up with some discussion of Marres, Lippmann, and Dewey.

THE MEANING OF *DINGPOLITIK*

In 2005, Latour served as co-curator of the art exhibition "Making Things Public." This was the second of his two curated shows at the Zentrum für Kunst und Medientechnologie (ZKM) in Karlsruhe, Germany, which is also the home institution of two of Latour's most provocative friends: the philosopher Peter Sloterdijk and the artist Peter Weibel. As with the first Karlsruhe show ("Iconoclash" in 2002) this one issued a handsomely illustrated catalog of essays,[3] in which Latour's introductory piece was entitled "From Realpolitik to Dingpolitik." The reader will recall that the early Latour looked very much like an advocate of brass-knuckled *Realpolitik*. In 2005, however, he distances himself from the concept, now describing it as "a positive, materialist, no-nonsense, interest only, matter-of-fact way of dealing with naked power relations" (RD 4) and objecting that "[a]lthough this 'reality,' at the time of Bismarck, might have appeared as a welcome change after the cruel idealisms it aimed to replace, it strikes us now as deeply *unrealistic*" (RD 4). Throughout the present book, we have seen that Latour tends to call upon nonhuman things for assistance whenever he seems to be most in danger of advocating a free-for-all human power struggle. The present case is no exception. What Latour now proposes is literally a *Dingpolitik* to replace *Realpolitik*, with the added metaphor of an "object-oriented democracy." Latour equates objects with *issues* while also claiming that much modern political philosophy has made great effort to avoid all mention of objects, "from Hobbes to Rawls, from Rousseau to Habermas" (RD 5). Despite this being an art catalog essay, a number of other points of political philosophy are raised, including Latour's praise of Lippmann's "stunning book called *The Phantom Public*" (RD 28) and a passing nod to Lippmann's admiring critic Dewey. But for our purposes here, the most useful aspect of Latour's essay is its closing summary of seven key features of the proposed new *Dingpolitik* (RD 31). We proceed point by point, with a brief commentary on each:

1. "Politics is no longer limited to humans and incorporates the many issues to which they are attached." As we have seen, the attachment of humans to nonhuman actors has been a pivotal feature of Latour's politics (and ontology) since his earliest career, and is what most separates Latour from Machiavelli and Hobbes. It also separates him from his flamboyant contemporary Žižek, whose bare-bones modernist appeal to the innate equality of speaking human beings seems to leave no political role for our attachments to multiple things. Nonetheless, Žižek's well-known hatred of "beautiful soul" politics at least entails that political actors must place their bets and show their hands rather than pretending to be above all political dispute, and this is a point that Žižek shares with both Latour and Schmitt.

2. "Objects become things, that is, when matters of fact give way to their complicated entanglements and become matters of concern." Though the term "matters of concern" is of somewhat recent date in Latour's writings (born perhaps in the late 1990s), the concept it describes was a key element of his ontology from the earliest years, as can easily be seen if we rewrite "matters of concern" as "matters of *relation*." Unfortunately, Latour's objection to matters of fact is not aimed solely at the arrogance of those who claim to have direct access to them, but also against the notion that there could be autonomous facts at all outside how they are registered by or affect other things. The unfortunate aspect of this strategy is that it cannot address the chief problem with the Hobbesian legacy to which Latour is a mostly satisfied heir: the inability to appeal to any authority beyond the Leviathan itself. Although Latour's Leviathan is a distributed network of humans and nonhumans in which sovereignty does not reside in any one privileged point, it remains a network that leaves nothing entirely outside it. This poses a problem for Latour's claim to take account of

a political "mini-transcendence" that would escape naked power plays by asking that the *polis* take account of previously neglected—though already networked—things.

3. "Assembling is no longer done under the already existing globe or dome of some earlier tradition of building virtual parliaments." Here we see the unfairness of critics who assume that Latour's distaste for the traditional Left entails a gradualist, reformist politics that would basically leave "neoliberalism" intact. Assembling will require entirely different instruments from the outdated ones at hand, as further emphasized by Latour's approving laughter at Sloterdijk's mocking notion of an inflatable "pneumatic parliament" for the recently invaded Iraq. (RD 7)

4. "The inherent limits imposed by speech impairment, cognitive weaknesses and all sorts of handicaps are no longer denied but prostheses are accepted instead." The target here seems to be the ideal speech situation advocated by Habermas, governed by inclusive rationality free from all forms of coercion. Given Latour's disagreement with the claim that rationality and coercion are utterly different in kind, the Habermasian model can only strike him as hopelessly *modern* in the bad sense of the term. The Latourian parliament must leave room for the "irrational" and for "power plays" no less than for ideal speech.

5. "It's no longer limited to properly speaking parliaments but extended to the many other assemblages in search of a rightful assembly." The reference here is not only to nonhuman actors, but also to humans who do not "speak" in the usual propositional sense of the term.

6. "The assembling is done under the provisional and fragile Phantom Public, which no longer claims to be equivalent to a Body, a Leviathan, or a State." The concept of the Phantom Public comes from Lippmann, of course. We will encounter it again shortly.

7. "And, finally, *Dingpolitik* may become possible when politics is freed from its obsession with the time of Succession." Recall that one of the pillars of Latour's critique of modernity was his distaste for any assumption that history proceeds from worse to better, with people gradually *believing* less and relying on *reason* to an increasing degree. For Latour as for his former teacher Michel Serres, time moves via spirals and eddies, forever reviving dead forms in new guise.

Keeping in mind these key features of *Dingpolitik*, we are ready to turn to Noortje Marres's innovative account of the Lippmann-Dewey debate.

MARRES ON LIPPMANN AND DEWEY

Marres gives a good summary of her fresh reading of Lippmann and Dewey in Chapter 2 of her dissertation, and a somewhat less detailed one in Chapter 2 of her book *Material Participation*. It is well known that Dewey's political theory, spelled out most explicitly in his 1927 book *The Public and its Problems*, is greatly indebted to two works by Lippmann: *Public Opinion* (1922) and *The Phantom Public* (1927). The two thinkers are often portrayed as polar opposites, as Marres describes:

> In such accounts, Lippmann represents the technocratic solution: he made the case that due to the complexity of current affairs governmental decision- and policy-making must have a strong component of expert advice, and allow for only a limited role for citizen consultations. This sobering argument is then contrasted with Dewey's radical proposal that the constraints on politics in technological societies precisely require an expansion of democracy.[4]

Against this usual view, Marres claims that there is "a striking similarity between the arguments developed by these two thinkers ... Both Lippmann and Dewey conceptualized democratic politics as a particular practice of issue formation" (p.35). While other commentators have noted that the two philosophers partially agreed in their diagnosis of what was going wrong with American democracy at the time, Marres goes a step further, trying to show that they "also developed strikingly similar critiques of the modern *theory* of democracy ... Lippmann and Dewey came to question the existing standards by which actually existing democracy is to be judged" (p.38). Lippmann was especially concerned with modern democracy's poor grasp of complex or mediated objects. Whether in wartime or at peace,

> it could not be assumed that the object of politics is known by those involved in public debate or political decision-making. It led Lippmann to make the following drastic inference: if it cannot be assumed that those involved in the debate have a good grasp of the affairs under discussion, then it cannot be expected that the opinions they form about them are pertinent. (pp.41–42)

In *Public Opinion* this led Lippmann to the verge of abandoning hope in democracy, though in *The Phantom Public* five years later his conclusions were not quite as grim (p.44). In the latter book, "Lippmann rejects the notion that for democracy to work ... it is necessary that citizens are competent judges on public affairs and have access to high quality information ... The emergence of a strange, unfamiliar, complex issue, he posits in *The Phantom Public*, is an *enabling* condition for democratic politics" (p.45). Since transparently accessible issues can be handled by existing institutions, they are less interesting and relevant for democracy than problems whose solution is less clear. "For Lippmann, public involvement in politics is thus sparked by the failure of existing social groupings and institutions to settle an issue. It is the *absence* of a community or institution that may deal with the issue that makes public involvement in politics a necessity. Because if the public doesn't adopt the issue, no one will" (p.47).

Lippmann had noted that the public's involvement in politics was not direct, but mediated by whatever indirect information it receives. "Dewey took over from Lippmann this notion that the relation between a public and its issues is secondary and indirect. But for Dewey the indirectness of this relationship does not prevent the public from being substantially implicated in the affair in question" (p.49). Indeed, many indirect political effects are highly significant ones, though they must be dealt with by different means than is the case with issues in which one is directly involved.

> As Dewey says, in these cases, if the issue is to be addressed, those who are jointly implicated in the issue *must organise* a community. What the members of a public share is that they are all affected by a particular affair, but they do not already belong to the same community: this is why they must also form a political community, if the issue that affects them is to be dealt with. (p.51)

Marres notes some backsliding on Dewey's part as *The Public and its Problems* progresses. Though early in the book he sticks to the notion that the community does not exist in advance but must be organized, in later chapters he seems to indicate that a shared community must exist beforehand: "Here, his earlier point—that a prime characteristic of the indirect consequences that call a public into being is that there is precisely no pre-existing community to settle the problems these consequences give rise to—is lost" (p.54). But Marres concludes that Dewey demands a pre-existing community only as a bulwark against the power of narrow private interests. "In this respect, it makes perfect sense that Dewey comes to posit a unified social community as a necessary condition for democracy. Such a community provides democracy with a location that can be successfully defended against the invasion of private interests, and it may provide the resources required to compel government to serve the public" (p.55). But Marres proposes that we downplay the usual focus on Dewey's concept of community, since "political democracy is *not* about the fulfillment that can be derived from participation in community life as such—that seems to me to be a moral challenge, not a political one. Political democracy is about taking care of the serious trouble in which those who do not necessarily share a way of life are collectively implicated" (p.56). Rather than a *moral* challenge, we might call community a *social* challenge, since for Marres the distinction between the social and the political is no less important than it is for Latour himself. Marres continues: "I want to emphasise that Dewey's account of the public's genesis suggests that members of political communities are not in [the] first instance connected by way of shared or opposing opinions and interests, but by issues" (p.57). Since issues often put "actors' whole being at stake" (p.58), Marres wittily notes that

> a public as it is organized around affairs may be most appropriately defined as a community of strange things. This elaboration of the Deweyian public also points towards another reason why it must not be understood as a sociable collective. Not only can a political community not be equated with a social community, the event in which modes of living prove irreconcilable [as between vegetarians and Kansas agribusiness splicing pig genes into tomatoes] is not exactly a situation that invites a leisurely exchange among those involved. (pp.58–59)

Since even the public cannot settle an issue directly and without mediation, "the solution that Dewey proposed as part of his theory of the state is … [that] the principal way in which a public can assure that an issue is dealt with is by *acquiring* the resources to do so. The task of a public is thus no less than to assemble an institutional arrangement that will allow the settlement of affairs" (p.59), a task that Dewey described as nothing less than "the discovery of the state."

The problem, as Marres sees it, is that "Lippmann and Dewey have surprisingly little to say about the *process* by which a public gets organized. In their writings, the public has a tendency to appear (and disappear) instantaneously" (pp.60–61). But they do tell us something very important in the negative sense, by forbidding the public to be treated as some sort of abstraction: "In their critiques of the Rousseauist assumption that only an abstract, general entity can perform public acts, Lippmann and Dewey emphasise that actual people or groups of people perform the role of the public" (p.61). And further, "both Lippmann and Dewey emphasised that actually existing individuals do the work of the public. Lippmann didn't tire of pointing out that a public can only be ascribed agency insofar as individual actors influence the course of an affair, by aligning themselves for or against the protagonists in the affair (which again are individual actors)" (p.63). Yet Dewey leaves us with a tension between what seems to be two different publics, "referring both to the set of actors that are affected by an issue, and to the set of actors who organize themselves so as to assure that the issue is addressed" (p.62). The danger of this ambiguity is that it suggests a "correspondence" model in which the public that gets organized is asymptotically obliged to match its membership as closely as possible with the public that is affected, when in fact it is never fully clear either at the beginning or the end of a political process who is affected by an issue and how. The political circle that Latour borrows from the pragmatists cannot function if the political actors and their goals pre-exist the process of forming a public around an issue.

The novelty of Marres's reading of the two figures becomes clear at the end of the chapter. As for Dewey, "it is somewhat ironic that Dewey's work is frequently mobilised in support of the definition of democracy as deliberative procedure … For Dewey, democratic politics could not be made sense of if the content of politics—the contingent but vital problems that it addresses and the settlement that is sought for them— was left out of account" (p.66). More briefly put, Dewey does not just philosophize about speaking and deliberating humans, but also about the objects that mediate human interaction, and thus for our purposes he can be treated as a kind of proto-Latour. And as for Lippmann, it hardly makes sense to read him in the usual manner as a technocrat, since much like Latour, Lippmann does not think the needed technocratic knowledge is attainable in the first place: hence, no Truth Politics for Lippmann. In the words of Marres, "Lippmann rejects the idea that adequate knowledge is a necessary condition for democracy … [He] adds that it is precisely under conditions of imperfect knowledge that we must engage in democratic politics" (pp.66–67).

Marres assesses the situation in her book *Material Participation* by saying that "the writings of John Dewey and Walter Lippmann develop a particular conception of the public as organized by material means, one which suggests that the material public is best understood as an *inherently* problematic formation."[5] Unlike many uses of the term "material" that merely employ it as a thin alibi for a thoroughly human-centric theory, Marres means this word in a truly object-centered sense. As she puts it, "the notion of the problematic situation ... is *not* an epistemological concept, according to which the problematicness of a situation would have to be understood as an artefact of it being 'perceived' or 'seen' as such. Rather, it foregrounds a kind of 'ontological trouble,'" to use Steve Woolgar's phrase (p.44). Stated even more plainly, "in [Dewey's] account, phenomena like clash and conflict, lack and need, loss and satisfaction, are most productively approached as dynamics that unfold 'on the plane of objects.'" Dewey holds that far from having an alienating effect on us poor disenchanted humans, the spread of technology leads to a "radical *multiplication* and excess" of publics. As Marres concisely puts it: "the joint implication of actors in problematic arrangements, technological, material, natural and otherwise, secures the proliferation of the entanglements called public" (p.46). Lippmann would surely approve of such entanglements, since he "explicitly challenged ... a 'horror of things' in modern democratic theory" (p.49). Marres is at pains to emphasize that "pragmatist theories of democracy in technological societies bring into view a material public that clearly differs from the object-centred publics that are associated with scientific liberalism" (p.55). These supposed object-centered theories are really nothing more than problem-solving technocracies of the sort called for by Karl Popper—theories that lose all sense of our permanent *ignorance* of the object and its impermeability by adequate knowledge. Moreover, there was a longstanding tendency among liberals to associate objects with science and therefore with consensus, such that all conflict and disagreement could only fall on the *human* side of the spectrum. But by turning the object from an epistemological object into an object of dispute, the pragmatism of the Marres variety closely approaches the theory of Latour. But Marres also seems to approach the views of Chantal Mouffe, who "shows that it is both possible to approach publics as taking form on the 'plane of objects' and to grant a formative role to dynamics of 'strife and conflict' in democracy" (p.57). Though it is not clear to me that Mouffe is as object-oriented a thinker as Latour, we saw earlier that she and Latour draw similar lessons from Schmitt, in a way that would make a full-blown Latour-Mouffe dialogue an intriguing prospect.

LIPPMANN, DEWEY, AND LATOUR

We now cite the following important passage from Latour for a fourth and final time:

instead of Aristotle, let's turn to the pragmatists and especially John Dewey ... [who], taking his cue from Walter Lippmann, [spoke of] "the problem of the public." Here is a Copernican Revolution of radical proportions: to finally make publics turn around topics that generate a public around them instead of trying to define politics *in the absence* of any issue. (RGDV 814–815)

Latour is so consistently critical of Kant's metaphor of the Copernican Revolution, and so dismissive of the modern adjective "radical," that we have to take notice when he uses these terms in a rare positive spirit. Though Latour denies that Kant pulled off the purifying revolution in the history of philosophy with which so many scholars credit him, he nonetheless grants Copernican status to the following political principle: "to finally make publics turn around topics that generate a public around them instead of trying to define politics *in the absence* of any issue." Since Latour uses "object" and "thing" as synonyms for "issue," let's rewrite the principle as follows: "Here is a Copernican Revolution of radical proportions: to finally make publics turn around objects that generate a public around them instead of trying to define politics *in the absence* of any object." Latour's call for an object-oriented politics is meant to remove politics from the domain of purely human interactions, a career-long strategy that Peer Schouten detected in Latour and Strum's remark that humans rise beyond baboons largely by way of nonhuman mediators. We recall Latour's amusing words from his 1996 article "On Interobjectivity": "while I am at the counter buying my postage stamps and talking into the speaking grill, I don't have family, colleagues, or bosses breathing down my neck. And, thank heavens, the server doesn't tell me stories about his mother-in-law, or his darlings' teeth" (INT 233). To use the increasingly archaic terms of modern philosophy, politics has more to do with the object than with the subject. This is not because stones and neutrons deserve to have votes or seats in Parliament, but because politics is not about human power struggles any more than science is about direct access to the real.

When Marres speaks of "issues and their trajectories," we can also think of the synonymous phrase "objects and their trajectories." Politics requires the existence of such objects. As Latour puts it: "Following Noortje Marres' reinterpretation of Dewey, de Vries redefines politics as neither a type of procedure nor a domain of life. Politics is not some essence; it is something that moves; it is something that has a trajectory" (RGDV 814). Perhaps the most interesting thing that Latour ever said about trajectories came in 2007 when he introduced the spectrum running from "Political-1" through "Political-5." Let's again replace the word "issues" with its synonym "objects" and see what Latour can tell us: "In the same way as stars in astronomy are only stages in a series of transformations that astronomers have learned to map, objects offer up many different aspects depending on where they are in their life histories." As we saw, objects for Latour generally pass in a series from vague background concerns (Political-1) to nascent problems for the public (Political-2), to the locus of sovereign intervention (Political-3), to the sphere of explicit political debate and problem solving (Political-4), and finally to banal problems of governance (Political-5). Naturally, the reverse movement is also possible, though surely not as common. The widespread fluoridation of drinking water in the United States was initially opposed by some as a communist plot, was later transformed into a fairly banal public health measure criticized mostly in the conspiracy theories of cranks, and is now once again under fire from a growing number of respected physicians. To summarize, fluoridation passed from Political-3 to Political-5, but has now probably moved back to the stage of Political-4. Much the same thing happened in the United States with the circumcision of male infants, which was viewed for decades as standard neonatal practice before later coming under fire as an industry too lucrative and unnecessary to be trusted. In this case, circumcision reversed course in much the same way as fluoridation, moving upstream in salmon-like fashion from Political-5 to Political-4. There are even numerous examples of Political-5 issues swimming against the stream all the way back to Political-3 as objects of sovereign intervention, such as alcohol in the United States during Prohibition. Whether an object can travel backwards as far as Political-2 or Political-1 seems more dubious, but perhaps some examples could be found. In any case, the trajectory of life stages of a political issue is surely one of Latour's most fascinating loose ends, though one that we must now leave aside in favor of a brief return to Lippmann and Dewey.

Perhaps the most interesting idea in Lippmann's *The Phantom Public* is that each issue/object generates a new public, instead of the same grey anonymous mass weighing in foolishly on every possible topic. This actually provides some grounds for optimism, since it eliminates the ridiculous expectation that the good democratic citizen must be informed about everything, and hence does not make democracy look like a massive failure every time someone loses touch with an issue. This topic causes especial distress in America, which still assumes it is supposed to educate its citizens for self-government, though "realistic political thinkers in

Europe long ago abandoned the notion that the collective mass of the people directs the course of public affairs."⁶ Speaking of a school text he had recently read, Lippmann objects that "the author of the textbook, touching on everything, as he thinks, from city sewers to Indian opium, misses a decisive fact: the citizen gives but a little of his time to public affairs" (p.14). The unfortunate reader of such a book

> cannot know about everything all the time, and while he is watching one thing a thousand others undergo great changes. Unless he can discover some rational ground for fixing his attention where it will do the most good, and in a way that suits his inherently amateurish equipment, he will be as bewildered as a puppy trying to lick three bones at once. (p.15)

Even Lippmann himself, one of the best-informed journalists of his era, cannot possibly live up to the official mandate of the democratic citizen: "for, although public business is my main interest and I give most of my time to watching it, I cannot find time to do what is expected of me in the theory of democracy; that is, to know what is going on and have an opinion worth expressing on every question which confronts a self-governing community" (p.10). Stated differently, "when we remember that the public consists of busy men reading newspapers for half an hour or so a day, it is not heartless but merely prudent to deny that it can do detailed justice" (p.109). The best one can possibly do as a student is to develop a general intellectual attitude and learn to notice a basic *pattern* in human affairs. However, "that pattern cannot be invented by the pedagogue. It is the political theorist's business to trace out that pattern. In that task he must not assume that the mass has political genius, but that men, even if they had genius, would give only a little time and attention to public affairs" (p.17). Here Lippmann shows an awareness of human ignorance at least as far-reaching as Latour's own. The various despairing efforts to produce well-informed democratic citizens actually have no right to despair, since they are hobbled solely by their own choice of a false ideal:

> I do not mean an undesirable ideal. I mean an unattainable ideal, bad only in the sense that it is bad for a fat man to try to be a ballet dancer. An ideal should express the true possibilities of its subject. When it does not it perverts the true possibilities. The ideal of the omnicompetent, sovereign citizen is, in my opinion, such a false ideal. (p.29)

In fact, our limited range of ability does not just pertain to politics, but extends to every aspect of our lives:

> The farmer decides whether to plant wheat or corn, the mechanic whether to take the job offered at the Pennsylvania or the Erie shops, whether to buy a Ford or a piano, and, if a Ford, whether to buy it from the garage on Elm Street or from the dealer who sent him a circular. These decisions are among fairly narrow choices offered to him; he can no more choose among all the jobs in the world than he can consider marrying any woman in the world. (p.35)

The public is made up of millions of such people, all of them only slightly more ignorant than their leaders and their sharpest public-affairs journalists. Abstractly pasting all such people together in a single amorphous blob called the public does not create a higher unity, as some philosophers have held. As Lippmann puts it, "the making of one general will out of many is not an Hegelian mystery, as so many social philosophers have imagined, but an art well known to leaders, politicians, and steering committees" (p.37). There is no genuine mass, but only what Lippmann calls a "deep pluralism."

> Against this deep pluralism thinkers have argued in vain. They have invented social organisms and national souls, and oversouls, and collective souls; they have gone for hopeful analogies to the beehive and the anthill, to the solar system, to the human body; they have gone to Hegel for higher unities and to Rousseau for a general will in an effort to find some basis of union ... We, however, no longer expect to find a unity which absorbs diversity. (pp.87–88)

This leads Lippmann to a conclusion that is not as cynical as it looks. "Before a mass of general opinions can eventuate in executive action, the choice is narrowed down to a few alternatives. The victorious alternative is executed not by the mass but by individuals in control of its energy" (p.38). Lippmann continues the theme: "We must abandon the notion that the people govern. Instead we must adopt the theory that, by their occasional mobilization as a majority, people support or oppose the individuals who actually govern. We must say that the popular will does not direct continuously but that it intervenes occasionally" (pp.51–52). And hence "it is idle, then, to argue that though men evidently have conflicting purposes, mankind has some all-embracing purpose of which you or I happen to the be the authorized spokesman. We merely should have moved in a circle were we to conclude that the public is in some deep way a messianic force" (p.57). Instead, "the ideal of public opinion is to align men during the crisis of a problem in such a way as to favor the action of those individuals who may be able to compose the crisis" (p.58). Stated differently, "it is the function of public opinion to check the use of force in a crisis, so that men, driven to make terms, may live and let live" (p.64).

Lippmann now touches base with the title of his book, which Marres showed us was borrowed from Kierkegaard. Against "the belief that there is a public which directs the course of events[,] I hold that this public is a mere phantom" (p.67). The idea is strikingly simple: "The public in respect to a railroad strike may be the farmers whom the railroad serves; the public in respect to an agricultural tariff may include the very railroad men who were on strike. The public is not, as I see it, a fixed body of individuals. It is merely those persons who are interested in an affair and can affect it only by supporting or opposing the actors." He picks up the theme once more in Chapter 10:

> the membership of the public is not fixed. It changes with the issue: the actors in one affair are the spectators of another, and men are continually passing back and forth between the field where they are executives and the field where they are members of a public ... [though] there is [also] a twilight zone where it is hard to say whether a man is acting executively on his opinions or merely acting to influence the opinion of someone else who is acting executively. (p.100)

Or again, "the random collection of bystanders who constitute a public could not, even if they had a mind to, intervene in all the problems of the day" (p.115). Not infrequently, they are in fact called upon to intervene. For when it is a question of "the hardest controversies to disentangle ... the public is called in to judge. Where the facts are most obscure, where precedents are lacking, where novelty and confusion pervade everything, the public in all its unfitness is compelled to make its most important decisions. The hardest problems are those which institutions cannot handle. They are the public's problems" (p.121). Despite Lippmann's passing reference to "the random collection of bystanders who form a public," the public is no random or even universal collection of humans, but a specifically different group in the case of each issue that arises. They are there, Lippmann said, for "the hardest problems ... which institutions cannot handle." His sparring partner Dewey will soon tell us that the public's task is precisely to create new institutions capable of handling such problems. If Lippmann represents the moment in Latour's *Politics of Nature* known as "taking into account," Dewey tells us a bit more about the complementary moment of "putting in order."

Dewey clarifies the nature of a public (deliberately in the singular) in the following terms: "the essence of the consequences which call a public into being is the fact that they expand beyond those directly engaged in producing them."[7] For this reason, "special agencies and measures must be formed if they are to be attended to; or else some existing group must take on new functions" (p.54). This all-important task is broader and more difficult than it sounds, since there is constant tension between the need to have new institutions to deal with new consequences, and the resistance of the already existing institutions:

> The new public which is generated remains long inchoate, unorganized, because it cannot use inherited political agencies. The latter, if elaborate and well institutionalized, obstruct the organization of the new public. They prevent that development of new forms of the state which might grow up rapidly were social life more fluid, less precipitated into set political and legal molds ... The public which generated political forms is passing away, but the power and lust of possession remains in the hands of the officers and agencies which the dying public instituted. This is why the change of the form of states is so often effected only by revolution ... By its very nature, a state is ever something to be scrutinized, investigated, searched for. Almost as soon as its form is stabilized, it needs to be remade. (p.56)

Dewey continues to emphasize the *experimental* aspect of politics:

> In concrete fact, in actual and concrete organization and structure, there is no form of state which can be said to be the best; not at least till history is ended, and one can survey all its varied forms ... And since conditions of action and of inquiry and knowledge are always changing, the experiment must always be retried; the State must always be rediscovered. (p.57)

An important related idea of Dewey's, thoroughly pragmatist in flavor, is the notion that we should not waste time looking for the supposed causal origins of the state, but should simply look to its consequences. "The wrong place to look ... is in the realm of alleged causal agency, of authorship, of forces, which are supposed to produce a state by an intrinsic *vis genetrix*" (p.60). Critiquing Hegel by name, Dewey adds that "the notion of an inherent universality in the associative force at once breaks against the fact of an obvious plurality of states, each localized, with its boundaries, limitations, its indifference and even hostility to other states" (p.61). This leads him to make the humorous aside that "it is peculiar, to say the least, that universal reason should be unable to cross a mountain range and objective will be balked by a river current" (p.63). It follows that "only the theory which makes recognition of consequences the critical factor can find in the fact of many states a corroborating trait." And yet, "in spite of the fact that diversity of political forms rather than uniformity is the rule, belief in *the* state as an archetypal entity persists in political philosophy and science" (p.64). Dewey finds this regrettable, since "the attempt to find by the 'comparative method' structures which are common to antique and modern, to occidental and oriental states, has involved a great waste of industry" (p.65). At times it has even led to outright metaphysical extravagance, with Hegel again prominent among Dewey's targets:

> The next dialectical conclusion is that the will ... is something over and above any private will or any collection of such wills: is some overriding "general will." This conclusion was drawn by Rousseau, and under the influence of German metaphysics was erected into a dogma of a mystic and transcendent absolute will ... The alternative to one or other of these conclusions is surrender of the causal authorship theory and the adoption of that of widely distributed consequences. (p.69)

Both Lippmann and Dewey view the public in local and transient terms, as formed by some novel issue/object that existing institutions are not equipped to handle. Latour's point of agreement with these authors is easy to see. Politics is not a purely human realm of power plays and language games, but results from the hybrid crossing of humans with things: one of the major themes of all of Latour's work, not just his political writings. Since even experts cannot fully sound the depths of things, let alone those non-experts who are affected or concerned by a given issue, ignorance lies at the basis of all human action. This is what links both Latour and Lippmann with Socrates, despite Latour's misreading of Socrates as an epistemology policeman, and Lippmann's misreading of Socrates as holding that virtue means knowledge[8] (precisely the opposite of what we learn from Plato's *Meno*).

The real question, we have seen, is whether Latour and Lippmann have *sufficient* respect for ignorance. Though Latour is fully convincing when he calls his politics object-oriented, simply recall what Latour and Dewey think objects to be. For Latour they are actants defined by their effects and relations rather than by some essential nature held in reserve; for Dewey, objects are consequences rather than hidden causal powers. In both cases we are in the orbit of pragmatism, which as a philosophy is respectable enough. However, the whole point of bringing objects into politics was to counter the widespread model of empty power plays without transcendent standards. Latour addressed this drawback of his early position by gradually building up the middle-Latour notion of "mini-transcendence" (in *Politics of Nature*) and finally the late-Latour claim that his entire philosophy is governed by an overarching morality (in *Modes*). But nothing can really be transcendent if it is stipulated to consist of its current effects, or even of the sum of its possible effects. Replacing the power play among humans with a power play distributed between things and humans merely displaces and retains the political dominance of power, and gives us no sense of what humans and things really are when *not* deployed in some relational network. As Leo Strauss might have put it, if only he had been on our side: "In principle, however, it is always possible to reach agreement regarding the effects of an object that is already fixed, whereas there is always quarreling over the objects themselves: we are always quarreling with ourselves only over what objects are."

8

Concluding Remarks

The previous chapter allows us to solidify our sense of how Latour differs from the other basic forms of modern politics discussed throughout this book. For Power Politics there is no object. The human subject breathes its own exhalations and is cooked in its own juice, making no contact at all with nonhuman surprises, since these would amount to unjustified chunks of transcendence. For Truth Politics there is also no object, since it is replaced by some definite model of what we *think* reality must be; all features of reality that do not fit this model are treated as needless ideological baggage that ought to be tossed from the train at the earliest hour. Objects are dismissed as the products of "commodity fetishism." It is said that "man is born free, and everywhere he is in chains," thereby converting every limit on human fulfillment into fetters manufactured in the degenerate smithy of society. Or in the right-wing version of Truth Politics, the philosopher has knowledge but must keep it to himself and a few elite students due to the violent stupidity of the general human mass, whose naïve beliefs must be flattered by any prudent thinker who wishes to avoid drinking the hemlock. In both cases it is held that everything is known, or at least *potentially* known in the manner of asymptotic progress. For Latour, by contrast, politics is provoked by objects that are never exactly "known," but are institutionally managed along a life cycle running from Political-1 through Political-5. Here, politics is primarily a matter of permanent surprise rather than of knowledge.

Shifting from Truth and Power to Left and Right, we can also see that for Left and Right alike there is no object. These are both modern, human-centered positions that embrace either a model of progress via the elimination of needless past constraints, or the cautious and pessimistic vigilance of those who have tracked the repetition of identical human sorrows from *Exodus* through Aeschylus, Socrates, Louis XIV, Burke, Talleyrand, Lincoln, Stalin, and Mao. In this sense Latour's object-oriented politics is perhaps more bold than the Left and more cautious than the

Right. At no point do we ever know what the political object really is; much like Socrates himself, Latour has a healthier respect for our basic ignorance than do Left or Right, Power Politics or Truth Politics. If Latour is on the proper track, then these familiar divisions are likely to disappear, to be replaced by others still unknown.

I began this book by speaking of four clues that would help us discover Latour's political philosophy, and four dangers that Latour must avoid. We can now review all eight of these points, thereby gaining a sense of what has been learned in the previous chapters.

First, we spoke of a need to divide Latour's political philosophy into three distinct phases. This division has proven to be useful. The early Latour takes great pleasure in wearing the silken costumes of Hobbes and Machiavelli, effacing all distinction between right and might. The middle Latour begins with the 1991 rejoinder to Shapin and Shaffer: "No, Hobbes was wrong!" Power Politics is now just as suspect to Latour as Truth Politics always was, and his interest turns to detecting whatever evades the current political collective. The late Latour of the *Modes* project finally puts an end to his previous tendency to identify politics with reality as a whole, since politics is now just one mode among numerous others.

Second, we marveled at Latour's career-long respect for politicians, who are normally despised by intellectuals. The reason for this should now be obvious as well. A good politician is one of the few people who does not try to replace the *objects* of her craft either with some epistemological model of what they ought to be or with a denial that there even *are* such objects beyond the workings of might.[1] In this sense, as seekers of mysterious objects, politicians might even be viewed as philosophers engaged in fieldwork.

The third clue was Latour's edgy 2008 statement at the London School of Economics that reactionary political philosophers are often more interesting than political "good guys" such as Rousseau. The reason for this is now clear as well. It is characteristic of the political Left to ascribe every deficit of the current human condition to some combination of ignorance, oppression, and conspiracy present in society. Although this model has proven liberating in numerous individual cases, it has more to do with epistemology and morality than with politics proper. Since the Right has little faith in the general upward trend of human history, being more inclined to view this history as a repetitious tragicomedy always coughing up the same heroes, lovers, and fools, it is less likely to dismiss the workings of politics as regrettable and accidental obstacles on the road to utopia. But while Latour is fascinated by reactionary political philosophers, he cannot be counted among their number. Not only does he lack their basic pessimism about human nature, and their conviction that the same human issues recur over and over again with no fundamental progress being made. More than this, he lacks the silent conviction of both Left and Right that human nature (whether good or bad) is a decisive political issue in the first place. For Latour, politics is a matter of objects at least as much as subjects.

The fourth clue was Latour's conviction that Lippmann and Dewey have brought about a Copernican Revolution in political philosophy. In Chapter 7, we reflected on the nature of this claim. Politics is a theater of issues/ objects about which we remain basically ignorant, and these objects are dealt with not continuously, by the entire mass of humans in the polity, but by different concerned groups each time an issue arises. We have now seen the compatibility of this idea with Latour's philosophical position more generally.

There were also four potential dangers facing Latour, and indeed facing any attempt at a political philosophy in the continental tradition. The first danger was that of outright *silence* about political themes. Strauss had pointedly observed that Bergson, Whitehead, Husserl, and Heidegger all had shockingly little to say about political philosophy compared with comparable figures from the past. By now we have seen that Latour by no means remains silent about political philosophy, which may even be regarded as one of the secret engines of his career.

The second danger was the opposite one of finding politics absolutely everywhere. We have seen that this particular problem haunted Latour for much of his career. The ultimate end to this danger comes only in *Modes*, where politics is finally contained and delimited as just one mode of existence among others.

The third danger was the temptation of flattering the Left, which has once again become the most fashionable political outlook in continental philosophy circles. While it may take a good deal of courage to face down capitalism amidst tear gas and billy clubs in the streets, it takes no courage whatsoever to shout down capitalism in intellectual gatherings of the early twenty-first century. This does not automatically mean that fashion has it wrong, but does mean that a certain conformism has set in among continental philosophers, with political biodiversity now reaching dangerously low levels. Latour's approach is fresh enough to increase such biodiversity, as long as his opponents are willing to engage his arguments rather than simply pillory them, whether "usefully" or not.

The fourth danger was that of turning all politics into nothing but a power struggle. By now we have seen that Latour becomes increasingly aware that Power Politics (on whose side he began) is no less flawed than Truth Politics (which he has always opposed). It is a separate question whether his appeals to "mini-transcendence," and his insistence that things-in-themselves be replaced by objects-not-currently-recognized-by-the-collective, are sufficiently robust to do justice to a reality that transcends power.

Bruno Latour is still hard at work determining the various consequences of his *Modes* project, and still very much invested in exploring the political implications of Gaia. Thus, I can hardly be sure that the present book will represent my last word on Latour's political philosophy. But I am sure of one point: it is no longer possible to associate Latour with a politics that can be characterized as Left, Right, Truth-Based, or Power-Based. His philosophical trajectory renders all four polarities equally impossible. Any discussion of Latour's political philosophy needs to begin here, and not with scattershot insults about bourgeoisie and neo-liberals.

Notes

A NOTE ON THE LIFE AND THOUGHT OF BRUNO LATOUR

1. William James, *Essays in Radical Empiricism* (Lincoln, NE: University of Nebraska Press, 1996).
2. Alfred North Whitehead, *Process and Reality*.
3. Graham Harman, *Prince of Networks: Bruno Latour and Metaphysics* (Melbourne: re.press, 2009), pp.85–95.

INTRODUCTION

1. Harman, *Prince of Networks*.
2. *Psalms* 118:22, New International Version.
3. Edward Gibbon, *The Decline and Fall of the Roman Empire* (New York: Modern Library, 2003), p.19.

CHAPTER 1

1. "Most cited authors of books in the humanities, 2007," Times Higher Education website, March 26, 2009. http://www.timeshighereducation.co.uk/405956.article
2. Harman, *Prince of Networks*.
3. Patrice Maniglier, "Qui a peur de Bruno Latour?" *Le Monde* website, September 21, 2012. http://www.lemonde.fr/livres/article/2012/09/21/qui-a-peur-de-bruno-latour_1763066_3260.html
4. For an especially hasty and vehement sample of this view, see page 51 of Ray Brassier, "Concepts and Objects," in Levi R. Bryant, Nick Srnicek, and Graham Harman (eds.) *The Speculative Turn: Continental Materialism and Realism* (Melbourne: re.press, 2011).
5. Leo Strauss, *What Is Political Philosophy?* (Chicago: University of Chicago Press, 1988), p.17.
6. During our aforementioned 2012 conversation in Rio de Janeiro, Latour was somewhat hesitant on the topic of political philosophy. Aside from expressing his youthful admiration for Hobbes, he merely expressed his considerable

respect for Schmitt and confirmed that, unlike many French thinkers of his generation, he never passed through a Marxist phase.

7. See Faye's work of intellectual propaganda, *Heidegger: The Introduction of Nazism into Philosophy in Light of the Unpublished Seminars of 1933–1935*, trans. M. Smith (New Haven: Yale University Press, 2011).

8. McKenzie Wark, "Accelerationism," *Public Seminar* blog, November 18, 2013. http://www.publicseminar.org/2013/11/accelerationism/

9. Stanley Rosen, *The Mask of Enlightenment: Nietzsche's Zarathustra*, second edition (New Haven: Yale University Press, 2004), p.5. As a student at Penn State during 1990–91, I heard Rosen say that he would die a happy man precisely because he knew all the possible philosophical positions that one might adopt.

10. Abraham Païs, in Stefan Rozental (ed.), *Niels Bohr: His Life and Work as Seen by His Friends and Colleagues* (Hoboken, NJ: John Wiley & Sons, 1967), p.218.

11. Peer Schouten, "The Materiality of State Failure: Social Contract Theory, Infrastructure and Governmental Power in Congo," *Millenium: Journal of International Studies*, June 2013, Vol.41, No.3, pp.553–574.

12. Jean-Jacques Rousseau, *Discourse on the Origin of Inequality*, trans. D. Cress (Indianapolis: Hackett, 1992).

13. Schouten, "The Materiality of State Failure," p.555.

14. Gabriel Tarde, *Monadology and Sociology*, trans. T. Lorenc (Melbourne: re.press, 2012). For my critique of Tarde, see Graham Harman, "On the Supposed Societies of Chemicals, Atoms, and Stars in Gabriel Tarde," in Godofredo Pereira (ed.), *Savage Objects* (Lisbon: INCM, 2012).

15. Gerard de Vries, "What is Political in Sub-politics? How Aristotle Might Help STS," *Social Studies of Science*, Vol.37, No.5, October 2007, p.781.

CHAPTER 2

1. James D. Watson, *The Double Helix: A Personal Account of the Discovery of the Structure of DNA* (New York: Norton, 2001), an example cited favorably in the opening pages of Bruno Latour, *Science in Action: How to Follow Scientists and Engineers Through Society* (Cambridge, MA: Harvard University Press, 1987).

2. Alfred North Whitehead and Lucien Price, *Dialogues of Alfred North Whitehead* (New York: Nonpareil Books, 2001), pp.123–124.

3. Brassier, "Concepts and Objects," p.53.

4. Leo Strauss, "Niccolo Machiavelli," in Leo Strauss and Joseph Cropsey, *History of Political Philosophy*, third edition (Chicago: University of Chicago Press, 2007), pp.316–317.

5. Alain Badiou, *Logics of Worlds: Being and Event 2*, trans. A. Toscano (London: Continuum, 2009), p.7 (Badiou's emphasis).

6. Brassier, "Concepts and Objects," p.51.

7. Bruno Latour, personal communication, November 11, 2005. Quoted in Harman, *Prince of Networks*, p.12.

8. Quentin Meillassoux, *After Finitude: Essay on the Necessity of Contingency*, trans. R. Brassier (London: Continuum, 2008).

9. Steven Shapin and Simon Schaffer, *Leviathan and the Air-Pump: Hobbes, Boyle, and the Experimental Life* (Princeton, NJ: Princeton University Press, 1985).

10. Ibid., p.344, cited in Latour, *We Have Never Been Modern*, p.26.

CHAPTER 3

1. De Vries, "What is Political in Sub-Politics?", p.803.

2. For further discussion see Graham Harman, "Relation and Entanglement: A Response to Bruno Latour and Ian Hodder," *New Literary History*, Vol.45, No.1, pp.37–49, 2014.

3. Martin Heidegger, *Bremen and Freiburg Lectures*, trans. A. Mitchell (Bloomington, IN: Indiana University Press, 2012).

4. Isabelle Stengers, *Cosmopolitics*, trans. R. Bononno, two volumes (Minneapolis: University of Minnesota Press, 2010).

5. The reference of the phrase "As I have argued elsewhere" is to Bruno Latour, *War of the Worlds: What About Peace?*, trans C. Brigg (Chicago: Prickly Paradigm Press, 2002).

6. John Tresch, "Mechanical Romanticism: Engineers of the Artificial Paradise", Ph.D. dissertation, University of Cambridge, 2001.

CHAPTER 4

1. Steve Jobs, "Steve Jobs on Apple's Resurgence: 'Not a One-Man Show,'" *BusinessWeek*, May 12, 1998. http://www.businessweek.com/bwdaily/dnflash/may1998/nf80512d.htm

2. As far as I know, I was the first to use the phrase "object-oriented" in a philosophical rather than a computer science context. "Object-oriented philosophy" first appeared in my doctoral dissertation at DePaul University, *Tool-Being*, defended in March 1999, which later became my first book. The first conference presentation of the term took place at Brunel University, Uxbridge, United Kingdom in a paper entitled (what else?) "Object-Oriented Philosophy." The date was September 11, 1999, Latour himself was in attendance, and despite his initial dislike for the paper, he immediately congratulated me by email for its catchy title. The paper is now available as Chapter 6 of my book *Towards Speculative Realism*.

3. Philippe Descola, *Beyond Nature and Culture*, trans. J. Lloyd (Chicago: University of Chicago Press, 2013), p.122.

4. For one of the classic overviews of the "zombie" theme, see David Chalmers, *The Conscious Mind: In Search of a Fundamental Theory* (New York: Oxford University Press, 1997).

5. Jacques Lacan, *Écrits: The First Complete Edition in English*, trans. B. Fink. New York: W.W. Norton, 2007.

6. Humberto R. Maturana and Francisco Varela, *Autopoiesis and Cognition: The Realization of the Living* (Dordrecht, The Netherlands: D. Reidel, 1980); Niklas Luhmann, *Social Systems*, trans. J. Bednarz with D. Baecker (Stanford, CA: Stanford University Press, 1995).

7. Bruno Latour, personal communication. October 5, 2013.

CHAPTER 5

1. Sande Cohen, "Science Studies and Language Suppression: A Critique of Bruno Latour's *We Have Never Been Modern*," *Studies in the History and Philosophy of Science*, Vol.28, No.2, 1997, pp.360–361.

2. Mark Elam, "Living Dangerously with Bruno Latour in a Hybrid World," *Theory, Culture and Society*, Vol.16, No.1, 1999, p.5.

3. The first of Braudel's three volumes on the topic is *Civilization and Capitalism, 15th–18th Century, Vol.1: The Structure of Everyday Life*, trans. S. Reynold (Berkeley, CA: University of California Press, 1992). But the detailed account of capitalism begins in Volume 2.

4. DeLanda, Manuel and Timur Si-Qin, "Manuel DeLanda in conversation with Timur Si- Qin" (Berlin: Société, 2012).

5. See Eyers's interesting question on page 138 of Bruno Latour, Graham Harman, and Peter Erdélyi, *The Prince and the Wolf: Latour and Harman at the LSE* (Winchester, UK: Zero Books, 2011).

6. Tom Eyers, "Think Negative!" *Mute*, April 7, 2011. http://www.metamute.org/editorial/articles/think-negative

7. Benjamin Noys, *The Persistence of the Negative: A Critique of Contemporary Continental Theory* (Edinburgh: Edinburgh University Press, 2012), p.80.

8. Brassier, "Concepts and Objects," p.53.

9. Noys, *The Persistence of the Negative*, p.94.

10. One plausible history of the term can be found in Jamie Peck, *Constructions of Neoliberal Reason* (New York: Oxford University Press, 2013), though I am not among those who find the book's analysis to be devastating.

11. Noys, *The Persistence of the Negative*, p.81.

12. Susan Hekman, "We have never been postmodern: Latour, Foucault, and the material of knowledge," p.435.

13. Olli Pyyhtinen and Sakari Tamminen, "We have never been only human: Foucault and Latour on the question of the *anthropos*," *Anthropological Theory*, Vol.11, No.2, pp.135–152, 2011.

14. Gavin Kendall and Mike Michael, "Order and Disorder: Time, Technology, and the Self." The article was published in the online journal *Culture Machine* in HTML format without pagination.

CHAPTER 6

1. Chantal Mouffe, "Introduction: Schmitt's Challenge," in Chantal Mouffe (ed.), *The Challenge of Carl Schmitt* (London: Verso, 1999), p.1.
2. Carl Schmitt, *The Concept of the Political*, trans. G. Schwab (Chicago: University of Chicago Press, 2007), p.26.
3. Jean-Jacques Rousseau, *The Social Contract and Other Later Political Writings*, trans. V. Gourevitch (Cambridge: Cambridge University Press, 1997). p.41.
4. Niccolò Machiavelli, *The Prince*, trans. P. Bondanella (Oxford: Oxford University Press, 2008), p.58.
5. Schmitt, *The Concept of the Political*, p.58.
6. Jean-François Kervégan, "Carl Schmitt and 'World Unity,'" in Mouffe, *The Challenge of Carl Schmitt*, p.54.
7. Schmitt, *The Concept of the* Political, p.65.
8. Leo Strauss, "Notes on Carl Schmitt, *The Concept of the Political*," appendix to Schmitt, *The Concept of the Political*, pp.99–100.
9. Schmitt, *The Concept of the Political*, p.58.
10. Strauss, "Notes on Carl Schmitt," p.111.
11. Tracy B. Strong, "Foreword: Dimensions of the New Debate Around Carl Schmitt," in Schmitt, *The Concept of the Political*, p.xviii.
12. Slavoj Žižek, "Carl Schmitt in the Age of Post-Politics," in Mouffe, *The Challenge of Carl Schmitt*, p.18.
13. Slavoj Žižek and Glyn Daly, *Conversations with Žižek* (Cambridge: Polity Press, 2003), pp.122–123.
14. Slavoj Žižek, *The Sublime Object of Ideology* (London: Verso, 1989), pp.5–6.
15. Chantal Mouffe, "Carl Schmitt and the Paradox of Liberal Democracy," in Mouffe, *The Challenge of Carl Schmitt*, p.38.

CHAPTER 7

1. Noortje Marres, "No issue, no public: democratic deficits after the displacement of politics," Ph.D. dissertation, University of Amsterdam, The Netherlands, 2005. http://dare.uva.nl/record/165542
2. I have learned a great deal from Marres as well, despite my ultimate disagreement with her orientation towards pragmatism. For Marres's critique of my own philosophical position, see Noortje Marres, "Nothing Special," in Deva Waal (ed.), *Drift wijsgerig festival* (Amsterdam: Drift, 2013), pp.9–19.

3. Bruno Latour and Peter Weibel (eds.), *Making Things Public: Atmospheres of Democracy*. Cambridge, MA: MIT Press, 2005.

4. Marres, "No issue, no public," p.34.

5. Noortje Marres, *Material Participation: Technology, the Environment and Everyday Publics* (London: Palgrave Macmillan, 2012), p.40.

6. Walter Lippmann, *The Phantom Public* (New Brunswick, NJ: Transaction Publishers, 1993), p.9.

7. John Dewey, *The Public and its Problems*, p.54.

8. Lippmann, *The Phantom Public*, p.20.

CHAPTER 8

1. See Graham Harman, "On the Undermining of Objects: Grant, Bruno, and Radical Philosophy," in Bryant, Srnicek, and Harman, *The Speculative Turn*.

Bibliography

RELEVANT WORKS AUTHORED, CO-AUTHORED, OR CO-EDITED BY
BRUNO LATOUR (ORDERED CHRONOLOGICALLY)

Michel Callon and Bruno Latour. "Unscrewing the big Leviathan: How actors macro-structure reality and how sociologists help them to do so," in K. Knorr-Cetina and A.V. Cicourel (eds.), *Advances in Social Theory and Metholodology: Toward an Integration of Micro- and Macro-Sociologies*, London: Routledge & Kegan Paul, 1981.

Bruno Latour and Steve Woolgar. *Laboratory Life: The Construction of Scientific Facts*. Princeton, NJ: Princeton University Press, 1986.

Bruno Latour. "The Powers of Association," in John Law (ed.), *Power, Action and Belief: A New Sociology of Knowledge? Sociological Review* Monograph No.32, pp.264–280, 1986.

Bruno Latour. *Science in Action: How to Follow Scientists and Engineers Through Society*. Cambridge, MA: Harvard University Press, 1987.

S.S. Strum and Bruno Latour. "Redefining the social link: From baboons to humans," *Social Science Information*, Vol.26, No.4, pp.783–802, 1987.

Bruno Latour. *The Pasteurization of France*, trans. A. Sheridan and J. Law. Cambridge, MA: Harvard University Press, 1988.

Bruno Latour. "How to Write '*The Prince*' for Machines as Well as for Machinations," Article Number 36 on website of Bruno Latour, http://www.bruno-latour.fr/article?page=6 (also available in Brian Elliott (ed.), *Technology and Social Process*. Edinburgh: Edinburgh University Press, pp.20–43, 1988. Page numbers cited in this book refer to the Latour website version.)

Bruno Latour. "The Enlightenment Without the Critique: A Word on Michel Serres' Philosophy," in Griffiths, *Contemporary French Philosophy*, 1987.

Bruno Latour. "Technology Is Society Made Durable," in John Law (ed.), *A Sociology of Monsters: Essays on Power, Technology, and Domination, Sociological Review* Monograph No.38, pp.103–132, 1991.

Bruno Latour. *We Have Never Been Modern*, trans. C. Porter. Cambridge, MA: Harvard University Press, 1993.

Bruno Latour. "Pragmatogonies: A Mythical Account of How Humans and Nonhumans Swap Properties," *American Behavioral Scientist*, Vol.37, No.6, pp.791–808, May 1994.

Bruno Latour. *Aramis, or the Love of Technology*, trans. C. Porter. Cambridge, MA: Harvard University Press, 1996.

Bruno Latour. "On Interobjectivity," trans. G. Bowker, *Mind, Culture, and Activity: An International Journal*, Vol.3, No.4, pp.228–245, 1996.

Bruno Latour and Emilie Hernant. *Paris Invisible City*, trans. L. Carey-Libbrecht, corrected by V. Pihet. Available online at http://www.bruno-latour.fr/virtual/index.html. Originally published in French as *Paris ville invisible*. Paris: La Découverte-Les Empêcheurs en rond, 1998.

Bruno Latour. *Pandora's Hope: Essays on the Reality of Science Studies*. Cambridge, MA: Harvard University Press, 1999.

Bruno Latour. "On the Partial Existence of Existing *and* Non-Existing Objects," in Lorraine Daston (ed.), *Biographies of Scientific Objects*, Chicago: University of Chicago Press, 2000, pp.247–269.

Bruno Latour and Peter Weibel (eds.). *Iconoclash: Beyond the Image Wars in Science, Religion and Art*. Cambridge, MA: MIT Press, 2002.

Bruno Latour. *War of the Worlds: What About Peace?*, trans C. Brigg. Chicago: Prickly Paradigm Press, 2002.

Bruno Latour. "What if we *Talked* Politics a Little?" *Contemporary Political Theory*, Vol.2, No.2, pp.143–164, 2003.

Bruno Latour. *Politics of Nature: How to Bring the Sciences into Democracy*, trans. C. Porter. Cambridge, MA: Harvard University Press, 2004.

Bruno Latour. "Whose Cosmos, Which Cosmopolitics? Comments on the Peace Terms of Ulrich Beck," *Common Knowledge*, Vol.10, No.3, pp.450–462, Fall 2004.

Bruno Latour. "Why Has Critique Run Out of Steam? From Matters of Fact to Matters of Concern," *Critical Inquiry*, Vol.30, No.2, pp.225–248, Winter 2004.

Bruno Latour and Peter Weibel (eds.). *Making Things Public: Atmospheres of Democracy*. Cambridge, MA: MIT Press, 2005.

Bruno Latour. "From Realpolitik to Dingpolitik, or How to Make Things Public," in Latour and Weibel, *Making Things Public*, 2005.

Bruno Latour. *Reassembling the Social: An Introduction to Actor-Network Theory*. Oxford: Oxford University Press, 2005.

Bruno Latour. "Turning Around Politics: A Note on Gerard de Vries' Paper," *Social Studies of Science*, Vol.37, No.5, pp.811–820, October 2007.

Bruno Latour. "Can We Get Our Materialism Back, Please?" *Isis*, Vol.98, pp.138–142, 2007.

Bruno Latour. "An Attempt at a 'Compositionist Manifesto,'" *New Literary History*, Vol.41, pp.41–490, 2010.

Bruno Latour. "Coming Out as a Philosopher," *Social Studies of Science*, Vol.40, No.4, pp.599–608, 2010.

Bruno Latour, Graham Harman, and Peter Erdélyi. *The Prince and the Wolf: Latour and Harman at the LSE*. Winchester, UK: Zero Books, 2011.

Bruno Latour. *An Inquiry into Modes of Existence: An Anthropology of the Moderns*, trans. C. Porter. Cambridge, MA: Harvard University Press, 2013.

Bruno Latour. "Facing Gaia: Six lectures on the political theology of nature," the Gifford Lectures on Natural Religion, Edinburgh, February 18–28,

2013 (unpublished version of February 19, 2013). Now available at http://www.bruno-latour.fr/sites/default/files/downloads/GIFFORD-SIX-LECTURES_1.pdf

Bruno Latour. "Biography of an inquiry: On a book about modes of existence," *Social Studies of Science*, Vol.43, No.2, pp.287–301, April 2013.

Bruno Latour. "War and Peace in an Age of Ecological Conflicts," lecture given at the Peter Wall Institute for Advanced Studies, Vancouver, September 2013. Available as article number 130 at http://www.bruno-latour.fr/article

Bruno Latour. "Another way to compose the common world," paper prepared for the session "The Ontological Turn in French Philosophical Anthropology," an Executive Session of the AAA Annual Meeting, Chicago, November 23, 2013. Available as article number 132 at http://www.bruno-latour.fr/article

Bruno Latour. "Let the dead (revolutionaries) bury the dead," published in a special issue of the Turkish journal of sociology *Birikim*, edited by Koray Caliskan. Cited in Noys, *The Persistence of the Negative*, and still available as of January 10, 2014 at http://www.translatum.gr/forum/index.php?topic=11884.0

WORKS OF OTHERS (ORDERED ALPHABETICALLY BY AUTHOR/ EDITOR)

Acuto, Michele and Simon Curtis (eds.). *Reassembling International Theory: Assemblage Thinking and International Relations*. Basingstoke, UK: Palgrave Macmillan, 2014.

Agamben, Giorgio. *Homo Sacer: Sovereign Power and Bare Life*, trans. Daniel Heller-Roazen. Stanford, CA: Stanford University Press, 1998.

Badiou, Alain. *Logics of Worlds: Being and Event 2*, trans. A. Toscano. London: Continuum, 2009.

Barad, Karen. *Meeting the Universe Halfway: Quantum Physics and the Entanglement of Matter and Meaning*. Durham, NC: Duke University Press, 2007.

Beck, Ulrich. *Risk Society: Towards a New Modernity*. London: Sage, 1992.

Beck, Ulrich. *Die Erfindung des Politischen*. Frankfurt: Suhrkamp, 1993.

Blok, Anders and Torben Elgaard Jensen. *Bruno Latour: Hybrid Thoughts in a Hybrid World*. London: Routledge, 2012.

Brassier, Ray. "Concepts and Objects," in Bryant, Srnicek, and Harman, *The Speculative Turn*, pp.47–65.

Braudel, Fernand. *Civilization and Capitalism, 15th–18th Century, Vol.1: The Structure of Everyday Life*, trans. S. Reynold. Berkeley, CA: University of California Press, 1992.

Bryant, Levi R., Nick Srnicek, and Graham Harman (eds.). *The Speculative Turn: Continental Materialism and Realism*. Melbourne: re.press, 2011.

Chalmers, David. *The Conscious Mind: In Search of a Fundamental Theory*. New York: Oxford University Press, 1997.

Cohen, Sande. "Science Studies and Language Suppression: A Critique of Bruno Latour's *We Have Never Been Modern,*" *Studies in the History and Philosophy of Science,* Vol.28, No.2, pp.339–361, 1997.

Cornell, Drucilla, Michael Rosenfeld, and David Gray Carlson (eds.). *Deconstruction and the Possibility of Justice.* New York: Routledge, 1992.

DeLanda Manuel and Timur Si-Qin. "Manuel DeLanda in conversation with Timur Si-Qin." Berlin: Société, 2012. Limited edition of 300 copies.

Derrida, Jacques. "Force of Law: The 'Mystical Foundation of Authority,'" in Cornell, Rosenfeld, and Carlson, *Deconstruction and the Possibility of Justice,* pp.3–67.

Descola, Philippe. *Beyond Nature and Culture,* trans. J. Lloyd. Chicago: University of Chicago Press, 2013.

Dewey, John. *The Public and its Problems: An Essay in Political Inquiry.* University Park, PA: Penn State University Press, 2012.

Disch, Lisa J. "Representation as 'Spokespersonship': Bruno Latour's Political Theory," *Parallax,* Vol.14, Issue 3 (2008), pp.88–100.

Elam, Mark. "Living Dangerously with Bruno Latour in a Hybrid World," *Theory, Culture and Society,* Vol.16, No.1, pp.1–24, 1999.

Eyers, Tom. "Think Negative!" *Mute,* April 7, 2011. http://www.metamute.org/editorial/articles/think-negative

Faye, Emmanuel. *Heidegger: The Introduction of Nazism into Philosophy in Light of the Unpublished Seminars of 1933–1935,* trans. M. Smith. New Haven: Yale University Press, 2011.

Gibbon, Edward. *The Decline and Fall of the Roman Empire.* New York: Modern Library, 2003.

Griffiths, A. Phillips (ed.). *Contemporary French Philosophy.* Cambridge: Cambridge University Press, 1987.

Harman, Graham. *Tool-Being: Heidegger and the Metaphysics of Objects.* Chicago: Open Court, 2002.

Harman, Graham. "Bruno Latour and the Politics of Nature," in Servomaa, *Humanity at the Turning Point,* pp.147–158.

Harman, Graham. "The Importance of Bruno Latour for Philosophy," *Cultural Studies Review,* Vol.13, No.1, pp.31–49, March 2007.

Harman, Graham. *Prince of Networks: Bruno Latour and Metaphysics.* Melbourne: re.press, 2009.

Harman, Graham. *Towards Speculative Realism: Essays and Lectures.* Winchester, UK: Zero Books, 2010.

Harman, Graham. "On the Undermining of Objects: Grant, Bruno, and Radical Philosophy," in Bryant, Srnicek, and Harman, *The Speculative Turn.*

Harman, Graham. "On the Supposed Societies of Chemicals, Atoms, and Stars in Gabriel Tarde," in Pereira, *Savage Objects.*

Harman, Graham. "Conclusions: Assemblage Theory and its Future," in Acuto and Curtis, *Reassembling International Theory,* pp.118–131.

Harman, Graham. "Relation and Entanglement: A Response to Bruno Latour and Ian Hodder," *New Literary History*, Vol.45, No.1, pp.37–49, 2014.

Harman, Graham. "Agential and Speculative Realism: Some Remarks on Barad's Ontology," *Rhizomes*, forthcoming 2014.

Harman, Graham. *Prince of Modes: Bruno Latour's Later Philosophy*. Melbourne: re.press, forthcoming 2015.

Heidegger, Martin. *Bremen and Freiburg Lectures*, trans. A. Mitchell. Bloomington, IN: Indiana University Press, 2012.

Hekman, Susan. "We have never been postmodern: Latour, Foucault, and the Material of knowledge," *Contemporary Political Theory*, Vol.8, No.4, 2009, pp.435–454.

Hobbes, Thomas. *Leviathan*, Oxford: Oxford University Press, 2009.

James, William. *Essays in Radical Empiricism*. Lincoln, NE: University of Nebraska Press, 1996.

Jasanoff, Sheila. "Breaking the Waves in Science Studies: Comment on H.M. Collins and Robert Evans, 'The Third Wave of Science Studies,'" *Social Studies of Science*, Vol.33, No.3, pp.389–400, 2003.

Jobs, Steve. "Steve Jobs on Apple's Resurgence: 'Not a One-Man Show,'" *BusinessWeek*. May 12, 1998. http://www.businessweek.com/bwdaily/dnflash/may1998/nf80512d.htm

Kafka, Franz. *The Trial*, trans. B. Mitchell. New York: Schocken Books, 1998.

Kendall, Gavin and Mike Michael. "Order and Disorder: Time, Technology and the Self," *Culture Machine*, November 2001.Top of FormBottom of Form Available online at http://www.culturemachine.net/index.php/cm/article/view/242/223

Kervégan, Jean-François. "Carl Schmitt and 'World Unity,'" in Mouffe, *The Challenge of Carl Schmitt*, pp.54–74.

Kymlicka, Will. *Contemporary Political Philosophy*. Oxford: Oxford University Press, 2002.

Lacan, Jacques. Écrits: The First Complete Edition in English, trans. B. Fink. New York: W.W. Norton, 2007.

Lévi-Strauss, Claude. *Structural Anthropology*. New York: Basic Books, 1963.

Lippmann, Walter. *Public Opinion*. New York: Free Press Paperbacks, 1997.

Lippmann, Walter. *The Phantom Public*. New Brunswick, NJ: Transaction Publishers, 1993.

Lovelock, James. *Gaia: A New Look at Life on Earth*. Oxford: Oxford University Press, 2000.

Luhmann, Niklas. *Social Systems*, trans. J. Bednarz with D. Baecker. Stanford, CA: Stanford University Press, 1995.

Machiavelli, Niccolò. *The Prince*, trans. P. Bondanella. Oxford: Oxford University Press, 2008.

Machiavelli, Niccolò. *Discourses on Livy*, trans. J.C. Bondanella and P. Bondanella. Oxford: Oxford University Press, 2009.

Maniglier, Patrice. "Qui a peur de Bruno Latour?" *Le Monde* website, September 21, 2012. http://www.lemonde.fr/livres/article/2012/09/21/qui-a-peur-de-bruno-latour_1763066_3260.html

Marres, Noortje. "No issue, no public: Democratic deficits after the displacement of politics," Ph.D. dissertation, University of Amsterdam, The Netherlands, 2005. http://dare.uva.nl/record/165542

Marres, Noortje. *Material Participation: Technology, the Environment and Everyday Publics.* London: Palgrave Macmillan, 2012.

Marres, Noortje. "Nothing Special," in Waal, *Drift wijsgerig festival,* pp.9–19.

Marx, Karl. *Das Kapital,* Vol.1, trans. B. Fowkes. New York: Vintage, 1977.

Maturana, Humberto R. and Francisco J. Varela. *Autopoiesis and Cognition: The Realization of the Living.* Dordrecht, The Netherlands: D. Reidel, 1980.

Meier, Heinrich. *Carl Schmitt and Leo Strauss: The Hidden Dialogue,* trans. J. Harvey Lomax. Chicago: University of Chicago Press, 1995.

Meillassoux, Quentin. *After Finitude: Essay on the Necessity of Contingency,* trans. R. Brassier. London: Continuum, 2008.

Mouffe, Chantal (ed.). *The Challenge of Carl Schmitt.* London: Verso, 1999.

Mouffe, Chantal. "Introduction: Schmitt's Challenge," in Mouffe, *The Challenge of Carl Schmitt,* pp.1–6.

Mouffe, Chantal. "Carl Schmitt and the Paradox of Liberal Democracy," in Mouffe, *The Challenge of Carl Schmitt,* pp.38–53.

Negri, Antonio and Michael Hardt. *Empire.* Cambridge, MA: Harvard University Press, 2001.

Noys, Benjamin. *The Persistence of the Negative: A Critique of Contemporary Continental Theory.* Edinburgh: Edinburgh University Press, 2012.

Peck, Jamie. *Constructions of Neoliberal Reason.* New York: Oxford University Press, 2013.

Pereira, Godofredo (ed.). *Savage Objects.* Lisbon: INCM, 2012.

Pyhhtinen, Olli and Sakari Tamminen. "We have never been only human: Foucault and Latour on the question of the *anthropos,*" *Anthropological Theory,* Vol.11, No.2, pp.135–152, 2011.

Rosen, Stanley. *The Mask of Enlightenment: Nietzsche's Zarathustra.* Second edition. New Haven: Yale University Press, 2004.

Rousseau, Jean-Jacques. *Discourse on the Origin of Inequality,* trans. D. Cress. Indianapolis: Hackett, 1992.

Rousseau, Jean-Jacques. *The Social Contract and Other Later Political Writings,* trans. V. Gourevitch. Cambridge: Cambridge University Press, 1997.

Rozental, Stefan (ed.). *Niels Bohr: His Life and Work as Seen by His Friends and Colleagues.* Hoboken, NJ: John Wiley & Sons, 1967.

Schmitt, Carl. *The Concept of the Political,* trans. G. Schwab. Chicago: University of Chicago Press, 2007.

Schmitt, Carl. *Constitutional Theory,* trans. J. Seitzer. Durham, NC: Duke University Press, 2008.

Schouten, Peer. "The Materiality of State Failure: Social Contract Theory, Infrastructure and Governmental Power in Congo," *Millenium: Journal of International Studies*, June 2013, Vol.41, No 3, pp.553–574.

Schouten, Peer. "Security in Action: How John Dewey Can Help Us Follow the Production of Security Assemblages," in Acuto and Curtis, *Reassembling International Theory*, pp.91–97.

Serres, Michel. *The Natural Contract*, trans. E. MacArthur and W. Paulson. Ann Arbor: University of Michigan Press, 1995.

Servomaa, Sonja (ed.). *Humanity at the Turning Point: Rethinking Nature, Culture, and Freedom*. Helsinki: Renvall Institute for Area and Cultural Studies, University of Helsinki, 2006.

Shapin, Steven and Simon Schaffer. *Leviathan and the Air-Pump: Hobbes, Boyle, and the Experimental Life*. Princeton, NJ: Princeton University Press, 1985.

Shaviro, Steven. *Without Criteria: Whitehead, Deleuze, and Aesthetics*. Cambridge, MA: MIT Press, 2009.

Stengers, Isabelle. *Cosmopolitics*, trans. R. Bononno. Two volumes. Minneapolis: University of Minnesota Press, 2010.

Stengers, Isabelle. *Thinking with Whitehead: A Free and Wild Invention of Concepts*, trans. M. Chase. Cambridge, MA: Harvard University Press, 2011.

Strauss, Leo. *What Is Political Philosophy?* Chicago: University of Chicago Press, 1988.

Strauss, Leo. "Niccolo Machiavelli," in Strauss and Cropsey, *History of Political Philosophy*, pp.296–317.

Strauss, Leo. "Notes on Carl Schmitt's *The Concept of the Political*," appendix to Carl Schmitt, *The Concept of the Political*, pp.99–122, 2007.

Strauss, Leo and Joseph Cropsey. *History of Political Philosophy*. Third edition. Chicago: University of Chicago Press, 2007.

Strong, Tracy B. "Foreword: Dimensions of the New Debate Around Carl Schmitt," in Carl Schmitt, *The Concept of the Political*, pp.ix–xxxi.

Tarde, Gabriel. *Monadology and Sociology*, trans. T. Lorenc. Melbourne: re.press, 2012.

Tolstoy, Leo. *War and Peace*, trans. R. Pevear and L. Volokhonsky. New York: Vintage, 2007.

Tresch, John. "Mechanical Romanticism: Engineers of the Artificial Paradise," Ph.D. dissertation, University of Cambridge, 2001.

Vries, Gerard de. "What is Political in Sub-Politics? How Aristotle Might Help STS," *Social Studies of Science*, Vol.37, No.5, pp.781–809, October 2007.

Waal, Deva (ed.). *Drift wijsgerig festival*. Amsterdam: Drift, 2013.

Wainwright, Joel. "Politics of Nature: A Review of Three Recent Works by Bruno Latour," *Capitalism Nature Socialism*, Vol.16, No.1, pp.115–127.

Wark, McKenzie. "Accelerationism," *Public Seminar* blog, November 18, 2013. http://www.publicseminar.org/2013/11/accelerationism/

Watson, James D. *The Double Helix: A Personal Account of the Discovery of the Structure of DNA*. New York: Norton, 2001.

Whitehead, Alfred North. *Adventures of Ideas*. New York: Free Press, 1967.

Whitehead, Alfred North. *Process and Reality*. New York: Free Press, 1979.

Whitehead, Alfred North and Lucien Price. *Dialogues of Alfred North Whitehead*. New York: Nonpareil Books, 2001.

Žižek, Slavoj. *The Sublime Object of Ideology*. London: Verso, 1989.

Žižek, Slavoj. "Carl Schmitt in the Age of Post-Politics," in Mouffe, *The Challenge of Carl Schmitt*, pp.18–37.

Žižek, Slavoj and Glyn Daly. *Conversations with Žižek*. Cambridge: Polity Press, 2003.

Index